Ghost-Watching American Modernity

GHOST-WATCHING
AMERICAN MODERNITY

Haunting, Landscape, and the
Hemispheric Imagination

MARÍA DEL PILAR BLANCO

Fordham University Press

NEW YORK   2012

Library of Congress Cataloging-in-Publication Data

Blanco, María del Pilar.
  Ghost-watching American modernity : haunting, landscape, and the
hemispheric imagination / María del Pilar Blanco.
    p.   cm.
  Includes bibliographical references and index.
  ISBN 978-0-8232-4214-6 (cloth : alk. paper)
    1. Comparative literature—American and Latin American.   2. Comparative
literature—Latin American and American.   3. American literature—19th
century—History and criticism.   4. American literature—20th century—
History and criticism.   5. Spanish American literature—19th century—History
and criticism.   6. Spanish American literature—20th century—History and
criticism.   7. Ghosts in literature.   8. Landscapes in literature.   9. Nationalism
in literature.   10. Haunted places.   I. Title.   II. Title: Haunting, landscape, and
the hemispheric imagination.
PS159.L38P55   2012
809'.897—dc23

                                                                    2011040568

Printed in the United States of America

14 13 12   5 4 3 2 1

First edition

A book in the American Literatures Initiative (ALI), a collaborative
publishing project of NYU Press, Fordham University Press, Rutgers
University Press, Temple University Press, and the University of Virginia
Press. The Initiative is supported by The Andrew W. Mellon Foundation.
For more information, please visit www.americanliteratures.org.

THE
AMERICAN
LITERATURES
INITIATIVE

Contents

Acknowledgments

Although the geographical scope of this book is the American hemisphere, its development was very much a transatlantic affair that began in New York City and culminated in various locations throughout the United Kingdom. I take this opportunity to thank people on both sides of the ocean for their support, friendship, and inspiration. At New York University, Gerard Aching, Ana Dopico, and Nancy Ruttenburg gave me intelligent and useful advice on my writing as well as on my career moves, and for this I'll always be grateful. Martin Harries, a master of haunted writing, has been a true model for me. I met some wonderful and supportive people when this project began to take shape, and I thank them here for their continued friendship: Anna Brígido-Corachán, Ifeona Fulani, Jennifer Kaplan, John Pat Leary, Emily Maguire, and Mariano Siskind. Along with his friendship, Chris Bongie has given me invaluable help on all life and career matters for well over a decade now. I thank him for always posing the most significant and challenging questions. I also give heartfelt thanks to Sheila Debrunner, Tim Shaw, Jean Beier Murphy, Mike Pingicer, Lavina Lee, Luke Andrews-Hakken, and Kat Driscoll, who, through visits and several forms of technology, have always made me feel closer to home, even when I was so many miles away. Beyond New York, I thank my supportive network of friends from so long ago with whom I've reconnected thanks to my adventures in research travels as well as my relocations: Roberto Frau, Anna Orenstein, and Jason Sánchez.

Across the pond in Britain, I am grateful to all my fabulous colleagues at UCL, within and outside of the Department of Spanish and Latin American Studies—among them Stephen Cadywold, Jo Evans, Gareth Wood,

Alex Samson, Claire Thomson, and Mi Zhou. I am indebted to Stephen Hart and Dilwyn Knox for all their encouragement during my early career as a lecturer. My deepest appreciation goes to Claire Lindsay, mentor extraordinaire, for her friendship and invaluable support. My graduate students have been marvelous interlocutors about the ways in which haunting works in literary narrative, and I thank them for spending so much time thinking about ghosts. I also express my gratitude to the lovely people I've met since my move to the UK in 2006, for their hospitality, brilliant conversation, good humor, and encouragement: Deborah Cohn, James Dunkerley, Peter Hulme, Julia Jordan, Peter and Lizzie Howarth, Jeremy Lane, Eric Langley, Sean Matthews, David McAllister, Gillian Roberts, Mark Robson, Heidi Scott, Karina Lindeiner-Stráský, and the legendary Phil Swanson. I give heartfelt thanks to Esther Peeren, impressive scholar and editor, with whom I share a book and a lot of common ground in matters of haunting. I also thank all the *Popular Ghosts* contributors, for showing me new ways of discussing the pervasiveness of ghosts in our everyday cultures.

A section of Chapter 2 ("Desert Mournings") was published in *Space, Haunting, Discourse,* edited by Maria Holmgren-Troy and Elisabeth Wenno (Cambridge Scholars Publishing, 2008). I thank them both for their permission to publish it here. At Fordham University Press, I thank Thomas Lay for his assistance throughout the many stages that the manuscript has gone through to reach publication. My gratitude also goes to the anonymous readers of the manuscript for both their criticisms and their enthusiasm for the project. I especially want to express my enormous appreciation to Helen Tartar, for taking an interest in this project and for seeing it through to publication. I'm very fortunate to have my book sponsored by the American Literatures Initiative and would like to thank all of those involved in this wonderful and much-needed venture. Very special thanks go to Tim Roberts and Teresa Jesionowski, for their attentiveness and thorough editorial work.

Finally, I return to the greatest source of support throughout these years, my transatlantic family network. Huge thanks to my mum-in-law, Janet, and the rest of the James clan, for making England (and the EU) feel like a second home so quickly. In Puerto Rico, Susan Homar inspired me to pursue literature as a career when I was half my present age. I feel so blessed for her continued affection and support. My parents, Carmen and Jorge Blanco, foremost role models and driving spirits, are always with me, despite the distance between us. Despite my getting older, I continue to get no bigger thrill than making them proud of me. My siblings, Jorge and Lula; their spouses, Julie and Andrés; and my four amazing nephews (Alex, Martín, Jack, and Sammy) have continually been the most comforting company as well as true models of intelligence, responsibility, and unconditional love.

The culmination of my gratitude goes to my *media naranja*, David James. I first laid eyes on him during the Q&A session at a conference, when he was making a characteristically lucid yet complex statement about Roland Barthes's *punctum*. From that day onward, he has punctuated every single moment of my life with his love, absolute brilliance, humor, and unfailing encouragement. The world is indeed smaller, and so much more amazing, since he came along.

Note on the Translations

I've included published translations for most of the texts written originally in Spanish. The rest of the translations are my own.

*He nodded. Kind of smiled. Then he did ask me a question. He said:
This mystery man you think killed that trooper and burned him up in his
car. What do you know about him?*

I don't know nothin. I wish I did. Or I think I wish it.

Yeah.

He's pretty much a ghost.

Is he pretty much or is he one?

No, he's out there. I wish he wasnt. But he is.

He nodded. I guess if he was a ghost you wouldnt have to worry about him.

*I said that was right, but I've thought about it since and I think the
answer to his question is that when you encounter certain things in the
world, the evidence for certain things, you realize that you have come
upon somethin that you may very well not be equal to and I think that this
is one of them things. When you've said that it's real and not just in your
head I'm not all that sure what it is you have said.*

—CORMAC MCCARTHY, *NO COUNTRY FOR OLD MEN* (2005)

Introduction

Haunting can take many forms: Alongside apparitions of supernatural shapes or beings that would otherwise be imperceptible, it can also mean the disquieting experience of sensing a collision of temporalities or spaces—an experience that is nevertheless riddled with doubt and uncertainty. Thus, to look for ghosts as a reader of literature and film is to study different perceptions of haunted landscapes as distinct from one another—and to vigilantly account, as a reader, for the spatiotemporal coordinates that merge to produce a site of haunting. To search for them within different texts that recount different experiences of modernity in the Americas in the nineteenth and twentieth centuries is to register (however slowly or doubtfully) an emerging sense of a diverse and changing experience of American landscapes, as well as to account for the constantly shifting set of perceptions of local, national, and transnational space that a given text may reveal.

Ghost-watching is a particular way of reading perceptions of space within a given text. Let us begin defining this compound word by saying that, within the action of a literary or cinematic text, to ghost-watch implies a vigilant perception of the landscapes depicted within it, as they may reveal a different, and haunted, dimension. Our ghost-watching commences with the site of the frontier and a story by a writer of multiple frontiers. Ambrose Bierce was born in 1842 on an Ohio farm and vanished in revolutionary Mexico at some point around 1914. His career famously spanned the fields of journalism, war stories, tall tales, and narratives of haunting. Bierce is an interesting figure with which to begin an exploration of hemispheric haunting, because of his career in frontier crossing as well as his open criticism of the invention of new frontiers brought on by U.S. expansionist policies in the late nineteenth century. When the Spanish-American War broke out in 1898, Bierce was a columnist for the San Francisco *Examiner*, then owned by William Randolph Hearst. As Jane Creighton notes, "Week after week Bierce blasted patriotic hysteria in the same pages of the paper that induced [the war], and supported intervention only as a necessary military response to the sinking of the *Maine* in the Havana harbor."[1] Bierce read Hearst's impassioned support for the Filipino insurgencies against Spain alongside the tycoon's "underlying interests in economic power and manifest destiny" (69), and he correctly gleaned in this support for the "underdogs" the United States' greater expansionist desire to replace Spain's imperial rule: "Whatever may be the future position of the United States in international politics," he wrote in an article on May 29, 1898,

> whether we shall adhere to our traditional policy of self-sufficient isolation, non-intervention in the affairs of the Old World and unquestionable dominance in those of the New; whether we are to remain content with continental possessions, or join in the general scramble for colonial expansion by treaty, purchase and conquest; however these momentous questions may be answered by events impossible to foresee, it is clear enough that we are conducting this war, if not with a view, yet in a way, to promote the larger scheme.[2]

As such, Bierce remains one of the most incisive commentators of inter-American relations at a time when U.S. borders would be revised and when (to paraphrase Ann Laura Stoler) the haunting of a burgeoning empire would materialize.

Bierce's concerns with borders manifested themselves both in his journalism and in his fiction, in international as in regional matters. A number of his ghost stories are set in the mid-nineteenth-century U.S. frontier, a wild landscape marked more by movement than by settlement, a place where memories and histories are difficult, if not impossible, to reconstruct. "The Boarded Window" (1891), for example, opens in the style of incisive reportage to set the scene for what unravels into a rather shocking tale of horror:

> In 1830, only a few miles away from what is now the great city of Cincinnati, lay an immense and almost unbroken forest. The whole region was sparsely settled by people of the frontier—restless souls who no sooner had hewn fairly habitable homes out of the wilderness and attained to that degree of prosperity which to-day we should call indigence than impelled by some mysterious impulse of their nature

they abandoned all and pushed farther westward, to encounter new perils and privations in the effort to regain the meager comforts which they had voluntarily renounced.[3]

Bierce's sprawling sentence wanders the abridged history of the equally sprawling narrative of westward expansion in the United States. The narrator telescopes in on a character named Murlock, who defied this rule of frontier "impulse," and died where he settled, in a "little log house, with its chimney of sticks," a "single door," and a single boarded window. As a child, the narrator listens to his grandfather relate the "earlier chapter" of an otherwise inconsequential and "true" story of a man who lived and died in one place. This "earlier chapter" is, in fact, the element of horror that surrounds the off-putting detail of a boarded window (228).

Bierce's story works within the frame of the history of the frontier to first pick out the anomaly of someone who stays behind and does not move with the current of that larger narrative of expansion, to then concentrate on the particular peculiarity of a sealed house. Thus begins the spinning of a tale of loss—of an "early" chapter that hovers over a "true" story. Murlock's wife had died before him (so goes the retold history by a narrator that several critics have deemed "unreliable"), a series of events that leads the narrator to conclude that Murlock's failure to continue moving west was due to his melancholia, "for what but the magnetism of a blessed memory could have chained that venturesome spirit to a lot like that?" (229). The death of the wife presents a problem for Murlock, because he "had had no experience in grief"; his "heart could not contain it all, nor his imagination rightly conceive it" (229).

The narrator interestingly combines an idea of "grief" with one of a fresh "imagination." Grief, he says, is an "artist of powers as various as the instruments upon which he plays his dirges for the dead, evoking from some the sharpest, shrillest notes, from others the low, grave chords that throb recurrent like the slow beating of a distant drum" (229). Evoking, perhaps, a recurrent motif in American frontier narratives—the beating of (Indian) drums, described in Lewis and Clark's expedition journals (1803–4) to Edgar Allan Poe's "A Tale of the Ragged Mountains" (1844)—our narrator provides an aural and rather florid dimension to the description of frontier loss that Murlock experiences. As it turns out, however, the "art" of Murlock's grief manifests itself in a mysterious and bleak encounter between his wife's dead body and the entrance of a panther (probably a cougar) through the single window of his cabin, at the time still open. The animal drags the corpse toward the window, a horrific scene that Murlock is able to discern through the "vivid illumination" provided by the flash of a rifle shot. Murlock loses consciousness, and upon waking during the time of day "when the sun was high and the wood vocal with songs of birds," finds the body of his dead wife by the window, lying in a pool of blood. Bierce's last two sentences reveal the story's surprising supernatural inflection: "The ribbon with which he had bound the wrists was broken; the hands were tightly clenched. Between the teeth was a fragment of the animal's ear" (231). The event of frontier nature entering Murlock's home inexplicably turns supernatural. Although one reader may interpret this turn of events as death apparently suspending itself, if only briefly, for the corpse to come alive to defend the homestead, another reading may be that the clumsy Murlock, so unacquainted with death and its rituals, had prepared his wife for burial too soon. This conundrum is further complicated by the existence of different versions of "The Boarded Window." Bridget M. Marshall has noted that at least four exist (from 1891, quoted here, 1892, 1898, and 1908). Bierce made amendments to phrases in the story at each moment of publication, every time complicating the possible verdict.[4] These revisions complicate matters in terms both textual and metatextual, and reveal to us the different dimensions that haunting may take: As readers we are haunted by the doubt of a haunting, and the multiple versions of the story haunt each other to add and remove layers of certainty to each other.

Now let us focus on the ways in which the author constructs a haunted frontier space. I want to suggest that place, grief, and imagination spell out an art of haunting for Bierce. The event of death produces, in the character who does not know about mourning, an imagination of a fierce event arriving from an afterlife, a tale of wild haunting that in turn becomes inextricably associated with that specific site on the Ohio frontier. The story of Murlock's frontier haunting is unique and strange in itself. That is, Murlock's experience in loss in the end emulates no other and is caught in that space of a single frontier that is soon erased and replaced by others, between multiple past and future American experiences. Alongside the focus on location and the history of the frontier that frames the story, what is remarkable about Bierce's invention is that haunting is not necessarily tied to mourning (as Murlock fumbles with the very notion of it), but to imagination, doubt, and anticipation instead. This new framework makes us wonder what shape haunting may take when it is not necessarily tied to a notion of trauma or memory, but rather to a sense of that anxiety surrounding the possible shape and location of the events of an *after*-life. The boarded window in the wall of Murlock's cabin is metonymic of a waiting—a vulnerability and exposure to what may come, even if the character remains in one place, although others may pass him by in search of "new perils and privations." One could argue that Bierce creates the character of Murlock as a symbol of frontier life, and a cipher for the questions that surround mourning in a location that is movable, unfixed.

Ambrose Bierce's own disappearance raises questions about how one
can mourn that which is constantly shifting location. His final movements
traced a trans-American tale that is itself haunted by his mysterious van-
ishing. The last known correspondence from Bierce, dated December 26,
1913, was written in Chihuahua, south of the U.S.-Mexico border. It read,
"As to me, I leave here tomorrow for an unknown location." Bierce's "afterlife" in Mexico became the subject of fiction in Carlos Fuentes's *El gringo
viejo* (1985). In this novel, Fuentes endows the ghost of the American writer
with a new wandering life in Mexico, as well as the capacity to incisively
reflect on the fraught history that transpired along the U.S.-Mexico border. On his arrival in Mexico, *Don Quijote* in hand, the aging Bierce looks
around the space immediately surrounding him to produce a massive
palimpsest of the history that had transpired in the country south of his
native United States.

> En la mirada clara del viejo se reunieron en ese instante las ciudades
> de oro, las expediciones que nunca regresaron, los frailes perdidos,
> las tribus errantes y moribundas de indios tobosos y laguneros sobre-
> vivientes de las epidemias europeas.

> [At that instant, in the old man's clear eyes were fused all the cities
> of gold, the expeditions that never returned, the lost priests, the no-
> madic and moribund tribes of Tobosos and Laguneros that had sur-
> vived the epidemics of the Europeans].[5]

Although this description of the living Bierce in the second chapter reacti-
vates a colonial past in the observation of the landscape immediately surrounding him, the novel opens with the character of Harriet Winslow beck-
oning forth Bierce's specter. This incantation, which recalls Rosa Coldfield's
in the opening of William Faulkner's *Absalom, Absalom!* (1937),[6] is not the
imagination of a simple ghost, but of an entire "mobilized past" ["un pasado
movilizado," 11] brought forward. Bierce's life is indeed imagined in terms
of continuous border crossing. As Colonel Frutos García, one of the burial
party for the "old gringo," explains, North American subjects "se pasaron
la vida cruzando fronteras, las suyas y las ajenas . . . y ahora el viejo la había
cruzado hacia el sur porque ya no tenía fronteras que cruzar en su propio
país" (13). ["They spent their lives crossing frontiers, theirs and those that
belonged to others, and now the old man had crossed to the south because
he didn't have any frontiers left to cross in his own country"] (5). The frontier obsession of Bierce's own characters in a story like "The Boarded Window" becomes the raison d'être of his fictional afterlife in Fuentes's novel.

In *Gringo viejo*, the crossing into the other locations of the American
hemisphere constitutes both a critical and existential evaluation of these

transnational spaces. This necessarily involves a "mobilization" of other temporalities into the present, and an electrification of the specters that move across these spaces in order to yield a critical history and literature. In its broadest sense, this book attempts to do just that: To think of ghosts and haunting not simply as useful metaphors for enduring and difficult memories of things past, but as commentaries on how subjects conceive present and evolving spaces and localities. My focus on this *present-pro-gressive* conception of haunting is not an attempt to reintroduce a notion of the "absent things" of an American life without past or culture to speak of, as Henry James did in his 1879 description of Nathaniel Hawthorne's American experience.[7] Instead, I want to make a case for reading texts from the Americas that elucidate a different definition of haunting—one that is marked by what is ungraspable about present, changing, and developing landscapes. *Ghost-Watching American Modernity* deals with the intersections of pan-American imaginations of haunting and location in a constellation of texts produced from the mid-nineteenth century to the mid-twentieth century, and asks what it is that ghosts facilitate in these narratives. I look at a constellation of works by authors from the American hemisphere—among them Domingo Sarmiento, José Martí, Henry James, W. E. B. Du Bois, Felisberto Hernández, Juan Rulfo, Clint Eastwood, and Alejandro Jodorowsky—and, in my readings, I focus on an understanding of haunting as a narrative phenomenon during a period when the Americas share a certain set of commonalities. As these countries began to emerge from colonial rule, they became increasingly navigable to their subjects through the modernization of travel, and the political and personal conditions of displacement and exile. This is also a period during which conceptions of modernity as a temporal phenomenon characterized by rapid change are felt in terms of spatial transformation. For centuries the national geographies of the Americas, as described by native sons and daughters (such as Domingo Sarmiento in Argentina, and Henry James and W. E. B. Du Bois in the United States) as well as travelers (José Martí in the United States), have been marked according to indexes of civilization, present or potential modernization, or conversely, stasis and retrogression. In nineteenth- and twentieth-century grand narratives of American modernity such as these, however, we see a second story emerge, one that is contemplative rather than fully assertive, marked by what Alexander Nemerov describes as the doubt surrounding the discovery of "a meaning definitive and clear" in what we see and what we can fully represent.[8] It is in this fissure of perception that I find my own definition of American haunting, and of the practice of ghost-watching.

In the texts studied in the following chapters, we gain a sense that pan-American and European writers of the mid-nineteenth century and beyond increasingly read modernity along the lines of urban, as opposed to rural, landscapes, and it is in the simultaneous life of these two spheres that *Ghost-Watching American Modernity* proposes that we watch for the textual eruptions of haunting. This dynamic version of haunting seeks to look at ghosts as representations not of occluded pasts, or buried secrets, but as manifestations of an increasing awareness of *simultaneous landscapes and simultaneous others* living within unseen, diverse spaces in the progressively complicated political and cultural networks of hemispheric modernization.[9] As I explain later in this Introduction, by "simultaneity" I mean a "now" moment that is happening in a different location (near or far) at the same time. My argument about simultaneous landscapes shares a set of qualities with Kevin Lynch's notion of cognitive mapping, which was later adopted by Fredric Jameson to explain the workings of ideology in postcapitalist society. In *The Image of the City* (1960), Lynch implores us to "learn to see the hidden forms" of the urban environment, to discover how to mediate between subjective perception and an imagined spatial totality that is absent to that necessarily limited appreciation.[10] Where *Ghost-Watching American Modernity* departs from Lynch is in its concern with developing a literary history of spatial representation; it is not a phenomenological study.

The consonances among these writers and filmmakers who share similar anxieties about a specific set of landscapes common to the experience of the Americas elucidate how we can establish readings of hemispheric simultaneities through the use of haunting. Rather than reading haunting and ghosts as past conundrums in search of closure, this book champions a perception of these phenomena in literature and film as experiments in a prolonged evocation of future anxieties and extended disquiet in multiple locations of the Americas. Put another way, the poetics of haunting is addressed here precisely in terms of how authors perceive and write the changing multicultural spaces of the Americas in the nineteenth and twentieth centuries.

Twenty years after writing "The Boarded Window" and a few years before disappearing in Mexico, Bierce defined the word "ghost" in his famous *Devil's Dictionary* (1911) as "the outward and visible sign of an inward fear."[11] A generalized view of ghosts would lead us to conclude that there is little that is inherently new, or modern, in the figure of a ghost. Fear, to rephrase the Spanish saying, is as old as time itself. These manifestations of the most intangible of feelings, whether rendered visible or not, have long survived in the history of world narratives. From figures that emerge in dark corners to progressive winds of political change (as in the case of the specter of communism that haunts Europe in the opening line of Marx and Engels's 1848 *Communist Manifesto*), it is clear that ghosts and haunting have acquired an infinite number of forms and meanings throughout the years. Although a certain typology of ghosts and their haunting actions persists in a multicultural popular imagination, ghosts often remain unwieldy figures and haunting actions perplexing events that resist prescribed interpretations, which, importantly, ask to be read according to their historical and geographic location. Returning to Bierce's definition of "ghost" in his dictionary, we can appreciate how this (so often terrifying) manifestation of an anxiety has been modified by the cultural anxieties that affect individual global literary traditions at any given time.

Such a statement, however, comes with a question: Is there such a thing as a specific ghost, or is the evidence of those anxieties across literary and cinematic traditions enough to theorize the generic commonalities of ghosts among cultures? In *Ghost-Watching American Modernity* I take the simple position that ghosts need to be read in their specificity. They are embedded in the story about a place. In addition, my focus on ghosts as sites of innovation for literary and cinematic form departs from previous attempts to analyze spectral figures according to thematic or narratological conventions. Therefore, it is not my intention to produce a pseudostructuralist account of the emergence of ghosts in a given number of texts (along the lines of Tzvetan Todorov's *The Fantastic*), for example, but to understand ghosts as figures of the transgeneric fictions we use to understand our cultures. In the fictions studied here, culture, location (both temporal and spatial), and language produce specific *styles of haunting*. In turn, as I argue, haunting becomes itself a *stylization of space*.

The specific relations between sites and moments of haunting are endowed with unique senses of anxiety. In turn, these anxieties refer to the different events and actions that the possibility of a ghost propels in a story—that is, how the characters react to this possibility and how the landscape in a story changes with the event of haunting. Although it may seem an obvious clarification, it is surprising to note how few critics working on haunting have actually produced readings that take into account the singularity of ghosts and apparitions, and how they constitute distinct transformations in terms of the narrative's form itself, opting instead to see these figures as traumatic symptoms of something that is often hidden, rather than actual presences that need to be reckoned with in a narrative. Many of these recent projects, greatly influenced by Jacques Derrida's *Specters of Marx* (1993), necessarily insist on the political potential of haunting, or what the philosopher calls a "spectropolitics." These particular ghost-reading exercises frequently run the risk of losing track of the locations or even histories that give ghosts their specificity, in favor of larger allegorical diagnoses of haunting. My own project is much more discrete in its analysis of depictions of haunted space among different inter-American texts. Although indebted to Derrida's groundbreaking work, which produced certain vocabularies that have updated they manner in which we speak about haunting in an academic context, I do not focus on his particular project of spectrality, interested as he is in the afterlives of Marx's materialism, and where the future is read in terms of messianic or apocalyptic politics. Instead, in *Ghost-Watching American Modernity*, I read the development of haunting within a text as a phenomenon that says something about the formal solutions writers discover and deploy when evoking the experience of perceiving specific locations. Ghosts and haunting should thus be considered not only as thematic preoccupations but also as problems of textual representation and innovation, when crises of perception provoke new advances in literary craft.

Given my principal interest in depictions of haunted space, throughout the chapters that follow I therefore heed the advice of Roger Luckhurst, who has pointed to the potential problems in reading haunting as a catch-all repository of critical tropes that in the end hover above the relationships between content and form, thus "elid[ing] object and instrument."[12] Writing of the "spectral turn" that academic discourse has taken in the past two decades (an academic turn of events in which I am nevertheless a participant), Luckhurst observes that "to keep a generalized account of temporal disadjustment [of the specter] . . . is . . . to miss the point of its contemporary insistence" (542). He continues:

> The spectral turn reaches a limit if all it can describe is a repeated structure or generalized "spectral process"—perhaps most particularly when critics suggest the breaching of limits is itself somehow inherently political. . . . If, as Derrida constantly proclaims in "Marx & Sons," the whole thrust of *Specters of Marx* is to aim for a "repoliticization" then surely we have to risk the violence of *reading* the ghost, of cracking open its absent presence to answer the demand of its specific symptomatology and its specific locale. (542)

Seeing the potential "emptiness" that may surround a generalized poetics and politics of haunting, Luckhurst ends his essay with this call to commence an interpretation of a ghost in its "specific locale." Indeed, what may seem like a very simple question—*Why* does this author introduce haunting precisely *here*, and *how* does s/he go about it?—may well prove to be a more useful exercise in understanding the particular anxieties of the living who are reacting to the spatial manifestations of modernization around them. In terms of my interest in focusing on spatial matters, I also found a useful model in Andrew Thacker's critique of the surge in academic work that plots literary geographies. In many ways parallel to Luckhurst's own discomfort with an all-too-expansive definition of the spectral as an ultimately *"vacuous"* (542) metaphor and/or allegory, in "The Idea of a Critical Geography" Thacker exposes the problems behind "geographical tropes" that interpret landscape and maps as metaphors and not as actual sites where we may be able to read "more complex questions about space and power" and where we could glean "how space and geography affect literary forms and styles."[13] Among Thacker's suggestions for a more responsible practice in plotting literary geographies I am most drawn to his connection between the interrelation between form and style, as described here:

> A critical literary geography would trace how social space intrudes upon the internal construction of spatial forms. *Literary texts represent social spaces, but social space shapes literary forms.* The term *textual space* could then refer to this interaction between spatial forms and social space in the written text. (63)

Although Thacker's invitation to read texts in terms of this dialogue between space and form is challenging and rich, it also presents a particularly daunting prospect to those of us seeking to question the literary forms in which haunting tends to be housed. Formations of haunted space are undoubtedly important in terms of how authors conceive and imagine their social space. As I will explain at greater length below and in the first chapter ("Unsolving Hemispheric Mystery"), we should be wary of linking ghosts and haunting to a set of specific literary forms, if those forms are understood in terms of conventions rather than possibilities. In this sense, each literary text analyzed here will be read as a specific experiment in literary or cinematic form, which is nevertheless conversant with, and even critical of, certain kinds of literary heritage. Ghosts and haunting exist in specific and unique ways within each of these texts. In *Ghost-Watching American Modernity*, I endeavor to keep a critical distance from generic markers such as "Gothic," "magical," or "fantastic" to describe the ghosts or events of haunting that are present in each of the texts. Therefore, a haunted Latin American space in any given text studied here does not immediately become a manifestation of "magical reality," for example. Instead, the landscape represented in that text gathers a set of questions about its transformation, about the social forces that affect those living there, and about why the experience of the geography of modernity should so often be narrated as a haunted one.

One of the main interventions that I wish to make in this book is a thorough metacritical interrogation of the growing number of analyses that deal with the representations of ghosts and haunting hailing from the American hemisphere. My definition of ghost-watching is therefore necessarily expansive: Alongside my close readings of literary and cinematic texts, I also closely follow the location of ghosts and haunting in criticism from the twentieth century, in order to question how these critical voices have envisioned the American hemisphere as a generalizable entity, as far as literature and film are concerned. The notion of a "hemispheric imagination" in this book thus includes a body of recent work from the Americas that seeks to make critical sense out of a transnational corpus of artistic work from the nineteenth and twentieth centuries, when the nations of the hemisphere begin to develop projects of autochthonous self-constitution.

Hemispheric Studies: A Disciplinary Question

As the book claims to undertake an exploration of this hemispheric imagination, it is also important to state my position in relation to the growing body of work devoted to these particular literary, cultural, and historical transnational networks. Although I share some assumptions with the majority of authors devoted to the field of "hemispheric American studies," I want to outline the differences between that canon and my own work. As Deborah Cohn (*History and Memory in the Two Souths*, 1999), James Dunkerley (*Americana*, 2000), Kirsten Silva Gruesz (*Ambassadors of Culture*, 2001), and Anna Brickhouse (*Transamerican Literary Relations and the Nineteenth-Century Public Sphere*, 2004) have pointed out in past decades of hemispheric critical enquiry, the nineteenth century marked a period of national constitution in the Americas, when the United States and the countries of Latin America and the Caribbean were constructing a sense of autochthony and broadcasting it within and outside the nation. From within the space of the nation, the definition of a subject presupposes certain exclusions: Who belongs to the modern American nation, who does not, which language is the language of the state, which spaces define a nation, and which others fall outside the scope of national modernity. These delineations, sparked by conflicts, wars, and international tensions, took place at a time when connections were forged among subjects traveling throughout the Americas—subjects who were continuously coming into contact with people of other national, historical, and linguistic provenances. Contemporary critics like those mentioned above (the list is far from exhaustive) have brilliantly identified sites of conflict and/or communion where these questions of national and hemispheric constitution are asked, contested, and in some cases overcome. Throughout the past decades, as the field of American studies has expanded to include matters of the historical and cultural coincidences of pan-American experience—what Russ Castronovo and Susan Gillman have explained in terms of "doubleness," or the realization that "American difference turns out to be rooted in its special comparability"—critics have noted the similarities in historical, political, and cultural formations of the countries of the hemisphere.[14] Writing about the United States South and Spanish America specifically, for example, Deborah Cohn cites the political and cultural struggles common to these expansive regions that deeply affect a sense of regional identity, among them "wars, racial and ethnic conflict, changing orders, urbanization and industrialization, struggles against metropolitan powers, [and] the worship of an idealized past."[15] Anita Patterson, in her 2008 book on "transnational modernisms," has pointed out the "shared history" of "colonial settlement, empire-building, slavery, cultural hybridity and diasporic cosmopolitanism."[16] Both Cohn and Patterson point to the different levels of doubleness that inform comparative readings of the Americas: That sitting alongside the study of the similarities among the Americas is of course a very complicated narrative of expansionism and so-called uneven development, which spells out the divergences rather than the parallels between North and South. Writing about the threat of "imperial modernity" in the late nineteenth century, Laura Lomas observes that "conflicts between American modernities begin . . . with the locked horns of dominant and peripheral societies in this hemisphere."[17] There is little room to argue with these critics' contentions, and my own readings in the following chapters will consciously address the historical factors that led to common experiences as well as stark discrepancies in countries north and south. The emergence of haunted narratives throughout the hemisphere, as we will see, reveals interesting connections within a diverse group of practitioners on different sides of the tensions that the critics above highlight in their own works.

Different from much recent works by scholars of hemispherism, which analyze matters of influence, cultural and linguistic translation, and political interaction among subjects across the Americas, however, my own approach to landscapes of haunting employs a level of close reading that necessarily pushes *Ghost-Watching American Modernity* into other territories of inquiry. My aim is not to demonstrate the Jamesian roots of an "ex-centric" writer such as the Uruguayan Felisberto Hernández,[18] for example, but rather to see how different authors present a constellation of the anxieties about urban space and belonging through recourse to modes of haunting (as will be explored in Chapter 3). I look at authors in terms of how they experiment with specific kinds of haunted space: the city, the desert, and the real and imagined frontier. Beyond producing an account of the cultural histories that inform the creation of these narratives of haunting—an exercise that would be closer to the historical research performed by critics such as Brickhouse, Gruesz, and Lomas—I am concerned with performing close readings that shed light on formal and figurative affinities among works by authors from different American traditions and different historical locations. I include an example to illustrate how my project is different from the works by critics cited above: In her impressive study of trans-American literary relations from the 1820s through the 1850s, Brickhouse traces the "genealogical narratives embedded within literary traditions that share a legacy of colonialism, slavery, and indigenous 'removals.'" She revises the period commonly known as the "American Renaissance" in an attempt to account for its "international and hemispherically American dimensions."[19] *Ghost-Watching American Modernity* is a discrete exercise in terms of comparability, as I do not claim to trace transnational literary genealogies as Brickhouse does. Hers is a historically focused study that spans three decades, whereas mine spans a century. I understand "modernity" as a lengthy period that manifests itself in simultaneous, yet distinct, ways across the Americas, and I choose texts that (as I will argue) share preoccupations with space and haunting. This book is also distinct from the work of the aforementioned critics in that the links established between and among authors are not necessarily biographical, existing through relationships of encounter, collaboration, and/or translation (as is the case, for example, with Gruesz's analysis of José Martí's translation of Longfellow's *Evangeline*). As such, this book is much more an experiment in close reading than it is in historiography.

In *Ghost-Watching American Modernity*, I approximate apparently dissimilar authorial perspectives that have at their core a preoccupation of dramatizing American landscapes as *presently and progressively haunted*. Although my corpus of authors often overlaps with those used by the critics cited above, given their positions as commentators of the evolving social reality of pan-American subjects in the nineteenth and twentieth centuries, my own work is different in that it specifically ponders the question of what it is that haunts these authors and their characters, what forms their ghosts and their hauntings take, and how this haunting is told. The discussion of each text in terms of its historical and cultural location provides the basis for analyses of how each author imagines and crafts a haunted landscape—in short, how haunting is progressively woven and placed in a story about a certain site. The scenes the authors studied here depict, as I will argue, are concerned with describing ghosts and various stylizations of haunting in terms of their simultaneity to (not their generational anticipation of) the living world. In other words, I read them as the emergence of alternative presences and landscapes within modern consciousness. Through these comparative readings of haunted landscapes, we find a different story of hemispheric American modernization—a ghost story—that nevertheless tells much about the way the present has been perceived in the past two centuries.

Caroline F. Levander and Robert S. Levine, editors of *Hemispheric American Studies* (2008), argue that it is necessary to conceive of analyses of American spaces beyond the scope of the nation, and "to consider regions, areas, and diasporan affiliations that exist apart from or in conflicted relation to the nation."[20] As mentioned, I explore the comparative stylizations of haunting within spaces found in all the countries of the American hemisphere: deserts, cities, and imagined, but deeply embedded, borders. Understanding "American" as a term that, among other regions, encompasses Latin America, the Caribbean, and the United States, I opt for a more fluid conceptualization of space and region that is not bound by rehearsed theories of national expression, although reference to them will be made throughout the text. Here, I read space and location in terms both literal and figurative. On one level, the American hemisphere is perceived as one landmass that comprises similar topographies that harbor distinct regional identities. On a second level, I read the different texts by authors from the United States and Latin American countries as singular enunciations, which nevertheless converse with other texts from neighboring American literary and cinematic traditions. Thus, *Ghost-Watching American Modernity* proposes an alternative canon of American haunted narratives, one that is spatially, rather than generically, organized.

The diverse spatial organization of the book allows me to read the different narratives according to the particularity of the spaces being represented. My chapters thus revolve around the following questions: Chapter 2 ("Desert Mournings") is informed by questions of how haunting is manifested in American desert narratives. Chapter 3 ("Urban Indiscretions") asks what forms hauntings take in narratives set in urban centers of the American hemisphere. Finally, the fourth chapter ("Transnational Shadows") considers the relationship between haunting and established and unestablished borders within a given national space.

Mine is not the first attempt to read ghosts hemispherically, that is, in terms of the "doubleness" of pan-American cultural and political history (to recall Castronovo and Gillman's analysis). In *The Usable Past* (1997), for example, Lois Parkinson Zamora frames her reading of ghosts from Mexican and U.S. literature around a narratological analysis of the genres of romance and magical realism (I will explore this in greater detail in Chapter 1, "Unsolving Hemispheric Mystery"). Alongside her use of structuralist notions of genre to understand literary ghosts, Zamora reads these figures as archetypes, or allegories of indigenous cultural memories.[21] Departing from Zamora's notion of hemispheric American haunting, I suggest a reading alongside what I call a present-progressive sense of self-identification as national and pan-American subjects. I contend that, in the imaginations of the authors studied here, haunting comes to mean a creative anxiety of perception that reflects how we understand modern identity through lived spaces, and not simply as a backward glance into the finished pages of a collective history. In addition to Lois Parkinson Zamora's contribution, a more recent intervention is Jesse Alemán's exploration of the *unheimlich* connections between U.S. romance literature and the ghosts of republicanism-turned-empire in Robert Montgomery Bird's *Calavar, or, The Knight of the Conquest* (1834), William Prescott's *History of the Conquest of Mexico* (1843), and *Xicoténcatl* (anonymous, 1826).[22] Alemán's essay is about history as much as it is a disciplinary intervention. Echoing Deborah Cohn and Jon Smith, Alemán writes that "instead of a happy hemispherism, the presence of the other felt and discovered within rather than outside of the borders of self, home, and nation generates an inter-American gothic anxiety" (78). At the heart of his critique is the notion that the two Americas are deeply connected by the questions surrounding racial and cultural others, and the events that shape their confrontations. Thus, Alemán argues that in the case of a text such as *Calavar*, the history of the conquest of the Aztec empire "haunts" the real events that were transpiring between Mexico and the United States during the 1830s. In an inspired move, Alemán riffs on the notion of "'inter-American' studies," where the prefix "inter" comes to mean not "between" but "to bury," in order to "emphasize the idea that the presence of the other in the nation is 'that which is concealed and kept out of sight' but always felt as a haunting history that must be excavated" (79).[23] I share with Alemán this insistence on haunting as that transnational, transcultural anxiety of the tensions that are occluded, but nevertheless palpable within the space of a given American nation. He is also right to let the ghost out of the prison-house of the haunted mansion of Gothic lore and into a more complicated nexus of hemispheric narrative relations. In *Ghost-Watching American Modernity*, however, I take issue with the ubiquity of the Gothic and its adjacent terminologies for a number of reasons, given my principal interest in finding ways to relocate the ghost and haunting within its specificity, and through discussions of literary form as well as of simultaneity. The Gothic, as it has been understood by genre studies, is a versatile genre embedded in the idea of the domestic, the familial, and the microcosm of the region. As I have argued elsewhere, the boundaries of the Gothic have long been traced through applications of psychoanalytic theory, and the ghost has continuously come to represent the reactivation and repetition of past traumas (what in Freudian terms is the "repetition compulsion"), and the unwanted return of the repressed.[24] We should ask, however, whether the only possible reading of the haunting presence of the "other" in any given hemispheric American text must refer to vocabularies that center on ideas of genre and psychoanalysis. We should also question whether there are sites where we may read for a more "naked" ghost that can be stripped of the languages of repetition and the trappings of generic conventions. If a disciplinary intervention that seeks to add new layers of textuality to the already burgeoning field of hemispheric American studies returns to conceptions of genre and psychoanalysis to explain how past histories are activated to reflect the haunted sense of our present(s), then we need to observe how American narrators are capable of crafting ghosts as agents of that which is yet to be fulfilled. In their introduction to a special 2003 edition of *Modern Fiction Studies* on the "trans-American imaginary," Paula M. Moya and Ramón Saldívar commend the search for a history that can account for the past of hemispheric relations but can look to the future as well. In the chapters that follow, I suggest a number of ways in which haunting can indicate how American authors write spaces that are in the process of being transformed, rather than simply describe locations where the past has been interred.

Because I use a hemispheric lens to discuss how haunting can link dissimilar literatures across the Americas, I should like to clarify some matters of corpus selection. Other scholars have discussed some of the works I analyze, in terms of haunting, memory, and hemispheric critique (most notably, Rulfo's *Pedro Páramo*, which is analyzed in both Cohn's and Zamora's monographs, and of course José Martí, who has been such a seminal figure in the development of this field of inquiry).[25] Many other figures discussed in *Ghost-Watching American Modernity*, however, have not often been placed in hemispheric company (e.g., Henry James, Clint Eastwood, and Felisberto Hernández). Some readers may be wondering why I have selected this particular group of authors while letting go of others. One particular question the reader may ask is why I have decided to go without figures the likes of Edgar Allan Poe, William Faulkner, Gabriel García Márquez, and Toni Morrison, all such excellent choreographers of haunting. I will briefly respond to these questions of selection. On one hand, much attention has already been paid to Poe, Faulkner, and Morrison and their haunted (often, "Gothic") landscapes. These authors are inherently important in this discussion, and the bountiful criticism on them has already begun a hauntology of the U.S. South. Teresa Goddu devotes a chapter and more to Poe in *Gothic America*, and J. Gerald Kennedy and Lilliane Weissberg have put together *Romancing the Shadow* (2001) to discuss matters of race, haunting, and the cultures of antebellum America in Poe's work. One need only look at the impressive collections put together by Lois Parkinson Zamora and Wendy B. Faris (*Magical Realism*), and Deborah Cohn and Jon Smith (*Look Away!*) to notice the preeminence of

Faulkner's and Morrison's positions in discussions of hemispheric American literature, not to mention their importance within discussions of the neo-gothic. Given their ubiquity and importance, there are moments when these two figures will be incorporated in my discussion, but they will not be central to the development of the following chapters. The reasons why I am not including Gabriel García Márquez will become evident in Chapter 1, namely that although I want to give attention to a different grouping of authors and their invocations of haunted landscapes, I am also trying to think of ghosts outside of the genre of magical realism. Even though this book does not claim to be a survey of all literatures of haunting across the Americas, I think there is room and the moment is right to establish other, different comparisons while reading them within the rich conceptual and historical framework of literary space. Although it may be unsurprising to the reader that I use Rulfo, my comparative readings of Martí's and James's chronicles of U.S. life within my canon constitute an entirely fresh take on hemispheric American haunting. These are well-known authors who are at center stage in discrete discussions of the American hemisphere (Rulfo and Martí) and analyses of haunting (James and Rulfo), but they have not often been read together in this way. But then again, the same amount of recognition has not been afforded to writers such as Bierce (whom I have looked at, however briefly, in the opening pages of the book), Felisberto Hernández, or even the eccentric film director Alejandro Jodorowsky.

All these authors are standing at a crossroads or on boundaries between national territories, genres, literary movements, and aesthetic tendencies. Martí and James comment on the U.S. landscapes before them, neither of them feeling as insiders would within the spaces that they represent on the page. Martí's chronicle writing and James's own account of his journey back to his native land outgrow the idea of a single literary genre. Eastwood and Jodorowsky, filming in deserts in the U.S. West in the 1970s over a century after the Mexican War (before which those deserts belonged to Mexico), deconstruct the cinematic Western at a time when the genre itself was undergoing a crisis and, we could add, its first death. Juan Rulfo and Felisberto Hernández—two writers whom so many others, from García Márquez to Julio Cortázar, claim as forebears—are in many ways solitary figures in a mapping of Spanish American artistic communities, standing as they do outside any particular literary vanguard group, but whose depictions of haunted landscapes are nevertheless at the forefront of formal and thematic innovation in the realm of Latin American literature of the twentieth century.

Although these authors have not been commonly read alongside one another, they nevertheless show consonances in how they write and/or film space as haunted. In addition, as I will explain in greater detail below, they come from different generic traditions, and I intend to move beyond period, linguistic, and generic boundaries. This is because I want to give primacy to haunting as a diversified experience of space, more than as a certain category of literature. Looking at them outside the scope of genre, there are times when I suggest how these authors themselves provide commentaries and critiques on genre (e.g., how James may be producing a reevaluation of frontier tales and early American travel writing in "The Jolly Corner"). But at the center of my discussion is a consideration of the pervasive anxiety shared by these authors about how to represent and occupy American *space* within the context and conditions of modernization. As a category, haunted location provides a nodal point for the intersection of different genres, complicating the borders of familiar categories such as the Gothic and magical realism.

In my efforts to read ghosts and haunting from a hemispheric American body of work, many of the quotes from literary texts in this book are treated bilingually. Given that the book is devoted to close reading of literary and critical texts from different locations in the Spanish- and English-speaking Americas, I include the original passages from texts written in Spanish. This way the reader is given access to the stylistic nuances intended by the authors that can so often be missed in translations. Although I offer published translations for most of the works cited, I have provided my own translations for some texts written in Spanish, those for which the English translations are nonexistent or have proven elusive (the sources of all published translations are cited in the endnotes). Even though this book does not focus on the histories of how texts are translated within the American hemisphere, it nevertheless strongly adheres to an understanding of these literatures as loci of linguistic as well as technical diversity.

From Theory's Garments to the Naked Ghost: A Second Disciplinary Question

Why ghosts, and why now? As expressed in my discussion of Luckhurst's critique of the "spectral turn" after the publication of Derrida's *Specters of Marx* above, reading haunting has become a popular academic enterprise in the past decades, and it is impossible not to wonder why. The fascination with the phantasmagoric elements of culture, heralded by Walter Benjamin's prophetically suggestive work in the first decades of the twentieth century, has spawned a great number of texts tracing the histories and multiple manifestations of haunting in photography, film, literature, and beyond. In the realm of critical theory, beyond deconstruction, the spectral has become a common signifier to explore issues of trauma and recurrence. Andreas Huyssen has made a list of "master-signifiers of the 1990s" that have become useful within a current academic field which we can call here a "traumatology": Some examples are "the abject and the uncanny, all of which have to do with repression, specters, and a present repetitively haunted by the past."[26] Huyssen expresses his dissatisfaction with the proliferation of these terms, as their insistence on continuing repetition engenders no particular way forward or out of trauma. What he proposes instead is a reading and understanding of productive memory in the arts, where it does not "collapse into trauma," a move that, in turn, would mark remembering "too exclusively in terms of pain, suffering, and loss. It would deny human agency and lock us into repetition." "Memory," he writes, "whether individual or generational, political or public, is always more than only the prison house of the past" (8). Huyssen's reflections on the preconceptions with which we analyze history's effect on the cultural imaginary pronounce our current need for readings that elucidate not only how we look to the past for answers about our present but also how we can set into motion a productive, and collective, sense of haunting in the present.

One could argue that one exercise in productive memory is Avery Gordon's prismatic *Ghostly Matters* (1997; second edition 2008).[27] Gordon's successful book has been a welcome addition to the canon of ghost studies, as it suggests an array of methodological pathways through which to apprehend issues of haunting. It owes much to Derrida's concept of "hauntology" (a new perspective, or ontology, that takes into account the relationship we have with the past and future specters that surround us, which Colin Davis describes as symptomatic of the "ethical turn of deconstruction").[28] *Ghostly Matters* is a disciplinary intervention as much as it is a performance of this critical communion with ghosts. On one level, Gordon espouses interdisciplinarity, given that haunting "is a generalizable social phenomenon of great import" that requires the writer to acquire the languages and methodologies from different quarters (7). On another, she applies her affirmation on the radically different "way of knowing" that is haunting, by performing conversations with her subjects of study. An illustration of this can be found in her chapter on Sabina Spielrein (chapter 1), a student of Freud's engaged with the exploration of the uncanny and who died during World War II. Gordon includes a paragraph where she writes/speaks to the long-absent Sabina, as a way of practicing what she preaches—that is, to converse with ghosts rather than treat them as other: "Dear Sabina, I'm uneasy about using your story, or the story of the place you were between, as a pretext for speaking about methodology and other matters, about needing or seeming to need a dead woman to enliven matters" (59). The method is an innovative one and could potentially be called "productive" along the lines of what Huyssen is promoting.

However, Gordon's style has the capacity to alienate readers (one critic literally notes its *unheimlich* quality when she writes that she is "not at all at home with [Gordon's] book"), although ravishing others.[29] Like *Specters of Marx*, *Ghostly Matters* offers an expansive definition of haunting that stretches beyond the individual subject. It offers us such definitions of haunting as "transformative recognition" (8) or, in her introduction to the second edition, "an animated state in which a repressed or unresolved social violence is making itself known, sometimes very directly, sometimes very obliquely" (xvi). The underside of this throbbing definition of haunting—one that is able to read across genres and media, from photography to literature—is that it incorporates multiple realms of theory (from historical materialism to structuralism and psychoanalysis) to produce a very redemptive, palliative but ultimately unmanageable conception of the ghost. "Haunting," Gordon writes, "always harbors the violence, the *witchcraft* and *denial* that made it, and the *exile of our longing*, the utopian" (207). It is these intersections of the magical and antidotal with the discussions of histories of the Middle Passage and the Dirty War in Argentina, as introduced in Toni Morrison's *Beloved* (1987) and Luisa Valenzuela's *Como en la guerra* (1977), that become rather more difficult to process. Gordon does a magnificent review of theorists such as Adorno, Horkheimer, and Benjamin, all of whom address the difficult-to-pinpoint phenomena that escape materialist and historiographic explanation, and seems to construct an architecture of haunting out of their own suggestive pronouncements. In this way, haunting comes to mean a whole host of things, from "profane illumination" (Benjamin) to "sensuous knowledge" (Marx). This multiplication of meanings is essentially problematic. Judith Richardson rightly warns that Gordon's text "hovers in rarefied literary and theoretical spheres . . . connect[ing] ghosts to issues of broad significance."[30] As one of the germinal texts published in the 1990s about the importance of reconsidering haunting as a worthy and diversified category for study, *Ghostly Matters* should be considered the culmination of an inquiry into the possibilities of hauntology, one that needs to continue to be revised, reconsidered, and debated. To me, the question of the naked ghost, the one that lives underneath the garments of theory, hovers over Gordon's text, for what would Gordon's ghosts look like without the variegated layers of theories with which she has cloaked them? Does the ghost continue to be located in the site of its emergence or does it decamp to a theoretical sphere? Although it may seem impossible for an academic writer to completely forgo the use of any theoretical apparatus, it nevertheless seems a productive exercise to move in the opposite direction and strip our readings of any given set of preconceptions as a way of seeing the ghost afresh, bringing it back to the drama of its apparition.

Location seems to be a key word in the search for a way out of a reading of haunting that makes ghosts more elusive than they already are. Judith Richardson has called for a reading of ghosts that "touch[es] ground."[31] In her book on ghost stories from the Hudson River Valley, she effectively explores "how hauntings rise from and operate in particular, everyday worlds." She sets out to raise arguments "from the ground up, cordoning off a territory and a stretch of time, and examining hauntings as they work *in place*" (4). Richardson's work, to my mind, marks a decisive step forward in the direction of studying the cultural manifestations of haunting in a productively historic manner. By focusing on the ghost stories specific to the area of the Hudson Valley in New York, she explores—through archive and without using psychoanalytic or trauma theories—how narratives of haunting adapt and respond to the generational, historical issues of "territorial possession," "cultural conflict," and "community formation" (7). Thus, by holding the ghost in place, as it were, Richardson is able to explore how, from one generation to the next, haunting comes to tell the important stories of belonging and "possessions" (a word that carries several meanings in her book) that inhabit a place. Significantly, Richardson's space-focused project is a conscious new stage in the critical readings of haunting. She intentionally corrects other scholarship that has attempted to explain ghosts and haunting through an inordinate amount of theoretical lenses. She reminds us that ghosts, and haunting, are embedded in our ways of telling stories about locations, thus affecting how we narrativize our relationships with a given place. Whereas Richardson looks at how new versions of haunting emerge in the specific location of the Hudson Valley, my aim is spatially more expansive (given not only my hemispheric focus but also the organization of my chapters according to urban, desert, or frontier spaces). In addition, although Richardson's project is based on folklore surrounding haunted locales, my corpus is not only linguistically and culturally but also generically more diverse. This conjunction of style, site, and historical moment when telling a story of haunting constitutes a different critical approach to the issue of ghosts in literature and film.

Genre: A Third Disciplinary Question

Ghost-Watching American Modernity crosses not only period but generic boundaries as well, in order to prove how questions of haunting have much to do with more pervasive crises of perception that abound in any literary or cinematic format, than to the strictures of generic composition. As I have been explaining above, ghosts have often been construed as identifiable markers of particular genres in the realm of literary criticism. When we think of the problems of genre, we are reminded of Derrida's important question about the classic genres of essay and novel: "Can one identify a work of art, of whatever sort, but especially a work of discursive art, if it does not bear the mark of a genre, if it does not signal or mention it or make it remarkable in any way?"[32] If we take Derrida's prompt, and apply it to conceptions of subgenres within a hemispheric American context, the question often becomes, "can we identify an American ghost story as something other than magical, other than Gothic?" For, what is the place of the ghost story in a national canon?

As I explore at length in Chapter 1, the case of American ghosts is both interesting and complicated. Where in the United States literary canon ghosts have commonly been studied within the rubric of the Gothic genre, in Latin America the trend has been to place them within the catalogue of magical realism's many marvelous and, problematically, culturally different occurrences. In *Gothic America*, for example, Teresa Goddu traces the history of the Gothic genre within U.S. literature, a trajectory of inclusion and exclusion where the "historically belated" gothic—"belated" in comparison with British literary history—has been sized up against the more favored and avowedly "*American*" genre of romance. Thus, a body of literature that Goddu describes as "transgressive" and "extremely mutable" is nevertheless relentlessly subject to a classification aimed at stabilizing the gothic as a definite genre.[33] To even mention genre, as Derrida points out and Goddu reiterates, means simultaneously to announce a "limit" and a "contamination," what the former calls the paradox of "degenerescent self-engendering" (74). This means that the identification of a genre always and already announces the impossibility of retaining its exclusivity and integrity. Issues of literary form and the regional contribute even further to the problems surrounding generic definition. In the context of the southern Gothic, Goddu remarks that "even when authors such as Edgar Allan Poe or periods such as the twentieth-century Southern Renaissance are associated with the gothic, they reveal the difficulty of defining the genre in national terms: the American gothic is most recognizable as a regional form" (3). This tendency to recognize a genre as in some way relating to a particular place should alert us to a tension between two very large areas of belonging: a literary generalization and a regional sense of place. This is not to say that the two categories—regionalism and genre—do not work together to denote the tenors and styles in which a story about a given place can be told. The larger question I want to raise by using my corpus of writers is whether a ghost in a piece of literature or film should always be described as proof that a certain genre, or subgenre, has manifested itself. As I hope to establish in the chapters of *Ghost-Watching American Modernity* as in the latter part of this introduction, we should be careful of using genre allocation as a way of explaining away a given (moment in

a) text, of closing up the circle of meaning in a work that begs to leave a difficult question open.

Let me now turn to some questions related to the classic genres (e.g., essay, novel, drama) and the inherently trans-generic composition of this book: I analyze short stories (James's "The Jolly Corner" and Hernández's "El acomodador"); a novel (*Pedro Páramo* by Rulfo); chronicles by José Martí and James's *American Scene*, a travel narrative; post-Western films by Eastwood and Jodorowsky; Du Bois's *Souls of Black Folk* and Sarmiento's *Facundo*, two essayistic, yet ostensibly multi-generic compositions. Haunting, I will argue, pervades this constellation of narratives in distinctive ways, for which it would be misguided to assign labels according to any given subgenre. Thinking in larger terms, they are organized according to very diverse generic formats. Some readers may raise the question of why I do not employ certain terminologies that at first glance would be very useful in a formal study of ghosts, as mine claims to be. One such term, which can be very useful to describe the spatiotemporal node that is a ghost, is the chronotope, as explained by Mikhail Bakhtin.[34] The chronotope is the temporal-spatial structure through which, according to Janice Best, "the symbolic and metaphorical patterns of a work" are advanced.[35] In *The Dialogic Imagination*, Bakhtin identifies major chronotopes (genres like novel and epic), and minor chronotopes, which denote specific intersections of time and space (e.g., the road). It serves as a structural function of a novel— it describes, for example, the temporal and spatial points of encounter that push forward the action of a novel. In this sense, the chronotope manifests itself quite blatantly and openly within the structure of a novel, or novelistic text: As Bakhtin would have it, it has markers and abides by a certain set of conventions. The chronotope is thus tied to an idea of genre. Although it would work to think of the ghost as an example of a minor chronotope, or chronotopic motif, which is a more localized narrative phenomenon, it would nevertheless need to be tied to the generic, or major, chronotope in which it appears. Given that my corpus is so diverse, Bakhtin's model would prove unhelpful here, as my aim is precisely to disentangle the ghost from discussions of genre. Moreover, it would seem unproductive to want to apply the label to my explorations of ghosts and the action of haunting as crises of perception, which I argue need to be read precisely outside of the rubric of generic conventions.

Answerable Haunting and Simultaneity:
Theories to Read the Ghost

My caution regarding the use of the chronotope as a model for reading the ghost does not mean that I will forgo the use of Bakhtinian conventions altogether. There are other Bakhtinian concepts that I employ in *Ghost-Watching American Modernity* that I consider extremely useful for the configuration of my own argument about haunting and the experience of space. Two decades before he wrote the essays that would constitute *The Dialogic Imagination*, Bakhtin began his career with a short essay that appeared in December 1919 titled "Art and Answerability." In this piece that predates his future preoccupation with the structures of novelistic form, Bakhtin works on a development of a neo-Kantian philosophy of art and morality, and the subject's position as a rational self encased within moral laws. Answerability, in this first essay, as in the unfinished *Toward a Philosophy of the Act*, which followed two years later, has to do with the moral relation between aesthetics and cognition of the world. A moral aesthetics would need to be participative, and would try hard not to conflate what Graham Pechey explains as the aesthetic "*product*" (the work of art) and the "answerable *act* of such seeing."[36] Bakhtin expresses a preoccupation with the inherently "guilty" relationship between art and life, outlining thus the responsibility that an aesthetic rendition has to the everyday life being represented. It is worth quoting the 1919 essay at length here to illustrate this call to mutual indebtedness between being in the world and the aesthetic.

> Art is too self-confident, audaciously self-confident, and too high-flown, for it is in no way bound to answer for life. And, of course, life has no hope of ever catching up with art of this kind. . . . When a human being is in art, he is not in life, and conversely. There is no unity between them and no inner interpenetration within the unity of an individual person.
>
> But what guarantees the inner connection of the constituent elements of a person? Only the unity of answerability. I have to answer with my own life for what I have experienced and understood in art, so that everything I have experienced and understood would not remain ineffectual in my life. But answerability entails guilt, or liability to blame. It is not only mutual answerability that art and life must assume, but also mutual liability to blame. . . . The true sense, and not the self-proclaimed sense, of all the old arguments about the interrelationship of art and life, about the purity of art, etc.—that is, the real aspiration behind all such arguments—is nothing more than the

mutual striving of both art and life to make their own tasks easier, to relieve themselves of their own answerability. For it is certainly easier to create without answering for life, and easier to live without any consideration for art.

Art and life are not one, but they must come united in myself—in the unity of my answerability.[37]

The critique of the "self-confidence" of art when it turns its back on life raises the question of what an attainable form of representation that can link experience and aesthetic representation *is*. This is important in the context of this book, because I am interested in exploring not only the ways in which authors approach haunting as a stylization of their everyday spaces, but also because answerability is deeply linked to a notion of the act of creation as embedded within the specific historic moment of its enunciation.

In addition, I am drawn to Bakhtin's concept of answerability, as delineated in his works from this period, because—within a much more fluid context that explores the relationships between art and its object, rather than generic conventions—it gives us a modern framework with which to approach *doubt* in the figures of the characters in a work of fiction (e.g., the dead in *Pedro Páramo*, Spencer Brydon in "The Jolly Corner") and the implied observer in a chronicle or essay (e.g., José Martí and Henry James), and the *incompleteness of experience* that becomes evident in the observation of haunting.[38] These two units have much to do with my own understanding of haunting as it occurs within the texts analyzed in the following chapters. Haunting, as I will explain, is linked to doubt because it depends on that crisis of perception expressed in questions surrounding a landscape ("what is there that I cannot see, but I nevertheless sense is there?"). Doubt is also a reminder of the unfinished business that is experience and its necessary open-endedness: It indicates a site of action that does not know its outcome or even its purpose. Doubt, Bakhtin reminds us, is "the basis of our life as effective deed-performing" and is therefore quite the opposite from a theorization of life, because to theorize is to imbue an event with a unitary meaning or "truth of the world."[39] Again, I find this to be a useful model with which to understand haunting as part of American landscapes affected by ongoing modernization. The subjects represented in the texts analyzed throughout this book are constantly questioning how different realities are infiltrating, and haunting, their own perceived landscapes, reducing the sense of certainty about the world that surrounds them. This tentativeness about one's location—the hauntedness of this perception of the everyday world—could well be described along the lines of Bakhtin's notion of "Being-as-event." An expression of "being" is intensely historic, in that it is dependent on the structure (or "architectonic") of location, of tone, or enunciation, and the moment of utterance. In this sense, I could argue that the ghost emerges as that which has a meaning in the past but that emerges again, reopening the question of its purpose and its meaning. In speaking of answerability and the idea of Being-as-event, we are thus open to a discussion of haunting in its proleptic potential.

Another term that will keep reemerging throughout *Ghost-Watching American Modernity* is *simultaneity*. In my comparative analysis of Martí and James in Chapter 3, for example, I discuss the form of their anxious contemplations of a multiethnic U.S. geography that they are having difficulty grasping in its wholeness. I describe these as "landscapes of modern simultaneity," because I find that at the heart of these two particular crises of perception is an awareness of the difficulty of accounting responsibly for those other subjects living beyond these writers' own visual horizons of comprehension. James's anxieties in *The American Scene* are mirrored in his work of fiction, "The Jolly Corner," where the repatriated Spencer Brydon (who has returned to New York after living for decades in Europe) imagines his ghostly double living a life simultaneous to his in his childhood home. I argue that the concept of simultaneity is an admission of modern haunting and ghostliness par excellence, because, although grounding one observer in a specific landscape, it forces an imagination of others in other locations.

We often think of simultaneity in temporal terms, but we should also look at it as an event in which two spatialities are confronted with each other. Although my aim is to explore this phenomenon at the level of literary and cinematic form, it is worth mentioning the more philosophical implications of a theory of simultaneity as it emerged in a period of radical modernization in the sciences, when relativity constituted a major shift in thinking about the experience of the self in the universe. From a different quarter in the post-Kantian (*Lebensphilosophie*) tradition, in 1922 Henri Bergson arrived at the problem of duration and different consciousnesses when pondering a single and "universal" physical time. The subject, according to Bergson, perceives duration as an "unfolding of the universe," where different consciousnesses may meet or overlap "at the fringes of their fields of outer experience."[40] However, underwritten in this concept of duration and simultaneity is the idea of distance, and incompatibility of perception. In other words, regardless of how much a subject may be able to control her or his spatial and temporal location, the locations of others are constantly moving, so that distance is understood in terms of "*degrees of impossibility.*"

In the system in which I live and which I mentally immobilize by conceiving as a system of reference, I directly measure a time that is mine and my system's; it is this measurement which I inscribe in my mathematical representation of the universe for all that concerns my system. But in immobilizing my system, I have set the others moving, and I have set them moving variously. They have acquired different speeds. The greater their speed, the further *removed* they are from my immobility. (53)

In this passage, Bergson is pointing toward a lack of a *shared* perspective of subjects inhabiting their present moments and locations, and which are progressively shifting their positions. And this, as I will be arguing, is what *haunts* the authors that I am studying: Spatially, they express the lack of conjunction in different views of, say, a national space. Thus, as I will analyze in Sarmiento's *Facundo* and Du Bois's *Souls of Black Folk* (Chapter 4), for example, the vistas of one individual—socially and racially constituted—are starkly different from those of another. It is in this divergence of perspectives within the supposedly unitary space of a nation that haunted space is demarcated.

Chapters 2, 3, and 4 are organized according to the idea of landscapes that coexist simultaneously (although not often in synchrony) in the Americas—the desert, the city, and the imagined borders that have come to define modern national belonging and unbelonging. Although these chapters are devoted to texts dealing with geographic spaces, I devote Chapter 1 ("Unsolving Hemispheric Mystery") to a discussion of the theoretical location that ghosts have occupied in literary studies. Looking closely at the interventions of authors such as Jorge Luis Borges, Alejo Carpentier, and Flannery O'Connor as well as contemporary literary critics, I discuss how ghosts have been assessed in texts from North and South, and how we may move toward a more honest (and naked) reading of their haunted specificity. In line with the transgeneric quality of the canon discussed in Chapters 2 to 4, my explorations of the theoretical treatment of ghosts in this chapter reflect my interest in carefully studying the ghost's location in a variety of discourses, be they fictional or otherwise. Indeed, my efforts to ghost-watch throughout diverse textual forms relate to my interests in promoting an understanding of close reading as an enterprise that should include critical interventions as well, given the momentum with which ghosts and haunting are entering our analytical discourses.

Thus, throughout the first chapter, I engage with a critical body of work, inquiring where and how we stand within a number of interrogations about literature, haunting, and space. In this sense, Chapter 1 is indeed a panorama of the critical scene of the multiple disciplinary fields that this project addresses. It sets the tone for what follows throughout the rest of the book, but it is also adamant in its search for new departures from the critical work that is available to us. As I mention above, similarly to the way the Gothic has found acceptance as the genre and mode of a southern U.S. literature (in authors from Edgar Allan Poe to William Faulkner) in late-twentieth-century criticism, we can say that magical realism has become the most widely accepted genre by which to measure Latin American literature. As mentioned above, Lois Parkinson Zamora established a hemispheric literary connection between authors north and south of the U.S.-Mexico border by making the case for a connection between magical realism as a genre and the already-established genre of the romance, which is traceable in U.S. literature to early authors such as Nathaniel Hawthorne. By solidifying the literary relationship this way, she is able to draw comparisons between ghosts in texts emerging from different traditions and cultural spaces through the literary commonplace of genre studies. Taking issue with this particular approach, I pose a question about magical realism: Can we consider it a uniform genre, and if so, is the analysis of the ghostly in Latin American literature possible only by embedding it within the realm of the marvelous and magical real?

Carefully looking at foundational authors of theories of the marvelous real and the twentieth-century southern Gothic such as Alejo Carpentier and Flannery O'Connor, respectively, as well as studies of genre such as Tzvetan Todorov's *The Fantastic* (1975), I scrutinize the ways in which we have studied ghosts in literature, and their uneasy attachment to any given genre. I propose to look at the ghost in its singularity, to locate it within a more expansive conception of hemispheric movements in the nineteenth and twentieth centuries, and to focus on the creation of space and landscape in pan-American literature of this transformative time.

Organized according to different spatialities, the rest of the chapters in *Ghost-Watching American Modernity* move from considerations of how each of these locations have been represented in American literatures of the nineteenth and twentieth centuries, to focused comparative readings of specific texts. Chapter 2 ("Desert Mournings") explores the work of apparently dissimilar twentieth-century authors—Juan Rulfo and Clint Eastwood—and their imaginations of ghost towns in Mexico and the U.S. West. Long-lost communities cast away in forgotten and recondite deserted wildernesses, ghost towns are exemplary sites of modernization read spatially: They are the remaining vestiges of booming enterprises and populations that have been transformed by the fluctuations of industry and migration in the American landscape. Importantly, however, they are spaces that exist simultaneously to the "successes" of modernity, and the crafting of their stories necessarily involves a parallel evocation of lively boom and unquiet afterlife. In this chapter, I read the dialectic correspondence between desert sites and the events of desertion by examining how both Rulfo and Eastwood explore the unmaking of communities in their respective configurations of ghost towns, north and south. Chapter 3, "Urban Indiscretions," is devoted to city spaces. It begins by offering a contrapuntal racial and spatial history of the development of American cities in the nineteenth and twentieth centuries in hemispheric literary imaginations of travel and regionalism, and how authors—among them Domingo Sarmiento, José Martí, and Henry James—write the city while envisioning simultaneous spaces made invisible by the multifarious fluctuations of modernity. I argue that these authors' literary projections of city spaces, explored in the "heterogeneous" form of the chronicle (to quote Julio Ramos's description of this type of writing), demonstrate an insistence on perceiving urban locales in terms of those other spaces that are not seen, yet are nevertheless present, in the domain of a country. This is a significant corrective to the now familiar argument that modernity needs to be read through the textual rubric of fragmentation. Arguing that the invention of haunted urban narratives answers to the need to account for the multiple landscapes of modernity, "Urban Indiscretions" culminates in a comparative reading of how selected fictions by Henry James and the Uruguayan author Felisberto Hernández dramatize the "indiscreet" desire to illuminate an alternative modernity through a play of a massive spatial imagination and the manipulation of urban interiors. Finally, "Transnational Shadows" (Chapter 4) moves from a discussion of regionalism to a wider contemplation of what it means for a nation to contain the shadowlands of a haunted frontier. Around the time when Karl Marx and Friedrich Engels were writing about the border-setting Mexican-American War of 1847, they translate the Hegelian sentiment that the Americas were, as of that time, the land of the "future," haunted by no menacing ghosts, darkened by no ominous shadows. As strategic metaphors, however, shadows pervasively haunt hemispheric American literature, noting thus the already prevailing presence of a disquieting past. This final chapter is a comparative exploration of the works of Domingo F. Sarmiento and W. E. B. Du Bois. Their works—*Facundo* (1845) and *Souls of Black Folk* (1903)—are read as reconsiderations of the limits of nation and belonging through the use of a trope of shadows. I argue that, by figuratively placing the shadow over the troubled national landscapes of Argentina and the United States in these particular times, both authors offer a topographically inflected account of the ghosts of unresolved racial strife and barbarism that haunt their civic imagination.

1 / Unsolving Hemispheric Mystery

In this chapter, I explore the impasse between the haunting of art and the art of haunting, its critical history and implications. I am particularly interested in seeing how genre—the delineation of artistic production into historical, ideological, and formal classifications—has come to haunt haunting. Given my interest in accounting for the links between haunting, landscape, and a hemispheric American aesthetic and critical imagination, a substantial part of this chapter focuses on how ghosts have been explained according to the logic of certain genres or subgenres. These genres and subgenres have in turn been employed to describe certain national and geographic conditions. More specifically, as we will see throughout this chapter, they have even been described as the preferred aesthetic conditions of particular regions within the Americas. This first act of ghost-watching thus involves an observation of the critical-literary spaces that harbor haunting presences, so that we can begin asking whether and how these critical landscapes have done justice to their appearance in literature and film.

Haunting is, without a doubt, enmeshed in the telling and retelling of mystery; the moment the verb is uttered as well as the moment a ghost comes on the scene, things have become strange and more than likely uncomfortable. Invariably, the stories of haunting signal a limit to our comprehension, or they supplant our understanding of reality with what Philip Weinstein calls "the loom" of another, and unforeseen, history.[1] Immediately we try to make sense of ghosts, to impose reason on the unreasonable, in order to restore a sense of "life" as we know it. We call these apparitions "supernatural," "fantastic," "marvelous," and we attempt to order them, so as to furnish that space that has been breached between the "realistic" and the artful. Before engaging in readings of specific instances where narrative presents us with a haunting, we must look at the complicated intersections of the telling and explaining of mystery (and haunting), as well as the ways in which these have been categorized. This will lead to an exploration of how these intersections have often become entangled in an impasse between history and creativity that necessarily will take us to an analysis of how we can begin to ask a different set of questions to address this sphere of the unbelievable and mysterious.

In her essay "Some Aspects of the Grotesque in Southern Fiction" (1960), Flannery O'Connor makes a distinction between the writer of reality (the one who writes about how natural, social, and economic forces shape lives) and the writer of mystery, whom she qualifies as the "writer who believes that our life is and will remain essentially mysterious"; the writer of mystery "looks upon us as beings existing in a created order to whose laws we freely respond," so that "what he sees on the surface will be of interest to him only as he can go through it into an experience of mystery itself" (816). She adds, about this writer of mystery: "His kind of fiction will always be pushing its own limits outward toward the limits of mystery, because for this kind of writer, the meaning of a story does not begin except at a depth where the adequate motivation and the adequate psychology and the various determinations have been exhausted." This writer writes about what "we don't understand" (816).

O'Connor explains that these two kinds of writers coexist (the "naturalist" and the writer of mystery), but there is a different affect for the writer who can no longer base himself on an idea of scientific truth or a psychological explanation that can rid the mind of an impenetrable question. As she argues, explanations of what is realistic, or close to what is easily perceptible, and what is mysterious, have been reaching points of exhaustion for a while. One only needs to look to writers such as Edgar Allan Poe and Nathaniel Hawthorne, who announce the limitations of reality in their stories and sketches early on in the nineteenth century. The word "adequate," which O'Connor uses in this passage to refer to the psychology that has been becoming more and more ineffectual for the mystery writer, is particularly interesting to me. I want to spin it into a different, yet parallel, direction. What is an "adequate" character or an "adequate" situation to write about in a story? Once you have reached the limits of what is "adequate," what situations and characters would you write about? On a large scale, what I am trying to address in this book is the question of the adequacy of ghosts in literary works that cut across received period boundaries between roughly 1850 and 1970. If a ghost is inserted in a story, novel, or essay, what is the author trying to achieve? Is s/he trying to produce a sense of fear, or an atmosphere where human existence is out of control, and there is no way to define what is alive and what is not? O'Connor, in her description of a "Christ-haunted" U.S. South, writes that ghosts "cast strange shadows" on literature: "It is interesting that as belief in the divinity of Christ decreases, there seems to be a preoccupation with Christ-figures in our fiction. What is pushed to the back of the mind makes its way forward somehow. Ghosts can be very fierce and instructive."[2] Later in the chapter, I discuss the negotiation of this Catholic faith and the belief in ghosts in literature, but my preliminary focus centers on O'Connor's idea of the "strangeness" of ghosts. O'Connor does not write fantastic or supernatural stories; her fiction uses the "concrete" by "the way of distortion" ("Grotesque," 816). She is, however, writing about a regional literature confronting history, a literature that often creates a distance between a writer and her/his audience, because the former will infuse life with something "wild" or freakish, although the latter has become a "tired" reader who "demands the redemptive act, that demands that what falls at least be offered the chance to be restored" (820). What O'Connor proposes is a literature that has no promise of restoration, because the history and space of the U.S. South, at the moment when she is writing, does not allow for this. The ghost-figure of Christ and the South in general are thus aligned in O'Connor's thesis of mystery, casting a shadow of strangeness and the unexplainable. If these figures are strange, then it means they are unsettling, and in being so they unsettle or shake the norms of what is possible in the act of writing.

How can we describe what happens in such a literature? The writer of mystery might begin describing something that appears to be an everyday experience, and then, when s/he finds that the description has reached an insurmountable limit, the decision is made that something else needs to happen. In this context, the writer might begin with a straight description of the setting or landscape and the characters, all looking much like those found in a "realistic" novel, but then there is a shift to the unexplainable.[3] The characters might be put in an unprecedented situation, and they will react to it in perhaps even more unexplainable ways. In the case of Flannery O'Connor's fiction, Hazel Motes (the suffering hero of *Wise Blood*, her 1952 novel) will wrap his torso in barbed wire to be "clean" of sin, to which his landlady will reply that, "it's not normal. It's like one of them gory stories, it's something that people have quit doing. . . . There's no reason for it." But, as Hazel replies, that problem and that torture nevertheless exist and have become visible. He replies, "They ain't quit doing it as long as I'm doing it" (224).

If we continue to think alongside O'Connor, writing about mystery is not just about writing whatever ugliness might be lurking underneath the surface of life; it is also about our apprehension of things that just happen, appear, and are, and that we must react to even if we lack guidance. The landlady's reaction to Hazel is representative of literary ghost sightings. She fights the idea of Hazel's mysterious and inscrutable sacrifice with a call to normalcy, but this does not prevent the tortured man from still existing in the room in her boardinghouse. As readers reading ghosts, we are all landladies, amazed that this incredible task has fallen on us, of figuring out just what to do with a wild situation that has spun out of control within the worlds that we thought we had made "normal."

As someone writing about the use of ghosts and questioning their usefulness in narrative, I have wrestled with the overflow of terminology that surrounds this scholarship of the unbelievable. Many of these terms—among which allegory, the uncanny, and the repressed are key nomenclatures—run into and at times uncomfortably struggle within considerations of genre, especially since many critics have made ghosts the exclusive property of a magical realist school in a Latin American and Caribbean context and the gothic school in the U.S. literary canon. (In film and literature, ghosts are also staples in the horror genre, which owes a lot to the gothic genre in its form, but which we must also consider in the context of a now multinational culture and industry of the "scary"). It would appear that ghosts haunt genre theory and genre haunts ghosts. For this reason, I would like to explore some of the problems surrounding these appropriations of the ghostly theme in order to propose a limit to classifications—or perhaps a disappropriation—of what seems to me to be a much more complex figure that should resist set lodging in any particular company. This will also lead me to a consideration of what it is that makes ghosts the subject of an anxiety of placement, especially in cultures where they are so pervasive, and where the word "haunting" has achieved the currency of a quotidian term used unquestioningly to point to the elusive or the immaterial, though without adequate scrutiny as to what that semantic pointing might formally or ethically entail. As we continue to domesticate the ghost (and haunting) in our everyday experiences, are we also trying to domesticate it by baptizing it into genre? Are we perhaps operating under the same anxieties as the landlady in *Wise Blood* in our own experience of literature, casting off certain strange occurrences that have no place anywhere else into the realms of "them gory stories"?

Disrupting, then, our assumption about literary poetics just as it disturbs the epistemologies of human perception, haunting poses questions as to what is accomplished by associating it with specific classifications or genres. In very crude terms, we must ask what classification into a specific genre accomplishes. How does a critical work that pronounces that a certain novel can become a bedfellow for a group of other novels move

a discipline forward? Certainly genre studies help us understand and discover connections (be they transthematic, transnational, or transhistoric),
origins, and genealogies, but what if these lines become forced into and
susceptible to historically unanchored prescriptions? Despite a pervasive
need to facilitate readers' conversations that reflect on the unsolitariness
of texts as a way to expand an understanding of literature that transcends
borders, what happens when this is done for the sake of an ungrounded
and at times irresponsible universalization of the themes put forth by a
single and specific work or author? I am not proposing that genre studies
have become ridden with a rigor mortis beyond avail; what I do want to
put into question are the ways in which critics engage in scholarship where
genre becomes a conclusion and classification their only mission. In order
to approach these questions from a range of perspectives, I look closely at
the scholarship surrounding the study of magical realism in the field of
Latin American literary studies in order to gauge the compatibility of different analytic motivations and preoccupations that inform our discernment of genre.

Faith in the Strange

Since its induction into the Latin American canon of defining terms
with Alejo Carpentier's famous prologue to his 1949 novel *El reino de este
mundo* (*Kingdom of This World*),[4] the *marvelous real* ["lo real maravilloso"] has avowed a (Latin) American exceptionality. When Carpentier
explains why the marvelous belongs so prominently to "our" America, he
justifies it in terms of an intersection of mythology with race, history, ontology, and to the (we suppose both topographic and literary) "virginity"
of the landscape: "Y es que, por la virginidad del paisaje, por la formación,
por la ontología, por la presencia fáustica del indio y del negro, por la revelación que constituyó su reciente descubrimiento, por los fecundos mes-
tizajes que propició, América está muy lejos de haber agotado su caudal
de mitologías" ["Because of the virginity of the land, our upbringing, our
ontology, the Faustian presence of the Indian and the black man, the revelation constituted by its recent discovery, its fecund racial mixing, America
is far from using up its wealth of mythologies"].[5] Carpentier's signature
use of the baroque sentence manages to include nearly all aspects of the
American condition in what is ultimately an invitation to write new stories about the continent. Throughout the essay, the author points out the
absence of an *"exhaustion"* of mythologies, as well as the American condition of not having *yet* "finished establishing . . . a retelling of cosmogonies"
(133–34). Roberto González Echevarría reads this as symptomatic of a re-
newed *mundonovista* movement, which "with greater or lesser militancy

and with the combined effort of figures with varying ideologies set out to define Latin America on its own terms and which actively endeavored to recover its past."[6]

Carpentier's vision is in many ways similar to Flannery O'Connor's interpretation of an exhaustion of psychology that can impel a fiction of mystery. Carpentier sees a continent that can provide enough mysteries to propel a new (yet unwritten) literature that homes in on the untrammeled mythologies of the Latin American and Caribbean context. Both O'Connor and Carpentier signal a representational limit where the psychological is not viable and where another, multivalent dimension is in turn beckoned. In fact, Carpentier's proposal in this essay is at many turns a rebuttal of the surrealist proposal of a literature that aims at representing the bewildering machinations of the human psyche. Carpentier accuses surrealist literature of being "a literary scheme" ["una artimaña literaria"] riddled with boring "well-known formulas" ["fórmulas consabidas"]. Wendy Faris and Lois Parkinson Zamora, in their introduction to Carpentier's essay in their volume on magical realism,[7] see these criticisms of the surrealist aesthetic as a denunciation of the conscription of the marvelous to the format of a manifesto. Quite paradoxically, however, Carpentier's essay itself very much resembles a manifesto with its politics of exclusivity that claim a total state of "the marvelous" throughout America. "¿Pero qué es la historia de América toda sino una crónica de lo real maravilloso?" ["What is the history of America if not a chronicle of the marvelous real?"] is his final persuasively rhetorical question.[8] The difference between this and Breton's statement lies in that, although the author of the *Surrealist Manifesto* proposed an introspective, self-reflexive cartography of the psyche, Carpentier's is an invitation to a representational discovery and colonization of a past history and a "virginal" landscape—an analysis that is *extroverted* and looking outside of the limits of the individual.

Another element that both Flannery O'Connor and Alejo Carpentier share in their respective explorations of the literature of bewilderment and strangeness is the functional importance of faith.[9] Though referring to entirely different applications of metaphysical systems, both writers see faith as a starting point for perception—a perception that will allow for represented situations to be seen in an altogether different light. In "The Fiction Writer and His Country," O'Connor writes of the privileged status of the Christian writer whose "belief in Christian dogma" secures a "respect for mystery."[10] Furthermore, in one of her letters from 1955, O'Connor writes that "a higher paradox confounds emotion as well as reason and there are long periods in the lives of all of us, and of the saints, when the truth as revealed by faith is hideous, emotionally disturbing, downright repulsive."[11] Thus, for O'Connor, reading and writing with a perspective of faith can have a disfiguring—though not disengaged from realistic—effect on a reality that is otherwise perceived disinterestedly (we recall her consideration, in her essay on the grotesque, of the "adequate psychology" that has been exhausted). Carpentier's "marvelous real" is there for anyone who can see it, but this "sensation" [*sensación*] can be accomplished only through a prefigured faith, which at one point he describes as being potentially "terrible" (132). The marvelous requires a "heightened spirit" ["una exaltación del espíritu"] that is capable of driving perception to a limit ["un estado límite"]. González Echevarría refers to this pronouncement as a Spenglerian "moment of faith" that precedes the "moment of reflexivity" evidenced in the European arts in the early twentieth century. (By the same token, I should add, it reflects Carpentier's indebtedness to the writings of Guillermo de Torre, who was one of the founders of *ultraísmo* in Spain. De Torre's groundbreaking *Literaturas europeas de vanguardia* (1925) proposed a revitalized definition of cosmopolitanism in the face of failed internationalism after the First World War.)[12] The idea of a sophisticated sense of faith to reassess the Americas raises a number questions: Who participates in this faith that Carpentier describes? In what ways could this privileged perception be transmitted and to whom? Is it a perspective that is best translated in a writing of reality or in fiction?

Stephanie Merrim, in her essay exploring the location and "intonation" of a wonder at the beginning of literary utterance that inevitably leads us into a difficult questioning of the histories of the American Souths, compares Carpentier's and O'Connor's uses of faith as ways to "predicate southern literature on the miracle that stands at the etymological root of the marvel (ad*mira*re)."[13] Merrim identifies a difference in gradation to this presupposed faculty: She qualifies O'Connor's vision as less "apocalyptic" than Carpentier's imperative belief in "the miracle." Merrim does not quite explain what she means in her use of the word "apocalyptic" and is perhaps distinguishing between these two authors in terms of levels of resignation to the world: Whereas in O'Connor faith is a privileged perspective of the individual that arrives gradually with experience of the world, Carpentier imposes on his reader an urgency to see the marvelous in the world. It would thus seem that Merrim is referring to O'Connor's positioning of the (Catholic) writer in a privileged position vis-à-vis the rest of the world, whereas Carpentier is calling for a generalized belief in the miraculous in reality (which, as I address above, Carpentier himself does not make entirely clear). However, Merrim returns to a leveling of these two perspectives when she states that

> the importance that both Carpentier and O'Connor ascribe to faith grounds their deeper realism in epistemology. That is to say, the

efficacy of marvelous or mysterious fiction depends on the belief—of those in the narrated world and hopefully of the reader—in the miraculous events that the text purveys. (326)

I would contend that the differences in Carpentier's and O'Connor's definitions of faith in the reader as in character need to be made more explicit. Although O'Connor is speaking of the specific faith in the more enclosed space of Christian dogma (Merrim herself writes that, for O'Connor, mystery entails "the descent of the Holy Spirit into daily lives," 326) and her fiction is centered on it, Carpentier's faith is an a priori that remains elusive, with a foggy and rather elite congregation.[14]

On the level of human perception, where one puts into question the identity of the perceiver of an unbelievable realm existing underneath a tenuous surface, this problematic faith poses an unsettling question about the directions in which the marvelous real and its avatar the magical realist genre can and should go. The farthest Carpentier delves into explaining the nature of this faith revolves around the "unexpected" act of happening upon the hidden mythologies and cosmogonies of the American space.

> Muchos se olvidan, con disfrazarse de magos a poco costo, que lo maravilloso comienza a serlo de manera inequívoca cuando surge de una inesperada alteración de la realidad (milagro), de una revelación privilegiada de la realidad, de una iluminación inhabitual o singularmente favorecedora de las inadvertidas riquezas de la realidad, percibidas con particular intensidad en virtud de una exaltación del espíritu que lo conduce a un modo de "estado límite." (131–32)

> [Many forget, although dressed up as cheap magicians, that the marvelous starts being unequivocally so when it emerges from an unexpected alteration of reality (the miracle), a privileged revelation of reality, from a nonhabitual or favorable illumination of the unanticipated riches of reality, perceived with a particular intensity by virtue of an exaltation of the spirit which drives to a sort of "limit state."]

Only in this state of "privileged" perception can one have access to the marvelous—and the ability to have access appears to be nothing short of a "miracle." From this troubling yet exclusive state of perceptual supremacy, the next logical step is to inquire how it will manifest itself and to which audience. This is an enormous question, undoubtedly, which González Echevarría addresses in a discussion of what I would call the "parallax views" of the marvelous real in Carpentier's figuration. I will quote the critic at length in order to provide a fuller illustration of his point.

To assume that the marvelous exists only in America is to adopt a spurious European perspective, since it is only from the other side that alterity and difference may be discovered—the same seen from within is homogeneous, smooth, without edges. The best efforts of well-intentioned academic criticism to use the label "magical realism" fall into this contradiction. The occultist tradition that reaches us from Romanticism may have some Latin American peculiarities, but not radically different characteristics. Perhaps one of these is precisely that writers such as Carpentier and Asturias have felt the need to proclaim magic to be here, attempting to evade the alienation of the European for whom magic is always there. But in this attempt there is a double or meta-alienation; it may very well be that magic is on this side, but we have to see it from the other side to see it as magic. What is particularly Latin American is the round trip, that utopia suspended between here and there—perpetual voyage charting a course to that always elusive Antilla. (*Pilgrim,* 128)

González Echevarría addresses the paradox of perception of the marvelous, although also pointing to the problematic appointment of the magical realist label to different cultural productions. The "round trip"[15] constitutes a weirdly irreconcilable displacement of something that is first claimed as autochthonous but then fails to be so as it travels into the territory of (self-) exoticization.

Sending Mystery to School

What becomes of the legacy of such a movement between realms of perception? Carpentier belittles Lautréamont's contribution to the field of fantastical letters by stating that he merely inspired an "ephemeral school of literature" (135), that is, surrealism, which is of course Carpentier's main bone to pick in the essay. However, Carpentier's vision of a new literature for Latin America—made *manifest(o)*, as I argued earlier, in the essayistic format of "Lo real maravillosamente americano"—has offered a justification and a name to a whole genre (magical realism) that at times seems to have become, through the prescriptions of literary critics as well as journalists, synonymous with Latin American literature as a whole. The questions left unresolved in Carpentier have proliferated and continued spinning out of cohesiveness as it has been conflated with magical realism, a literary genre that, even in 1977, González Echevarría describes as existing "in a theoretical vacuum" (108). The polarity between America and Europe that Carpentier established has been retained in order to maintain an idea of Latin American difference. Ángel Flores, in his seminal essay from

1955, "Magical Realism in Spanish American Fiction," makes no mention of Alejo Carpentier, but instead lists authors (including Borges, Bioy Casares, and Mallea), all "meticulous craftsmen," who mark the "inception of a genuinely Latin American fiction" that is "uniquely civilized, exciting, and, let us hope, perennial."[16] In his *The Dialectics of Our America*, José David Saldívar understands Carpentier's major quandary in his formulation of the marvelous real to be "how to write in a European language—with its Western systems of thought—about realities and thought structures never before seen in Europe."[17] Reminiscent of González Echevarría's idea of marvelous realism's obligatory "round trip," Saldívar is also aware of Carpentier's indebtedness to European schools of thought, but perceives them to be more of a springboard to an original and *mestizo* American expression.

At the present moment, however, the genre of magical realism and Carpentier's phenomenology of the marvelous real appear to be tearing at the seams of transcontinental application, their cultural and compositional specificity surrendered to an uncritically affirmative notion of its emancipatory potential. The proverbial "estado límite" that Carpentier dreamed of is still fraught with an irreconcilable tension between the realms of ideology and anthropology, mythology and realism, fiction and nonfiction, form and content. It is therefore no surprise that there has been a proliferation of academic work centered on the problems of magical realism: Many critics have been taking the genre to task, whereas others have stopped addressing it as a viable topic of research, and there are still many other scholars operating under the spell of the boundlessness of its applications. In *Exhaustion of Difference* (a title that refers to the arrival at the hermeneutic limits of the tensions listed above),[18] Alberto Moreiras establishes how magical realism emerges from Fernando Ortiz's idea of "transculturation," a model that, throughout its history, has suffered from the same contradictions.

> As a radical concept, insofar as it is oriented toward a possible restitution, preservation, or renewal of cultural origins, and not toward a mere phenomenology of culture, transculturation runs into the theoretical wall that marks its conditions of possibility as heterogeneous with respect to itself. The critical concept of transculturation, paradoxically enough, seems to originate not in the anthropological concept but rather in a different, nontransculturated realm of (unexamined) truth: the realm of ideology. There is no critical transculturation without an end or a limit of transculturation, through which end the critical concept of transculturation appears as something other than or beyond what it is purported to be.[19]

Moreiras attributes the collapse of transculturation to a flourishing of the paradoxes centered on the very purpose of this critical term: the tense difference between a project of "restitution" of a past and that of an actual phenomenology. Suspended between loss and presence, transculturation has become a critical medium used to establish a reading of Latin American difference that can range from the geographical to the cosmological, which is no doubt a long and uneasy journey for a single theory.

Magical realism, transculturation's travel companion in the representational dimension of fiction, has been critically hailed as being responsible for an equal amount of emancipations. Christopher Warnes, who has also announced a limit to the responsibilities appointed to this genre, interprets the current status of critique of magical realism as a "deployment of a hermeneutic of vagueness."[20] The fault primarily lies, according to Warnes, in the "common refusal to define magical realism in formal terms" (6). After providing numerous examples of different ways in which critics have anointed texts from different cultural and historical contexts with this popular label, he argues for a more cohesive justification of inclusion into the genre, although also making the more provocative argument that perhaps critics "have vested interests of a thematic or conceptual nature in perpetuating this vagueness" (7). He asks, "If we do not know with any certainty what magical realism is and how it functions, then how can we be sure of the basis for our comparisons between texts which may operate very differently, emerge from different contexts, and have very different purposes in mind?" (7). As it seems, the impetus for a poetics of "difference" at the origins of the magical real is caught now in a problematic of a universalization of difference that is lacking in rigor. The meanings and ramifications of difference necessarily compel us to ask: What are the benefits and limits of a critique of heterogeneity? At what point does difference turn upon itself and become a universal value?

Warnes pauses to look at recent work by Wendy Faris, significantly titled *Ordinary Enchantments: Magical Realism and the Remystification of Narrative* (2004), in order to examine the extent to which critics claim to have a grasp of how magical realism is formally constituted when in fact they sacrifice the analysis of form in favor of a hopelessly teleological reading. Warnes delineates this deficiency in the following passage:

> Faris goes to great lengths to identify what magical realism is, where it can be found, and to describe the "cultural work" she sees it doing. Her approach thus . . . specifically uses the term *magical realism* in order to attend closely to the formal qualities of particular texts. . . . But, rather than pursuing precision of analysis into thematic terrain, Faris eschews cultural and historical specificities in

favour of a reading of magical realism in which the mode is held to perform a "remystification of narrative" leading to a re-enchantment of the Western reader, and a kind of shamanistic narrative healing. . . . What is extraordinary about Faris's claim is that she asserts that *all* magical realism, regardless of context or authorial intention, necessarily plays these roles because of its form. Such an ahistorical, universalizing approach is bound to perform a discursive violence on its object of study. . . . The "irreducible elements" of these texts—as of all magical realism—can be understood only through close scrutiny of the cultural, material and historical conditions under which they were written, yet the hegemony of form and genre in Faris's study precludes such readings. What is left are the vaguest, most indeterminate and incorroborative of notions: spirit, mystery, the sacred. (10)

Although Warnes is pointing to specific instances of the breakdown of genre theory where form has been sacrificed to make way for "indeterminate" notions that recall Carpentier's elusive idea of "faith" in the magical, Seymour Menton attacks Faris's book as "disregard[ing] literary history, preferring to rely heavily on a huge and ungainly number of literary theorists from Jacques Derrida and François Lyotard to Homi Bhabha and Gayatri Spivak," and also taking liberties with "chronological limits."[21] The web of complications becomes even larger when form clashes with literary history, which in turn clashes with an ever-expanding host of theories, not to mention historical and cultural specificity. Warnes seems to have faith in a definition and application of the magical realism label, but, in his essay, he goes to great lengths to show how the last decades in literary criticism have fallen short of establishing responsible explanations, much less ethical applications. His apt subtitling of magical realism as the "hermeneutics of vagueness" signals a moment of serious reflection around what seems to have become a Gordian knot of philosophical and terminological determinants.

The Location of Borges

Menton himself is an old hand at theorizing magical realism,[22] and in his review of *Ordinary Enchantments*, he criticizes Faris for confusing the magical real and the fantastic. He gives the example of Faris's erroneous classification of *Aura*, by Carlos Fuentes, where "once the protagonist crosses the threshold and enters the fantastic world inhabited by Aura and the Dickensian old lady Consuelo, the total environment becomes fantastic rather than realistic, thereby negating the novel's classification as magical realist."[23] Herein lies yet another prevalent complication for those who have theorized this genre: the establishment of boundaries between the fantastic and the magical real in fiction. In *Pilgrim at Home*, González Echevarría dismisses generic theorization of magical realism as "an effort" to describe something that could otherwise be called fantastical (109). Yet, contemporaneously with González Echevarría, Menton was attempting to establish the differences between the two concepts. In his 1982 essay, "Jorge Luis Borges, Magic Realist," he aims to disprove Borges's classification of his own work in the epilogue to the 1949 edition of *El Aleph* as belonging to the "género fantástico," in order to propose that there are certain exceptions to this rule which make him a "magic realist," as the title of the essay resoundingly affirms. Locating Borges in the map of twentieth-century Latin American literature is a particularly interesting, if not dizzying, endeavor: Although some critics are cautious about classifying his varied oeuvre under a specific genre, others take him for a magical realist through and through. Lois Parkinson Zamora, for example, devotes a thought-provoking chapter on the assumption that Borges, along with García Márquez, are the two "most influential of magical realists" in the American literary scene.[24] An exploration of the travels of Borges in the canon of Latin American letters allows us to see the different types of debates surrounding the magical realist genre.

Menton proposes that, "whereas 'lo fantástico' is a genre, a type of literature that may be found in any chronological period, Magic Realism is an artistic movement or tendency that began in 1918 as a direct reflection of a series of historical and artistic factors and continued in varying degrees of intensity until approximately 1970" (411–12). This explains his current criticism of Faris's transgressions in her own work on the issue, but it also leads us into yet another muddle with magical realism, namely the differentiation between genre and artistic movement. In 1967, when Luis Leal published "El realismo mágico en la literatura hispanoamericana," he refuted Flores's coinage of the magical realist movement with the idea that it is "more than anything else, an attitude toward reality."[25] Movement, genre, attitude: As we continue to travel through the history of late-twentieth criticism, the task of defining magical realism is complicated on both historical and conceptual levels.

Whereas González Echevarría separates Franz Roh's 1925 conceptualization of *Magischer Realismus* in painting and Alejo Carpentier's "real maravilloso"[26] because the former is a strictly pictorial representation where magic reveals itself in everyday objects and the latter believes in an unexpected magical dimension found in a continent's history and geography, Menton believes in establishing a connection between the Argentine (an "English-oriented one at that") Borges and the German painters Georg Schrimpf and Christian Schad, or the North Americans Charles Sheeler and Grant Wood to "finally" prove what "Magic Realism" is.[27] The critic discards magical realism's indebtedness to a Latin American supernatural imaginary (he states, "Magic Realism, involved as it is with the improbable rather than the impossible, never deals with the supernatural," 412), in favor of a European definition where magic is discovered in the everyday, thus making no differentiation between Roh's project and that of the Latin American writers of "Magic Realism." It is rather troubling that Menton would opt for this particular genealogy without at least acknowledging a Latin American literary history that traces desires to create an autochthonous literature (*costumbrismo* being one nineteenth-century example). Indeed, he performs critical oversights similar to those of which he would accuse Faris in his review two decades later.

Perhaps not surprisingly, Menton's New Critical approach to Borges as a magic realist is based on the latter's choice of words in his stories (his definition of "magic realism" is reminiscent of Flores's description of the linguistic craftiness of the authors he included in his 1955 essay, where Borges was, of course, the main example). Menton appears to take the oxymoronic label "magic realism" literally when he proposes his main thesis in this article: "One of the most incontrovertible indications of Borges' identification with Magic Realism is his constant use of oxymoron from his first stories of 1933 up through what is generally considered his best story 'El Sur' (1952) and beyond." He explains, "Oxymoron, strictly speaking, is the juxtaposition of apparently self-contradictory words such as 'cruel kindness.' Varying degrees of oxymoron are present in most of the titles of the [*Historia universal de la infamia*] volume's seven principal stories" (415). As part of his essay's denouement, Menton traces the oxymoronic structure to Argentina's "basic oxymoron-like antithesis of civilization-barbarism that has prevented Argentines from developing a true national consciousness" (424), a conceptual opposition that, according to him, explains cultural clashes throughout the history of Argentina, from "the triumph of brute force over innocent ivory-tower intellectualism, the triumph of the Perón dictatorship over the Argentine intellectuals, paralleling the Rosas dictatorship's persecution of the Unitarian intellectuals in the 1830's" (425). No allusion is made to the origins of this representational construct in the nineteenth century with Sarmiento's *Facundo* (discussed in Chapter 4 of this book), and Menton chooses not to invite a more nuanced interpretation of Argentine history.[28]

Stephanie Merrim, in her essay on "Wonder," describes Borges's "El Sur" as "more properly 'fantastic' literature" that "obliges the reader to hesitate between a 'real' and an 'unreal' solution" (328). Before continuing on to discuss Merrim's suggestive propositions in this essay, I want to stop at this juncture where the fantastic and the marvelous/magical are at odds.

To summarize our examples: In 2005, Menton describes Fuentes's *Aura* as "fantastic," because the main character crosses the threshold of a house and he effectively enters a new world of doubles, dark magic, and strange stagnation within a specific past. Merrim describes "El Sur," Borges's story of a man named Dahlmann who takes a train south and back in time—a journey that rattles with uncertainty in the reader's mind because Dahlmann has also just emerged out of a disorienting illness, or so we think— as more "fantastic" because of this very rattling of uncertainty around the lines dividing the realms of the unreal and the real (we experience a similar uncertainty, for example, with Henry James's problematic governess in *The Turn of the Screw*). Menton, as delineated above, describes this story as "Magic Realism." Here is his explanation:

> The key to an understanding of the literal interpretation lies in Borges' much greater affiliation with Magic Realism than with either Surrealism or the fantastic. . . . Borges has a Magic Realist world view. Truth is stranger than fiction and the most unexpected and amazing events may take place. . . . The juxtaposition of self-contradictory words or phrases, oxymoron, is not only Borges' favorite stylistic device, it is one of the basic structures of many of his stories. Although critics have generally divided "El Sur" into two parts, before and after Juan Dahlmann's release from the hospital (literally or through hallucination), it is more significant to note the juxtaposition throughout the story of an overly precise, objective, expository style and the transformation, without distortions, of reality into a dream world. (421–22)

Citing Borges's professed greater affinity with Jungian theory than with Freudian theory, Menton perceives the magic realist worldview as closer to representations of archetypes and the "relative insignificance of the individual human being" as well as the "simultaneity of past, present, and future" (419). In his reading of Borges, Menton counters an interpretation based on Dahlmann's "hallucination" in favor of a strictly linguistic approach highlighting the binary "oxymoron," which, to his mind, cancels out any apparent "transformations" or "distortions" in the telling of the story. His examples of Borges's use of oxymorons are not convincing (in the story's line "Las tareas y acaso la indolencia lo retenían en la ciudad," Menton perceives an oxymoronic standoff between "tareas" and "indolencia," 422), and, as I explain above, he extrapolates this textual "oxymoron" to perform an interpretation of the story as a critique of the larger "civilization-barbarism" oxymoron that, to him, defines the history of Argentina's national constitution. According to Menton, the story "is obviously intended to be a metaphor of Argentine history," representing "the triumph of barbarism over civilization" (425).

This interpretation, as stated earlier, chooses to accept Sarmiento's binarism at face value, without problematizing its status as part of a romanticization of nationhood more than being simple and "straight" historical narrative (which Doris Sommer would convincingly argue years later in *Foundational Fictions*). This in part could explain Menton's view of a lack of transformation or distortion in "El Sur"; he understands magic realism as the status of "reality being stranger than fiction," without taking into account how Sarmiento's binarism is part of a wider fiction of Argentine history. Needless to say, his sweeping claim that an oxymoron holds the key to a nation's history throughout a whole century is a problematic conclusion in an essay contesting literary genre.

The textual contest between the fantastic and magical realism thus compels us to reconsider the position of the reader in relation to classifying Borges's story, a story that Merrim uses as the basis for her association of "El Sur" with the fantastic. Are we supposed to read "El Sur" without at least a hint of puzzlement, given that the reader, like Juan Dahlmann, may well be pushed to wonder whether a threshold has been crossed (a threshold similar, perhaps, to the one in *Aura*)? Let us suppose that many of the problems surrounding definitions of what is "fantastic" or what is "marvelous" or "magical" revolve around issues of readerly hesitation and surprise. Tzvetan Todorov writes that "a genre is always defined in relation to the genres adjacent to it,"[29] which is precisely the type of exercise that critics such as Menton and Merrim are performing with regards to the fantastic and the marvelous/magical real. We are now faced, however, with the confusion that has ensued when literature has exceeded a single genre and plays with a number of approaches to these "reactions" (to continue using Todorov's terminology) of hesitation and surprise. Todorov's influential yet overly regimented approach to these reactions is based on the units of reader and character. The fantastic, he maintains, "lasts only as long as a certain hesitation: a hesitation common to reader and character, who must decide whether or not what they perceive derives from 'reality' as it exists in the common opinion" (41). Todorov thus accounts for a certain complicity between the reader and the character, and it is this description of the "fantastic" that Merrim uses in her interpretation of "El Sur." However, let us consider Todorov's follow-up point.

> At the story's end, the reader makes a decision even if the character does not; he opts for one solution or the other, and thereby emerges from the fantastic. If he decides that the laws of reality remain intact and permit an explanation of the phenomena described, we say that

the work belongs to another genre: the uncanny. If, on the contrary, he decides that new laws of nature must be entertained to account for the phenomena, we enter the genre of the marvelous. (41)

If we were to follow Todorov's guidance on the matter, then we could arrive at the conclusion that the fantastic is only experienced on a first and single reading of a text that harbors an ambiguous division of the real and the un-real.[30] This imperative decision of defining what can be explained through "real" and "natural" systems of thought, as opposed to supernatural—after the initial reaction of hesitation and surprise—thus breaks the alliance between the reader and the character, and interrupts the afterlife of a text. That is to say, Todorov's definition of the fantastic orders the reader to be done with a story that begets uneasiness. He admits that the fantastic genre "leads a life full of dangers, and may evaporate at any moment" (41). After suggesting that one option is to study the fantastic in fragments, a practice that would suspend the arrival at the conclusion of the narrative, Todorov's solution to this "danger" is to give the fantastic life through its attachment to the other two genres cited above, namely the uncanny and the marvelous, where the entrance of the supernatural is eliminated as an option in the former, but not in the latter.

The conquest of the supernatural in narrative fiction seems to be another major element in this business of defining one genre of the "unbelievable" against another, which appears to result in a spiral in Todorov's analysis. He writes, "There exists a curious coincidence between the authors who cultivate the supernatural and those who, within their works, are especially concerned with the development of the action, or to put it another way, who seek above all to tell *stories*" (162–63). This, Todorov continues, leads to an inquiry "into the very nature of narrative," which he defines as a "movement between two equilibriums which are similar but not identical" (163). The entry of the supernatural into a narrative—which Todorov indeed perceives as "narrative raw material"—defies a "fixed law" that disrupts the flow of narrative events. (Incidentally, Todorov uses the example of the *Arabian Nights* to illustrate this point, which is the book that Dahlmann is reading on his voyage south in Borges's "El Sur.") Thus, Todorov explains:

> If the supernatural is habitually linked to the narrative of an action, it rarely appears in novels concerned only with psychological descriptions and analysis (the example of Henry James is not contradictory here). The relation of the supernatural to narration is henceforth clear: every text in which the supernatural occurs is a narrative, for the supernatural event first of all modifies a previous equilibrium—which is the very definition of narrative. . . . Whether it is in social

life or in narrative, the intervention of the supernatural element always constitutes a break in the system of pre-established rules, and in doing so finds its justification. (166)

Todorov's admission at the end of his text that the supernatural supplies narrative with its eventuality places this process of narration at odds with his favored genre of the fantastic, which has more to do with the "reaction." The text is thus broken down into separate units of reader, character, and writer, and, as Todorov would have it in his structural analysis of genre, these are mutually exclusive. The statement that the supernatural resembles narrative, however, does provide cause for reflection regarding the position of the author as well as the moment of creation. Todorov writes that the marvelous has "always existed in literature" (whereas the "more interesting" fantastic "has had a relatively brief lifespan" [166]). Could we suppose, then, that the decision of the author in creating events to tell a story is in itself a supernatural inflection? Or, to put it differently, is the creation of a story that contains a set of artificial events with no grounds in a "natural" perception of real life a supernatural event?

What do we do with an argument like this in a study that sets out to delineate—and, one would hope, clarify—the features of a genre? Where does it take us? Although his concept of the reaction is useful in a reader's discernment of the "fantastic," the supernatural vein that runs through the narrative creation (which Todorov attempts to explain away with his structured concept of the marvelous) collides with the concept of narrative as a whole. Surely, "to tell *stories*" may well be the impetus at the core of all narrative performance—even a psychological narrative tells of events. In his explication of what he calls the *"exotic marvelous,"* Todorov writes that the "implicit reader is supposed to be ignorant of the regions where the events take place, and consequently he has no reason for calling them into question" (55), a statement that recalls the paradox in Carpentier's formulation of "lo real maravilloso," where, as González Echevarría explains, it takes a European perspective to be awestruck by the Latin American desires for an autochthonous expression.[31] This alleged absence of a "reason" to question in the act of reading, be it in a piece that has been deemed "marvelous" or "fantastic," is irresponsible in its closing down of the circle of "implicit" readers, not to mention the potentiality of exploring a text that is at first perceived as "exotic." Many of the problems of genre theory are thus presented here: That is, the problematic claim that some genres are avowedly more ripe for questioning, more "interesting" for analysis than others, while causality (or, the events that push a narrative forward) remains under the dark telos of the supernatural, a category that Todorov is not quite sure what to make of in terms of the reader's reception. The single text—the particular story—appears to be sacrificed to classification in Todorov, and the problem of ideology, so important to other genre theorists, is a nonissue.

A good way out of the quandary of Borges's location is to go to the writer himself. Let us consider Borges's 1932 essay "El arte narrativo y la magia" ("Narrative Art and Magic"), where the author understands narrative to be magical in its own right, due to its ordered limitation and its "frantic" harmony. He writes:

> La magia es la coronación o pesadilla de lo causal, no su contra-dicción. El milagro no es menos forastero en ese universo que en el de los astrónomos. Todas las leyes naturales lo rigen, y otras imaginarias. . . . Esa peligrosa armonía, esa frenética y precisa causalidad, manda en la novela también.

> [Magic is the crown or nightmare of the law of cause and effect, not its contradiction. Miracles are no less strange in this universe than in that of astronomers. It is ruled by all of the laws of nature as well as those of imagination. . . . That dangerous harmony—that frenzied, clear-cut causality—also holds sway over the novel.][32]

Borges understands narrative as the construction of a nonfragmentary causality, and, like Todorov, he aligns it with a magical realm. Magic is thus not the obverse of reality for Borges, and, more importantly, it does not *interrupt* or break down a fictional structure into constitutive, generic fragments: Whereas the "natural" is for him an "incessant" movement of "endless uncontrollable causes," narrative is a "lucid and determined" whole (115; 82), a universe onto itself. According to González Echevarría, this move harkens back to Aristotle's foundational philosophical argument of the *Poetics*, where, the same way "the cosmos is ruled in its movement by a series of potential actions that remit to an immovable prime mover," narrative "should reflect the same principle of composition." González Echevarría places Borges's argument in its historical context, at the moment when the early twentieth-century avant-garde sought to create separate realms for art and the real.

> In one way or another, with variations in the mode of presentation of that reflection, all versions of realism assume such a specular relation between art and the world. The whole avant-garde was pitted against that realistic bias. But instead of breaking the mirror to create a series of discontinuous images, Borges polishes it to make it reflect more keenly a complete and ordered image—an image, however, which is not a reflection of a real order, but a whole in itself. . . . Borges's marvels are not concrete and static, but dynamic functions of the self, of

the being that emerges from his fictions, a sort of minor Aristotelian god who thinks himself and invents a world. The term "magic" no longer neutralizes the transcendental element implicit in such a vision, but underlines it. (*Pilgrim*, 119–20)

Borges's argument is thus very similar to Todorov's acknowledgment at the conclusion of *The Fantastic*: To create a narrative fiction is, like magic and the supernatural, an invention of a sequence of events with an inherent coherence. The important difference between them lies in each author's understanding of magic and where it should be placed in the realm of poetics, if at all. The "transcendence" that magic commonly prefigures, as González Echevarría explains, goes hand in hand with poetic invention in Borges's view. Whereas Todorov arrives at this question almost by accident and hurriedly puts it away, for Borges it is the core of an understanding of narrative's development. If, for Borges, magic occupies and embraces the whole of poetic art, what currency does genre possess for contextualizing writing in which the magical is purposefully evoked as a particular improvement on the limitations of mimetic representation?

The Romance of Criticism

One indeed may argue that Borges's formulations about narrative art and magic are generalizations of cosmological proportions, but, from a different angle, we could also say that in superseding genre he is inviting us to see a universe in each text, each eliciting equal amounts of curiosity in the reader. Warnes admits that "generalizations may be necessary, but their accuracy and appropriateness need to be measured against text and context, rather than against the category itself."[33] This points to the pervasive tension that exists between the critical language that has been set in place in our tradition and the desire to transform the ways of looking at a text.

In her essay "Wonder," Stephanie Merrim performs the double task of criticizing the forms and functions of the magical realist genre, although referring to generic qualities (namely, those of the baroque and the fantastic) to describe Borges. She cites Borges's "Tlön, Uqbar, Orbis Tertius," as a parodic example of the vertigo that can be induced by classification, which she calls a "baroque expansion *ad absurdum*" (316). Merrim's reference to the magical realist genre is not performed with the vehemence of a Menton, where Borges is described, to use Warnes's language, "against a category" of magical realism, rather than the text and its context. Her actual coup de grace in this essay is the way in which she signals toward the element of wonder or "asombro" in the literature of Borges and Faulkner. Focusing on this reaction of amazement at the origins as well as the development of the poetic discourses in the work of these two authors, Merrim traces a more historically nuanced line of comparison that links texts without binding them together through snug comparisons. In the Platonic model of *admiratio*, from which Merrim's argument departs, wonder is the "intellectual energy" as well as the "beginning" of all philosophical inquiry. Faulkner and Borges, however,

> lace wonder with the fearful edge inherent in amazement, *asombro*. They wrench wonder from epistemology and mimesis and insert it in history, refunctioning and overloading it. Their catachrestic deployment of wonder, the wounding of its meaning(s), is the language of crisis. (312)

Whereas in Plato philosophy begins with wonder, Merrim argues that in the works of Faulkner as well as Borges's fictions toward the latter part of the 1930s, it is "*history*" that "begins in wonder" (314). She traces the genealogies of wonder in "southern literatures" in the Americas—traceable to the writing of the conquistadors, as Stephen Greenblatt shows in *Marvelous Possessions* (1991)—to arrive at crisis points in the histories of southern modernities. According to Merrim, it is in these instances that anticolonial nationalist discourses such as José Enrique Rodó's *Ariel* (1900) and the Twelve Southerners' *I'll Take My Stand* (1930) revert to "self-exoticizing methods," "choosing a profile that is eccentric, odd and off-center" in order to "define themselves over/against northern titans" (321). In Borges's "El Sur," Merrim reads an allegory of this exoticizing mood, where the protagonist Dahlmann "has mythologized Argentina's recent past into a heroic era," locating "the glorious past in the South of Argentina, in his military ancestors, and . . . in the family ranch that allegedly awaits him there" (323). Dahlmann, however, must negotiate between his literariness and his military past, and opts, "either in his mind or in actuality," to "dissociate himself from modernity and from his fetters to undertake a journey to the yearned-for South" (324).

This reading of Borges's story sets off Merrim's elegant critique of magical realism, for in the South, Dahlmann "enters a magical, palliative, truly inalienable and unseizable zone" trapped between "reality and fiction" (324), which resembles the zone where the history of southern literatures seems to be caught at present. Merrim asks, transforming Carpentier's famous query: "What, in the public eye, is the history of southern literatures if not a chronicle of the marvel of the real?" (325). Emerging from the polemics surrounding the genre to ask a question about the ethics of blending history and discourse, she arrives at the conclusion that "the triumph of the wonderful," which has come to describe these literatures, "can backfire."

While . . . the ontologizing of the marvelous both salves wounds and creates them afresh, marvelous realism's epistemological claim gives rise to utopian projections that can occlude or betray the cultural and political clashes—among them, ongoing strife between Norths and Souths—that endure to the present day. In its erasure of binaries, marvelous realism provides a sweet and easy resolution of persisting conflicts. It presents the wounds of history as *always already resolved*. The emollient myth that presses the marvelous into its service twists into a reductive panacea. . . . Marvelous realism resolves history into a palatable, crisis-palliating story diametrically opposed to Faulkner's classically inflected yet unregenerate tragic story of the South. (328)

Set against the practice where critics see in magical realism a poetics of "always already resolved" wounds, Merrim looks to Faulkner's *Absalom* where "differences and shibboleths are *always about to* surrender and coalesce into a harmonious unity," but refuse to, and to Borges's pronouncement, in *Otras inquisiciones*: "esta inminencia de una revelación que no se produce, es, quizá, el hecho estético" ["this imminence of a revelation that doesn't reveal itself is, perhaps, the aesthetic event"] (329). I have cited Merrim's suggestive essay at length, because it performs the close textual analysis that other critics seem to avoid, and because it takes us into a palpitating problem within the texts that have been tucked under the all-too-comfortable rubric of the magical realist genre. The problem of the "revelación que no se produce," of the moments of reading that promise clear visualization, yet in the end emit valuable, difficult questions (rather than saccharine and alienable readings of otherness), makes the practice of criticism more worthwhile. In so many instances, the theorization of the genre of magical realism has perceived mystery as a matter of unquestionable enchantment rather than as the wound that we find at the root of Merrim's thesis.

Wendy B. Faris, taking a cue from David Young and Keith Hallaman, the editors of the 1984 anthology of magical realist fiction,[34] describes magic as an "irreducible element" in these narratives, as I noted earlier in my discussion of Warnes's critique of her work. These magical moments are then interpreted as "a liberating poetics," or an "erosion of the boundaries between self and other," but we are never quite sure how that leap from the unexplainable, irreducible elements in fiction to the possibility of political, ethnic, cultural, and historical shifts becomes feasible. In her reading of Toni Morrison's *Beloved*, for example, Faris considers Beloved's apparition as one such irreducible element, and asks, "What force causes Beloved to reappear . . . ? We really cannot say" (112). I now take my cue from Philip Weinstein who, in a parallel discussion of Morrison's fiction of apparitions, asks: "Does it matter?" ("Cant Matter/Must Matter," 373). Perhaps a more valid question should be: "What does this apparition *do* (to the text, to fictions inspired by historical accounts of the horror of slavery in the United States, and to Sethe, Denver, and Paul D.)?" In claiming magic to be the unsplittable atom of contemporary international fiction, critics such as Faris read the literature of "otherness" as altogether positive alternatives to a stolid and calculating realism.

> In addition to its disruption of realism and reimagining of history, perhaps another reason why magical realism has played an active role in literary decolonization is that many of its texts reconfigure structures of autonomy and agency, moves that destabilize established structures of power and control. Individuals merge or identities are questioned in other ways, and mysterious events require us to question who or what has caused them. This aspect of magical realism aligns it with modernism and postmodernism, of course, which also conflate individual identities, but it uses the additional resource of irreducible elements of magic to understand those conflations. (111)

In this critical vein, the genre of realist fiction, according to Faris, has come to be understood by "writers of colonized societies" as "the language of the colonizer" (102). This interpretation of realistic literature as a monochromatic category *against* which this "decolonizing" genre of magical realism is defined begs for a more thorough and expansive definition of realism across time. Which constitutive realist texts is she retrieving and affiliating with, and from which tradition?

Realism's past accomplishments, then, can fall into neglect only when criticism defines the realist project retrospectively in terms of its inadequacies. Amy Kaplan's work on North American realism, for instance, sets out to analyze what realism has accomplished, noting how its aims have been met with critical skepticism, given the more widely accepted alliance of the genre of romance with U.S. fiction:

> The association of the romance with a uniquely American culture has displaced realism to an anomalous and distinctly un-American margin of literary criticism, which has necessarily viewed its literary mode as a failure. Reproducing [Henry] James's "absent things" in different theoretical guises, studies of American realism have repeatedly reinforced the ahistorical assumption of an impossible or flawed relationship between American literature and society.[35]

Kaplan calls attention here to a critique of trends in the field of criticism. In her reading of the history of criticism of American realism, she perceives a repetition, in the early twentieth century, of Henry James's initial remark of the state of the nation, which, despite being a century old, has continued to enrapture contemporary critics.

Something similar happens with much contemporary critique of magical realism: Carpentier's problematic (and performative, as González Echevarría argues) notion of Latin America's exceptionality in its other-ness appears to have established itself quite comfortably in the work of critics such as Faris, as well as her coeditor Zamora.[36] Faris contributes to the widespread advocacy of the hugely emancipatory capabilities of a magical realist school, although failing to produce the historically in-formed readings of realistic texts, as championed by Kaplan. Her critique of realism as the direct opposite of magical realism fails to account, among other things, for what Kaplan terms the "utopian moments" of realistic narratives, where the novels "imagine resolutions to contemporary social conflicts by reconstructing society as it might be" (12). They also fail to account, I might add, for the instances in realist and even naturalist fiction where the unbelievable enters the narrative, such as, for example, the mo-ment in Theodore Dreiser's *Sister Carrie* (1900) when articles of clothing phantasmagorically speak to the eponymous heroine in a Chicago depart-ment store ("Ah ah! the voices of the so-called inanimate. Who shall yet translate for us the language of the stones?").[37] Out-of-the-ordinary pas-sages such as the one in Dreiser's novel make us call into question our pre-conceived notions of realism's rigid affiliation with "post-Enlightenment empiricism" (Faris, "Question of the Other," 102).

The problem here can very well lie in what Kaplan describes as the crit-ical attachment to the connection of *romance* to American letters (which, as she explains, accounts for the failure of an American social realism). Romance has come to be accepted as more pertinent a foundational genre for the Americas based on the notion that these nations of the so-called "new" world, as opposed to Europe, were still in a state of invention in the late nineteenth century—standing on un-solid ground of sorts, where class systems, which had become so established in the European social imaginary, had not yet become cemented in the social psyche. The ro-mance genre in the Americas is thus, according to most critics, informed by a preoccupation with the politics and desires of nation building. This is one critical stance. Doris Sommer, in her *Foundational Fictions*, ex-plains how in U.S. literature, the genres of novel and romance have re-mained separate, whereas in Latin American literature they have become conflated.

> In the United States . . . the label [of romance] has traditionally dis-tinguished an ethico-political character of our most canonical books of fiction. And in Latin America, romance doesn't distinguish

between ethical politics and erotic passion, between epic nationalism and intimate sensibility. It collapses the distinctions.[38]

We could perhaps argue that this view of the American alignment with the genre of romance, and the subsequent "homelessness" of realism in its cultural landscape has in its turn historically allowed for a negation of realism as a viable means to read the nations of the New World in critical approaches to literature. Interestingly, however, Sommer points to the possibility of the words "romance" and "novel" getting lost in translation when she discusses Sarmiento's reading of James Fenimore Cooper, in which the former refers to the latter as a *"romancista"*: "Referring to Cooper as a *romancista* might simply have been a gallicism for 'novelist'; and Mrs. Mann [Sarmiento's translator] duly translates it both as 'romancer' and 'novelist.' The difference between these terms is an Anglo-American, not a Romance language tradition" (25). Sommer's observation—informed both by history and a devil's advocate–like reference to translation—points to the multiple obstacles one encounters in the naming and matching of generic categories in the American hemisphere, thus making it difficult to identify the whole of literature in these continents with a clear set of corresponding genres.

The necessity for a more aesthetically attuned and particularizing approach becomes ever more pressing as one continues to explore the recent evolutions of criticism of magical realism. Earlier in the chapter, I make mention of how Lois Parkinson Zamora, without a doubt one of the major contemporary champions of magical realism, refers to Borges as one of the two most influential magical realists in Latin American literature. Following this statement, she goes on to trace the generic connections between romance and magical realism in the literature of the Americas. She does so through Borges via his critical veneration for Nathaniel Hawthorne, whom he posits as the "beginning" of U.S. literature. Zamora's approach to romance is very different from Sommer's, and indeed she does not reference Sommer's work in *The Usable Past.* What Zamora sets out to do, through a conceptual rather than a historical reading closer to Sommer's project, is to consolidate the connections between these two writers in such a way that Borges's "universalizing" project of archetype becomes nearly indistinguishable from Hawthorne's.

> Because neither Borges nor Hawthorne used indigenous culture to any significant extent in his definition of America . . . both felt the lack of a significant American past when compared to that of Europe. And both worried about the present. Hawthorne opposed the prevailing mid-nineteenth-century ideologies of individualism and nationalism, as Borges opposed similar ideologies in Perón's Argentina eight decades later. (89)

In conjunction with this controversial comparative exercise,[39] Zamora extensively cites Borges's essay on Hawthorne, where the Argentine author draws comparative lines of his own between the literary North and South, stating that whereas Latin American literature is most concerned with "dictionaries and rhetoric," U.S. literature (starting with Hawthorne) deals more in "fantasy." At this juncture, Zamora makes a puzzling move in her criticism.

> Clearly, Borges wrote this essay before the flowering of magical realism in Latin American literature. It was precisely 1949 [the year in which Borges published "Nathaniel Hawthorne"] in which magical realism was first described as *lo real maravilloso* and designated an indigenous American phenomenon by Alejo Carpentier. (93)

Several issues come to mind when reading this passage: One is Zamora's observation that Borges was in some way unable to describe Hawthorne effectively, given the not-yet-current "real maravilloso" adjective. Second, she makes no differentiation between Carpentier's term and magical realism, and actually fails to mention Arturo Uslar Pietri's own hand in refreshing Franz Roh's term two years before 1949. If we are to believe that Borges is here committing an act of (self-) oversight, what became of his locus as García Márquez's partner in magical realism? In other words, what happened to Borges's own hand in the field of fantastic/magical/archetypalizing literature, which preceded the auspicious date of 1949? And what do we make of the two very different definitions of "magical realism" that emerge when speaking of Borges and Carpentier alongside each other? Certainly, the latter was most interested in positioning the indigenous element as a central factor of his marvelous real, whose aim, in many ways, is to "define" the nations of the literary south, and yet Borges, according to Zamora, is not.

We should return to Doris Sommer and apply her own observation of how genre is susceptible to becoming lost in translation as it travels between the continents of the American hemisphere. Zamora's methodological aim in connecting Hawthorne and Borges, is to justify an equation between magical realism and romance, in order to position her hemispheric reading of ghosts in literature. Hawthorne is traditionally regarded as a romance writer, and Borges, as I have tried to establish, exists in a more elusive generic-critical space. In an analysis of Borges's reading of the haunted dimensions in Hawthorne, Zamora arrives at the conclusion that, despite the differences between the two genres, "Borges' appreciation for Hawthorne points to the similarities of magical realism and romance rather than their differences, and to their shared project: the expansions and redefinition of our conceptions of subjectivity, against the limitations of Cartesian (and Freudian) consciousness, Hegelian historicism, and scientific rationalism" (96).

As I mentioned earlier, Zamora is arriving at a reading of both genres in terms of individual and community, and how ghosts affect these, but she adheres to Northrop Frye's structuralist model of genre in *Anatomy of Criticism*[40] to validate a reading of Latin American literature through an Anglo(-American) spectrum of "venerable" literature, which in many ways is reminiscent of Sommer's comment on the translations and travels of the literary generic in the Americas. Zamora concludes her section on Borges and Hawthorne with the following proposal: "Twentieth-century magical realism is a recent flowering of the more venerable romance tradition that Frye describes" (97). Her project of reading hemispheric ghosts in a comparative context depends on Frye's own acknowledgment of the ghost as a feature of romance, which in turn serves as her own descriptive mapping of magical realism, a genre "with ghosts aplenty" (82). Following Frye's location of the use of ghosts in literature within the "low mimetic" genre of romance, where "a ghost as a rule is merely one more character,"[41] Zamora explains that

> Frye does not mention "magical realism," of course, since the term was not yet current in literary criticism in 1957, when *The Anatomy of Criticism* was published. Nonetheless, we see immediately that what we now call magical realism corresponds to Frye's second category, romance, where ghosts are expected inhabitants of reality who may . . . enter without affrighting us. (97)

This conclusion certainly follows Zamora's earlier classificatory claim, where she asserts that "to qualify as a ghost a literary apparition need not have arms and legs or, for that matter, be limited to two of each" (78), a taxonomy that could very well clash with Frye's. And yet, Zamora feels the necessity to salute Frye as the voice of authority to legitimate her comparative project of Latin American and U.S. literature through the lens of a genre he does not acknowledge or know of. Here I turn to the final question, which has haunted this chapter on the haunting of genre: Why must we rely on piling up one literary category over another in order to read ghosts in literature?

Mapping the Ghostly

Zamora's project in her chapter on haunting in the Americas has undoubtedly haunted my own, given that on the surface they may appear similar, even down to the authors analyzed (we both share an interest in analyzing Juan Rulfo's *Pedro Páramo*, for example). Yet her work in this particular chapter returns to an urge to come up with generic allegiances among hemispheric American texts. Her most recent monograph, *The Inordinate Eye: New World Baroque and Latin American Fiction* (2006)—a stunning book that traces the baroque from its European origins to its American manifestations—compels us to entertain an alternative location for Borges alongside other Latin American neobaroque artists, namely Carpentier, Frida Kahlo, and García Márquez.[42] Carpentier himself pronounced Latin America "the chosen territory of the baroque" in his later essay "The Baroque and the Marvelous Real" (1975).[43] In a way similar to his multivalent description of America in his original 1948 essay on the marvelous real, Carpentier links race and aesthetics in "The Baroque and the Marvelous Real," developing a consonance between Latin America's profuse *mestizaje* and the baroque's *horror vacui*. Zamora explores the various connections between Carpentier and Borges (for example, their respective associations with Alfonso Reyes in the 1920s) to identify different strains in the manifestations of the baroque in twentieth-century Latin American literature. Yet, the results are very different, as Zamora observes: Whereas Carpentier adhered to the baroque aesthetic in his project of Latin American self-definition, Borges dissociated himself from it, perceiving it as a style he practiced in his early oeuvre and to which he did not care to return. Still, Borges was (not surprisingly) extremely well versed in Góngora and Quevedo, and his later stories have an affinity with baroque works, which Zamora meticulously analyzes in an interartistic study of illusionism through an exploration of Borges's use of mirrors, labyrinths, and trompe l'oeil.

Although Zamora's reading of Borges's more "baroque" elements is intelligent, provocatively rigorous, and conversant with more recent readings of Borges's form and style such as Stephanie Merrim's, there is still that insistence on classification and generic taxonomy that appears to be answering to a larger anxiety of placement of Latin American letters. She proposes a study of Borges that enriches a reading of "Baroque modes of expression, and vice versa," one that is more interested in "affinities rather than influence," but as she continues her analysis she turns to grouping and working by analogy, finally to count Borges as one of a group of writers that he nevertheless "felt compelled to distance himself from" (237). On the whole, Zamora's project in *Inordinate Eye* corrects the pliability of influence and affinity to which she commits her readings in *Usable Past*; this could possibly have to do with basing her project exclusively on a historically cohesive group of Latin American artists and intellectuals. She pauses to examine the histories of artistic influences much more closely and admits to the invariable difficulty of placing Borges anywhere, as he "always includes the means to deconstruct any single reading of his work"

(237). However, I would underline that the act of grouping according to affinities of influence, of creating a category among which we can count certain writers as part of a particular generic grouping, contradicts the more nuanced act of playing with affinities among the works of a heterogeneous community. Zamora seems to be conscious of this when writing that "in order to encompass this variety [of writers that range from Carpentier to García Márquez to Elena Garro to Borges], it is important to allow for play among terms, techniques and intentions. By doing so we will be able to entertain some generalizations about this alternative form of modernity."[44]

Any act of criticism involves a "play with terms." And by offering a critique of the etymologies of the magical and the fantastic, I have tried to demonstrate how this play needs to be conscious of its own history and the responsibilities implicit in the processes of naming and grouping, from which surreptitious subcanons are prone to emerge. Any act of criticism also necessarily involves a play with generalizations that span generations, especially when it is committed to imagining new worlds that illuminate new or neglected communities of writers, while hailing modern readers as respondents to these worlds. But there are also the different universes enclosed within each text, as Borges reminds us, to which we must attend and, in so doing, run the danger of prioritizing the particular at the expense of theorizing the general.

In writing about ghosts, those unruly figures that—despite the perilous histories of the making and breaking of genres that attempt to tackle them—literature "ain't quit doing" (if we return to Hazel Motes's haunting intransigence in *Wise Blood*), one always returns to the question of their presence and purpose within a text. Each ghost carries a revelation as well as a simultaneous occlusion, a "play" of antinomic implications out of which the general does not necessarily show or unravel itself. Stephanie Merrim is helpful here in the direction her analysis takes toward the moment of near "indifferentiation" in works that are full of what Philip Weinstein in turn terms "history that hurts." "Indifferentiation"—that incomplete aspiration of synthesis and integration, to which Merrim alludes in her discussion of the terrible binaries that haunt Faulkner's *Absalom, Absalom!*—is a process packed with a dual projection into the past as well as into an indeterminate future. That is to say, it is not only a history punctured with the event/affect of wonder but also a *history that wonders*—about what is yet to come and the distance that must be traversed in that process.

Likewise a ghost, as an image or signal of that wound, tells a story of a past, and through a progressive process of wonder, is also an expectation placed upon a future. In this respect, ghosts serve as agents of wonder. The event of haunting can be read within the frameworks that genre theory has set out to delineate (for example, the effects of surprise and incredulity brought on by the replacement of what we take as "realistic" with its opposite). However, haunting should also be read outside of the framework of a "usable past," as an equal projection of an as-yet mysterious future. A reading of ghosts and haunting in the Americas necessarily invokes a critique of modernity by a troubled or troublesome past.[45] What I am proposing, however, is an interpretation of haunting that looks into the realms of possibility of that portentous wound that not only faces the past but gapes open toward an undetermined future as well.

While signaling an impasse between the present and other temporalities, representations of ghosts meditate on the multiple meanings and outcomes of death. Ghost stories are reflections on the finality of death and simultaneously constitute a deviation from an interpretation of death as the period or endpoint that closes a narrative of existence. As a negative mirror image of life and the processes of living, the representation of haunting seeks to invent the events that follow death, departing from a premise that death does not matter. Haunting announces that action continues otherwise. The acceptance of this premise, however, represents an opening up of a different, unfinished story altogether, rather than the simple resolution that bodily death would allow.

In *Moby-Dick, or The Whale* (1851), Herman Melville implicates his narrator Ishmael in precisely this paradox of the continuation of action after death in "The Funeral" (chap. 69).[46] In terms of the action of the novel, this chapter recounts the dropping of a whale carcass back into the ocean after the whalers have stripped its body of all the material that can be used for human profit. This act constitutes, according to Ishmael, a "most doleful and most mocking funeral" (336), given that, as the men look on, sharks and fowls inevitably take part in a further desecration of the whale's carcass. Recognizing this, Ishmael eulogizes the whale in the first part of the chapter: "Oh, horrible vulturism of earth! from which not the mightiest whale is free" (336). However, following this utterance, at the chapter's midpoint, Ishmael's register switches to one of prophecy, signaled by the predictive "Nor is this the end." What had been an oratorical narration of the negativity surrounding the "mocking funeral" is punctured by the oracular "Nor," which in turn cancels the anterior clause of conclusion: Instead of marking the end, it points to death as only a zero-point that is subsequently followed by a powerful projection of the whale's afterlife. The "end" is thus immediately followed by a different story: "Desecrated as the body is, a vengeful ghost survives and hovers over it to scare" (336). The onset of this invention of haunting then populates the negative side of the actions of the living, resulting in a topography ruled by the living's circumventions of the sites whose haunting they are responsible for creating: "And for years afterwards, perhaps, ships shun the place" (337). Maps of human activity—marked by use-value—thus exist simultaneously with those indeterminate ones that are traced according to the unquantifiable economy of the fright of prophecy. Melville is here tracing a theory of ghost stories as compositions of different worlds that are determined by a future-oriented vision of socialization with the legacies of death.

Within this proleptic spectrum, haunting and ghosts do not necessarily participate in the making of the utopian fantasies that the multiple theorizations of the magical realist genre have claimed. In her reading of Rulfo's *Pedro Páramo*, for example, Zamora sees the novel working, on one level, as a "traditional romance" portraying the ambivalence of a "nostalgia for a lost innocence and a longing for a future ideal," which, to her, is encapsulated in Rulfo's use of the Mexican Revolution (117). Turning to Rulfo in Chapter 2, I will argue that the existence of the future in terms of "ideals" or utopia is no more present in *Pedro Páramo* than are "alternative constructions of community" (116), and the common projection of a poetics of "easy answers" is something that the proponents of magical realism need to become more wary of in their formulation of subversive collectivities. What we *do* have to cope with in a novel like *Pedro Páramo* is the wound of a deserted landscape seeped in a prolonged disquiet, where a pandemonium of voices engages in continuous and continuing discourse after death. Such is the logic with which Rulfo frames the Mexican Revolution, figuring in the novel more as an agent of desertion rather than as a utopian idealization of a communal future. In this sense, spectrality and haunting align Rulfo with the other authors in this book, for whom ghosts contain a present-progressive element with a projection into an indeterminate, and not necessarily resolved, future. To look at haunting as an event of questioning, rather than one of restoration and resolution, forces us to read narratives in terms of the (oftentimes violent) open-ended socialization of life with its possible legacies. This socialization plays with the suspension between revelation and occlusion—an expectation of human permanence that is simultaneously threatened by its fragmentation—stretched out in a manner of indefinite and mysterious disquiet.

2 / Desert Mournings

The desert was one prodigious graveyard.
—MARK TWAIN, *ROUGHING IT* (1872)

Thoughts about how desert landscapes come to be crafted in the arts reveal a tension among a number of national and ideological discourses that, tangled throughout time and innumerable disseminations, often cloud the specificity of their histories. The people of Israel crossed the desert for forty years, and Christ crossed the desert for forty days, and thus the Judeo-Christian myth of the ascetic life has taken hold of how we perceive the emptiness and psychological import of wandering into these spaces of ascribed nothingness. Buddhist scriptures, as Aldous Huxley reminds us in his essay "The Desert," compare an "emptiness of space" with a mind ready for the advent of enlightenment, an enlightenment that comes from great, and limitless, silence.[1] Moving forward across the centuries, we find many examples of the imagination of desert expanses in English and French romantic literature that have dealt with this spatial tabula rasa as a site for renewal, reinvention, and regeneration. Exemplary of orientalist fiction, Flaubert's *La tentation de Saint Antoine* emerged as a result of the author's travels in North Africa at a time when many of his contemporaries in the world of arts and letters found inspiration that resulted in the elongation of the line connecting the religious figures of the Old Testament and the Desert Fathers with their own particular expeditions.[2] Into the twentieth century, one need only look to a writer such as U.S. expatriate Paul Bowles, whose novel *The Sheltering Sky* represents the North African desert as a site where one may redefine sexual freedom for the world-weary Westerner through problematic performances of native possession.

"The wonderful thing about the desert is that visually and imaginatively it is so close to the other geographic correlatives of freedom," writes

Catharine Savage Brosman. "Freedom" is an interesting word when speaking about how representations of the desert unravel imaginations of the subject in landscape. Many conditions come to mind: How is freedom possible in the realms of the unbearable? Where does one cross the line between seeking freedom and becoming lost? If the desert of ascetic lore is the closest one comes to death in life, where does one inhabit this freedom: in or after life? Furthermore, whose freedom? Is it the freedom of a community or of the solitary traveler?

The capacity for enjoying desert freedom, in the artistic tradition of the European romantics, is an individual's project. Drawing from the strong Christian tradition of this myth, the landscapes of desert and wilderness become synonymous with the equally limitless capacity of self-reflection through an escape from what in the sixteenth century Fray Luis de León termed "el mundanal ruido," or the "worldly noise" of cities. As James E. Goehring has noted of early literature about Christian saints, those

> who populated the landscape came to embody the Christian theme
> of alienation from the world by reversing the classical conceptions of
> city and desert. They appear in the desert as the biblical saints, per-
> fecting the demands of the Gospel, and in their perfection, prefigur-
> ing the world to come.[3]

Epiphany through alienation, perfection through a breaking away from community, the preparation in life for an afterlife—such are the causal concatenations that arise from the myth of the desert as a distillatory landscape. The theater par excellence for the performances of solitude and silence, this mythic desert is prefigured by an act of escape and a renunciation of the (also mythic) city. This escape consequently entails an erasure of the muddle of images and sensations of urban life, in order for the subject to become an embodiment of the city dweller's absolute opposite, a portrait of human blankness, a journey to amnesia. But, what does "freedom" mean to a person who has shed the knowledge of its opposite?

If the desert myth ignites ideas of the possibility of experiencing the opposite of society's conditions, we may begin to strike associations with other imagined spaces of difference. Can the myth of the desert be described as the epitome of utopian space? What is the geography of utopia? David Harvey explains that the "figures of 'the city' and of 'Utopia' have long been intertwined."

> The connection long predates Sir Thomas More's first adventure with
> the utopian genre in 1516. Plato connected ideal forms of government
> with his closed republic in such a way as to fold the concepts of city
> and citizen into each other and the city-state of Phaecia depicted in

Homer's *Odyssey* has many of the characteristics later alluded to by More. The Judeo-Christian tradition defined paradise as a distinctive place where all good souls would go after their trials and tribulations in the temporal world. All manner of metaphors flowed from this of the heavenly city, the city of God, the eternal city, the shining city on a hill.[4]

Where utopias were imagined as closed societies that function ideally within walls, the desert has stood as the site of the "trials and tribulations" of the world that nevertheless entail a preparation for (somewhat ironically) the paradisiacal "eternal city." As Huxley notes, the eremite's desert experience—which only a few can endure—becomes a "de-tensioner and alterative" (72), an individual's act of de-edification after the flight from closed communities and fenced landscapes.

The concept of the idealized landscapes of utopia as necessarily enclosed leads to a consideration of how the spaces *outside* these enclosures converse with those within, and under what terms. Michel Foucault's famous definition of the "heterotopia"—first coined in *The Order of Things* (1966), it reappeared posthumously in *Diacritics* in 1986 in the essay "Of Other Spaces," an unpublished lecture from 1967—is important in our consideration of the myth of the desert as a site that is geographically opposed to the historical imagination of utopias. As Harvey explains, Foucault first conceived heterotopias only in terms of "discourse and language," and later tried to "give the term a material referent" (183). He developed a list of actual sites that function heterotopically: the cemetery, the garden, the carnivals outside of cities, and the ship, the perfect site for this other function.[5] In *The Order of Things*, Foucault first defines the heterotopia against the utopian space, stating that, although utopias "have no real locality, there is nevertheless a fantastic untroubled region in which they are able to unfold." Utopias entail highly elaborate landscapes—"cities with vast avenues" and "countries where life is easy"—even despite the hindrance that "the road to them is chimerical." Heterotopias, in contrast, are "disturbing, probably because they secretly undermine language." Where utopias "permit fables and discourse," heterotopias "desiccate speech, stop words in their tracks," "dissolv[ing] our myths and steriliz[ing] the lyricism of our sentences" (xix).[6]

This first definition of the other space in terms of language and the representation of myth is a useful springboard for our present discussion of the desert as an imagined space. The desert as a site of atonement that is far from being "untroubled" still allows for "fables and discourse," as I have been arguing. The paths of silence of the desert space of the Judeo-Christian and romantic imaginations, although "desiccat[ing]" speech" at the level of narrative experience (that is, what the character in a desert tale goes through in the solitude of the landscape), have constituted a proliferation of a rather unified myth rather than a dissolution. The solitude thus encased in this myth, renouncing any sense of community or relation, seems to oppose a utopian or heterotopian model of location or human process. However, the desert's story does not end here.

Envisioning and Imagining American Deserts

The historian Tulio Halperín Donghi complains that, in *Facundo* (discussed in Chapter 4), the Argentine Domingo Sarmiento "liked to compare the disconcerting trajectory covered by Latin America from the time of the declaration of independence until the middle of the nineteenth century with the forty years' wandering of the Israelites in the desert."[7] In this text, as we shall see, the author reads the desert as an encroaching menace upon the cities, which were the only possible sites of civilization and history. Modernization thus translated spatially into a "conquest" of the desert space. Caught between ancient myth and the problems of national transition, the landscape of the desert in this context becomes a riddle of storytelling and historical process—a tortuous link between subjective development through penance and the invention of the complicated webs of modern nationhood.

American deserts, north and south, present an interesting twist in this mythologizing tale of the desert as ascetic space. This is not to say that desert sites in the Western hemisphere somehow expel, or are immune from, mythic appropriation—far from it. Rather, the mythopoetics of topographic wilderness have evolved formally and thematically through a number of transformations that have worked, on the one hand, to keep abstract notions of the desert intact, and, on the other, to fill the desert's discursive void, substituting its semantic impoverishment with historical tales that recount the expansion of modern civilization. These two narrative strains are not mutually exclusive of one another. As Richard Slotkin makes clear, the concept of "regeneration through violence" is often rehearsed to describe the fictions of the expansion of the United States in the seventeenth to nineteenth centuries. The imagination of the vast American wildernesses and deserts as empty in the literature of conquest and colonization constitutes a *writing over* of the material processes of expansion with the age-old myth of spiritual renewal among solitudes and silences.

The symbolization of American desert landscapes has redefined what it means for writers to depict and project scenes of regeneration.[8] The representation of such landforms has yielded a variety of afterlives to the human element that crosses the desert, making this site a preferred location for recycling the discourse of possibility for the subjects who endure its terrain.[9] Through this myth, history is posited as the negative of the desert sphere, where the latter compromises and inverts the rules of eventual accumulation that define "civilization." In his travelogue *The American Scene* (discussed in the next chapter), Henry James describes a train voyage from the "Far West" through Chicago and on to New York City as a return to history.

> It is still vivid to me that, returning in the spring-time from a few weeks in the Far West, I re-entered New York State with the absurdest sense of meeting again a ripe old civilization and travelling through a country that showed the mark of established manners. . . . [A]nd history, as we moved Eastward, appeared to meet us in the look of the land, in its more overwrought surface and thicker detail, quite as if she had ever consciously declined to cross the border and were aware, precisely, of the queer feast we should find in her. . . . It was doubtless a matter only of degrees and shades, but never was such a pointing of the lesson that a sign of any sort may count double if it be but artfully placed.[10]

Here James describes "history"—which we can define schematically as a narrative of time through space—by means of a portrayal of the emergence of topographic features, of "overwrought surface and thicker detail." This synchronization of "surface" details with the narration of events across time is then able to "count double" if cast into the realms of artistic representation—that is, if it is processed from mere landscape to imagined, "artful" realms. At that moment, James can only envision history and manners as possible where he can perceive an architecture of human enterprise, although in the West he had not been able to envisage any approximation to that capacity for historical, or artful, narrative.[11] Thus James is noting the signs of "history" written over in the densely populated, progressively urbanized vistas met upon his entry into New York State. Nevertheless, a question arises here: Could we reverse James's declaration of the place where artful signs may dwell and think of the desert as a site where a narrative of history may *also* be represented? It would be important to question whether we have the adequate vocabulary to address the semiotic "thickness" of the desert, which is undoubtedly a different kind of density, one that exists in an ascribed emptiness.[12] By doing this, we could then argue that the signs that have been imposed on the desert may also "count double."

Twenty years after the publication of James's *American Scene*, and in a different American context, young Jorge Luis Borges reflects on the phenomenon of intersecting signs and landscapes in his short essay "La pampa

y el suburbio son dioses" ("The Pampas and the Suburb Are Gods"). Here
Borges understands the Argentine desert and the "arrabal" (the impover-
ished suburban area at the edges of cities like Buenos Aires) as "two godly
presences," "two realities of such reverential efficacy that the mere enunciation of their names is enough to swell any verse and to lift our hearts with
an intimate and intractable joy."[13] These two landscapes are always and already symbolic spheres: The act of representing them conjures "archetypal
things" ["cosas arquetípicas"] that are "not subject to the contingencies of
time" ["cosas no sujetas a las contingencias del tiempo"]. The desert landscape of the pampas is thus a spiritual "totem," which Borges defines as the
"accepted generalization of things that are co-substantial with a race or
an individual" ["acepción generalizada de cosas que son cosustanciales de
una raza o de un individulo"] (21). A geography that belongs to a culture,
the pampas thus stand as topographical presence, as well as a mightily
significant *word* that functions as both "sound" and "echo": "esa palabra
infinita que es como un sonido y su eco" ["that infinite word that is like a
sound and its echo "] (21).

Interestingly, the author's reflection is informed by various transnational references to thinkers such as Charles Darwin (who had explored
the pampas in his travels to the Southern Cone). Borges criticizes Darwin's
scientific rigor during his voyage to South America (as noted by W. H.
Hudson in *The Naturalist in la Plata* from 1892), where the Englishman
notes that the horizon over a plain can cover only "a distance of two miles
and four-fifths" ["distancia de dos millas y cuatro quintos"], something
that "completely annihilates the greatness one imaginatively prescribes to
a great plain" ["aniquila enteramente la grandeza que uno le imagina de
antemano a una gran llanura"] (23). Borges rejects this claim by, again, as-
serting the confluence in "vision" of reality and symbolization—the landscape that "grows with/through memories" ["crece con sus recuerdos"].
Thus, where the areas in the western United States stand as unrepresent-
able for James, who perceives no particular or accountable signs beyond
the frontier with the urbanized East, for the young Borges contemplating
the native landscape, the desert is already and necessarily understood as
a fusion of the values of "indubitable" space, memory, and symbol in the
imagination of the Argentine individual. It is a space that, along with the
"arrabal" at the city's margins, the author "feels like wounds" that "hurt
equally": "Es indudable que el arrabal y la pampa existen del todo y que los
siento abrirse como heridas y me duelen igual" (24). Borges's allusion to the
"wounds" of landscape that are formed in the poetic realm helps account
for a meeting between the totemic dimensions of the spatial imagination
of the desert plain and the human enunciation of memory and experience abiding within it. He insists on the participative dimensions of such

spaces: As national patrimony, the pampas and the "arrabal" are sites of belonging for the Argentine, places within which the national subject can travel in a dual process of poetics and reality.

This chapter is guided by questions of how we come to interpret the ways in which these "wounds" are portrayed in the spaces of American deserts in modern literature and film. Moments of solitude, solace, and regeneration in so many of the texts that have the desert as their chosen mise-en-scène (or better, a mise-en-abîme), converse with the possibilities of community and humanity in these landscapes, exposing their multiple and often devastating outcomes. American deserts, in their complicated histories as landscapes of violence, dispossession, and transience, have thus come to be symbolized as sites that host both rejuvenating and sinister forms of expanse. Moreover, deserts have been represented as places whose proverbial emptiness is something that can be *achieved* through the elimination of different human agencies.

The actions of haunting, as I will argue, constitute valuable points of mediation between these two opposing sides of the myth. They pose a troubling and negative "thick detail" that signals an altogether different idea of regenerative landscape. The imagined desert ghost towns I will explore later in the chapter—namely Juan Rulfo's Comala in *Pedro Páramo* (1955) and Lago in Clint Eastwood's *High Plains Drifter* (1972/3)—offer alternative interventions, negotiating as they do between topographical emptiness and the tumult of impending or actual death. Synthesizing scenic and corporeal manifestations of dread, these distinctive texts participate in that additional dialectic between the regenerative stillness of *desert* landscapes and human acts of *desertion*. Haunting becomes in this interplay of absence and abandonment nothing less than the proleptic dimension of regeneration, performing the disquieting reentrance of human history as an agent of the landscape's ongoing renewal. As discussed in Chapter 1, the analysis of haunting's disquietude should overcome the limitations of genre analysis and allocation, critical processes that often run the risk of inducing a suspension of history. It is not my intention to read these two very different texts comparatively in order to make them comply with a desert model of universal and transtemporal haunting; instead, I see them as separate expressions of how the dialectics of desert and desertion compels us to pay closer attention to the specificity of imagined sites.

Neither do I intend to write a utopia over these imaginations of desert spaces by exploring the proleptic dimensions of haunting. As my opening chapter made clear, it is a critically disingenuous and dehistoricizing move to frame the desert as a site where a possible *melting* or *fusion* of the nation's past, present, and future may be conceived in solely allegorical or archetypal terms. Although a more useful category, to classify the desert as a heterotopia may also prove disingenuous. Foucault reminds us that heterotopias are real sites that exist within our everyday worlds, and in this sense, they are everything but mythical. However, the very act of assigning a heterotopic function to the desert as a way of performing a spatialization of otherness may well run the risk of mythologizing difference itself. In Lois Parkinson Zamora's reading of Rulfo as a magical realist writer, the desert myth is taken at face value as the archetypal backdrop to the "romance" of ghostly types and lends itself to a reading of landscape as eternally ancient. The desert becomes in itself the animistic and alternative cosmology to Western values and temporalities. She contends that Rulfo's *Pedro Páramo* reflects "the cosmology of the Nahuatl-speaking peoples of the central and northern highlands of Mexico," while the dead that inhabit the earth of Comala stand as Day of the Dead "*calaveras*" (skulls) that, in traditional popular Mexican culture, "celebrate the pleasures of the living" and "mock our [living] follies."[14] In Zamora's analysis, the archetypal emptiness of the desert turns into a repository for a problematic collapsing of multicultural histories of human agency and violence. This particular interpretation of the desert opts for a refreshing, and carnivalized, Mexican otherness that stands against "post-Enlightenment" values. Zamora thus uses genre to write over Rulfo's story of broken community with a misplaced anthropological use of myth.[15] We should ask whether it is possible to read the desert for itself and its specificity rather than for its amenability to preconceived philosophical and methodological objectives. This directly leads to the question of whether we can read the ghosts that have been inscribed into the fictions of this landscape as historically specific figures, and not simply as eternal archives—or infinite libraries (to give it a Borgesian twist)—of a continent's or a nation's past.

Landscapes of Modern Simultaneity

I could argue that the imagination of the desert is irresistible because it is one topography of our modern natural space that feels ancient, as well as yet-to-be done. In this sense, the desert has been perversely allegorized (although not, in this case, in the Benjaminian sense of immediately "becoming obsolete") and has become vulnerable to attributions of immense meanings and suspensions of human history. The spectacle of the desert has a variety of outcomes for the observer: Although it can conjure the shock of simultaneity of landscapes in one spectator, it can also create the fantasy of the desert as *another* world. In other words, although one non-desert dweller may see in the imagination of the desert the unseen space of an ongoing modernity, another might perceive it as a retreat from modern time and space.

This first case of simultaneity is something that troubled the Cuban José Martí when he went to see Buffalo Bill's "Wild West" in the 1880s (episodes that will continue to be discussed in the next chapter).[16] Described by Joy Kasson as "an engaging outdoor display of exotic animals and individuals demonstrating skills and enacting fictions," the Wild West exhibition "was immediately recognized as a remarkable theatrical innovation, bringing the stage play together with other entertainments such as the circus and sportsmen's exhibitions."[17] As Richard Slotkin explains, the "show" was meant to be "educational," and thus never called a "show," but simply the "Wild West," a "name which identified it as a 'place' rather than a mere display or entertainment."[18] This insistence on location rather than spectacle, Slotkin argues, in reality constitutes "its landscape" as a "mythic space, in which past and present, fiction and reality could coexist; a space in which history, translated into myth, was reenacted as ritual" (166). The "Wild West" thus becomes the movable representation of that space beyond urban recognition through the processes of "magnificent spectacle" (Martí's descriptive phrase in the title). It represents the transportable conflation of myth and true history thanks to a process of transplanted *evidence* for the urban spectator who does not know that simultaneous landscape to the west.

When looking at tableaux from the desert on display at the exhibition's tents, Martí describes that faraway and unseen landscape with its "mountain trees petrified in the active silence of the centuries: the mountains seem like centuries, centuries huddled in strings, seeing the world simmer and change" ["árboles petrificados en las montañas en el silencio activo de los siglos:—siglos parecen ser los montes, siglos acurrucados en hilera, a ver hervir y transformarse el mundo"].[19] Martí's attention to that "active silence" of passing time in the desert wilderness, of centuries that tower into mountains, recovers an idea of human agency in the emptiness—an agency that runs parallel to the "history" that James saw in the "thick detail" of the East. In Martí's imagination of the desert within the context of a spectacle, the landscape and its inhabitants (the indigenous populations, also on display), are active witnesses of the boiling points of history's movements.

Martí's impressions about the Buffalo Bill show in New York represent a site for the hemispheric confluence of narratives that not only observe but reflect on the simultaneous conceptions of the landscape on a national scale. His North American chronicles, written during his exile in New York from 1880 into the 1890s for major newspapers in Latin America, describe scenes of life and culture as they were transpiring in the "gigantic" United States in an innovative style combining reportage and poetic experimentation. The chronicles give the reader a sense of hemispheric simultaneity insofar as Martí's Latin American audience was able to witness life unfolding elsewhere at the same time that their own daily rituals and stories transpired. As Susana Rotker explains, "In Martí's time the awareness of modernity suffuses everything," so that "journalism becomes the ideal medium through which to contact, day to day, the flow of a new society."[20] Here we are reminded of Benedict Anderson's work on formal and spatiotemporal simultaneity as a form of constructing nationalism in the modern age. In *Imagined Communities*, he explains how after the ancient ontological-religious conception of time as a way of understanding the world (what he calls "simultaneity-along-time") began depleting itself— through, for example, a democratization of print cultures—the semantics of simultaneity takes a new shape: "What has come to take the place of the mediaeval conception of simultaneity-along-time is, to borrow again from Benjamin, an idea of 'homogenous, empty time,' in which simultaneity is, as it were, transverse, cross-time, marked not by prefiguring and fulfilment, but by temporal coincidence, and measured by clock and calendar" (24). Interestingly, Anderson exemplifies this "temporal coincidence" in the "two forms of imagining which first flowered in Europe in the eighteenth century: the novel and the newspaper," forms that help construct an "idea of a sociological organism moving calendrically through homogenous, empty time," which is analogous to "the idea of a nation, which also is conceived as a solid community moving steadily down (or up) history" (26). Anderson believes that, even if a person in a nation does not meet all of the citizens living within it, "he has complete confidence in their steady, anonymous, simultaneous activity" (26). Martí poses an interesting case in this consideration of Anderson's idea (which is mostly grounded on a temporal notion of simultaneity). The former's chronicles, in their status as literature within the format of dated reportage, constitute a point of contact between the novel and the newspaper, two forms of literature that, according to Anderson, reassure "that the imagined world is visibly rooted in everyday life" (35), creating "that remarkable confidence of community in anonymity which is the hallmark of modern nations" (36). In the case of Martí's coverage of events in the United States from a point of view of exile, it seems to me, the notion of "community in anonymity" is complicated by spatial and racial divisions, as is explicit in the Buffalo Bill chronicles. For Martí, to speak of temporal simultaneity does not mean the same thing as spatial simultaneity: His writing consists of a coming to grips with precisely the opposite of "community in anonymity," because the everyday lives of cultural others are too often and too easily obscured. With a subject like the Buffalo Bill "Wild West," one must come to grips with the question of how we can read modernity when it comes packaged as a spectacle of its immediate, diverse, and spatially expansive pasts and presents.

As critics from Rotker to Laura Lomas have argued, Martí's readings of the United States in the chronicles epitomize the keen observations of an exiled cultural outsider, constituting what Rotker calls a complicated "gesture of relocation."

> It begins with the difficulty of constructing a location from the margin. Then it must also construct a discourse that can be understood by Spanish America, which it in turn modifies as his place of belonging. . . . He writes from the margins of the gaze—not with the attitude of inferiority expected of the subject confronted by Empire, but with a transforming will. He does not seek to subject or be subjected, but to *create*. (104)

Martí's chronicles are thus sites of *invention* via critical contemplation. Surpassing the rudimentary ambitions of the journalistic essay, they acquire a certain aesthetic force by synthesizing social and metaphysical aims, combining "referentiality" with the transcendental (88). The Buffalo Bill chronicle from 1886 represents the author as a spectator reflecting on his own anxieties of seeing, expressing a significant amount of admiration that is still able to recognize the "stunned fantas[y]" ["absorta fantasía"] of the spectacle of dispossession of the land from its "natural owners" by the "conquerors of the jungle" (68). This process is perceived to extract the "soul" from the "scarcity and squalor of urban life" to the point at which, "involuntarily," it can "excite" the self to rise upon the stands. I quote this paragraph at length as an illustration of Martí's consciousness of the powers of spectacle.

> Y así va viendo la absorta fantasía, con fruición de enamorada, los lances nativos de aquella existencia original y grandiosa: así asiste en todo el fulgor de la verdad al desalmado combate entre los dueños naturales del país y los conquistadores de la selva; así se va sacando al alma mansamente de la poquedad y escualidez de la vida ciudadana,—cuando un espectáculo estremecedor, involuntariamente excita a ponerse en pie sobre las gradas, cual si fuera vergüenza quedarse holgando en los estrados de la vida cuando cruzan ante nosotros, con la majestad del trabajo y el peligro, los que bregan en sus entrañas. (68)

> [And with the resolution of a woman in love, the stunned fantasizing progressively makes out the native lances of that original and grandiose existence; so in the glimmer of truth she tends to the cruel combat between the country's natural owners and the conquerors of the jungle; so the soul is gently extracted from the scarcity and squalor of urban life—when an overwhelming spectacle excites one to rise involuntarily upon the stands, as if it were embarrassing to loiter on

the sidelines of life when we have before our eyes those who, with the majesty of work and danger, live within its bowels.]

Here we have the chronicler critically perceiving the spectacle of the "Wild West" as a mediation between one national site of "squalor" with the "majesty of work and danger" residing magnificently in another. Sheer *spectacle* stands in the way of any compulsion to naturalize the scene as incontrovertible: In alluding to the "involuntary" euphoria experienced by the viewing public, Martí appears to be pointing to larger and more troubling questions of agency (or the loss thereof) in the narratives we construct about landscapes to the west.

The conclusions to the two Buffalo Bill chronicles are valuable in the ways in which both author and reader cope with the repercussions of literary witnessing. Although I discuss the conclusion to the earlier 1884 chronicle in Chapter 3, in this chapter I want to focus on how Martí ends his longer 1886 chronicle. The spectacle subsides, though life continues "palpitating for a long time in the circus that empties little by little" ["Queda la vida palpitando largo tiempo en el circo que se depleta poco a poco"], and the "droves of the curious begins to vanish along the pine paths, like blood issuing from veins" ["el curso de curiosos va perdiéndose a lo largo de los pinos, cual sangre se sale de las venas"] (68). This alignment of the images of the spectators' exit with the severed vein constitutes an unsettling aftereffect of the noisy and colorful revelry that has just transpired in the exhibition. The following and final paragraph imagines the personification of this disquietude: the "downcast Indian doctor" ["el médico tristísimo"]—a melancholy subject who appears earlier in the chronicle, and who does not participate in the revelry of the circus, instead entering into the pine path "like a king in his palace"—his figure "made gigantic" ["agigantada"] by the "shadow" that rises and extends over the "horizon." He looks on at the disappearing white people, his two "bony hands" crossed over his chest, his "shield" at his feet, his "eyes dry, and his complexion earthy":

> Pero junto al más recio y lejano de los pinos, agigantada por la sombra sobre el horizonte su figura enhiesta erizada de plumas, mira a la gente blanca que desaparece, el médico tristísimo, sobre el pecho ambas manos huesudas, el escudo a los pies, los ojos secos, y la faz terrosa. (62)

> [Next to the sturdiest and farthest tree, his lofty plumed figure enlarged by the shadow cast over the horizon, the downtrodden Indian doctor, with his bony hands over his chest, shield at his feet, his dry eyes and earthen face, gazes at the white people as they disappear.]

Curiously, as Slotkin observes, the program to the 1886 "Wild West" describes the "history of the West" as the "'lengthened shadow'" of Buffalo Bill (169). Whether intentional or not, Martí leaves the Latin American reader with that image of the extending shadow of the Native American figure instead of evoking Buffalo Bill's mythological immensity in the final part of his chronicle. He subverts the intended narrative developed by the show's organizers and inserts the melancholy of dispossession through a figure that remains powerful in his permanent liminality—on the severed vein that separates the mythology of the frontier and the reality of exile, along the margin that divides the simultaneous landscapes and cultural realities of the modern United States.

Martí's formal and critical invention in the space of the chronicle works on the separate registers of the social and the metaphysical. He questions an idea of a unified national psyche through the textual invention of landscapes of simultaneity. The tensions between these spheres of different "thickness" (if we think back to James) are evident in the reality of the "suffering provinces" in Latin America, as he calls them in his essay "Nuestra América" from 1891. His chronicles lead us to an understanding of U.S. expansionism as a movement covered in the overwhelming armature of universalizing narratives—something Martí will then work to redress in his conception of "*nuestroamericanismo*" (the ideology of "our América" made famous in the above-mentioned essay). In this oratorical essay, Martí inserts the values of national self-invention into a narrative of Latin American unity.

> Cansados del odio inútil, de la resistencia del libro contra la lanza, de la razón contra el cirial, de la ciudad contra el campo, del imperio imposible de las castas urbanas divididas sobre la nación natural, tempestuosa o inerte, se empieza, como sin saberlo, a probar el amor. Se ponen en pie los pueblos y se saludan. «¿Cómo somos?», se preguntan, y unos a otros se van diciendo como son. . . . Entienden que se imita demasiado y que la solución está en crear. Crear es la palabra de pase de esta generación.[21]

> [Tired of useless hate, of the resistance of the book against the lance, reason against the altar candle [*cirial*], the city against the countryside, of the impossible empire of divided urban castes over the native nation, by turns tempestuous or inert, they unknowingly began to try love. People stand up on their feet and salute themselves. "What exactly are we?" they ask, and they tell one another what they are like. . . . They understand that we have imitated for too long and that salvation is in creating. *Crear* [to create] is the password of a generation.][22]

This national self-creation is marked by a recognition of simultaneous landscapes that had been suffused with a rhetoric of opposition in the hemispheric north and south: the fragmented national landscape overcome through the creative process of participatory crafting of a recognizable American *us*. Martí's Buffalo Bill chronicle represents an instance in which the (spectacular) experience of dichotomous landscapes, represented as such, haunt one another. It also displays the author as he tries to make sense of how the past is represented and made spectacle, and how one can revise it and thus bring it back into panoptic focus.[23] The chronicle illustrates what it means to watch out for ghosts of the present, that is, to be vigilant of the coexistence of simultaneous communities in those landscapes beyond the reaches of our immediate perception.

Spectacles of the Desert: From Literature to Film

Film is arguably our most haunted medium. As Gilberto Pérez has beautifully shown, this form of representation relies on what he calls "our acceptance of absence," as well as a specific understanding of temporality, whereby the cinematic image is forever coming into being although also announcing its pastness.[24] Film taunts our reliance on permanence, as figures on the screen can appear, disappear, and reappear without warning. As scenes focus on a slice of cinematic "reality," spectators are left out of the experience of an environment outside of the image's frame. This recognition of an outside that is beyond our perception is itself an acknowledgment of a disquieting sense of incomplete understanding. We could argue that the absence of the film medium itself is intensified when the image represented is that of an empty landscape, a desert.

The desert landscapes in the history of film are perhaps the best-known spectacles of the tensions between fictions of emptiness and representations of violence. The offspring of the Buffalo Bill shows, the Western genre (especially in its golden era from the 1930s to the 1950s) has often given us the curious melding of the campaigns of expansion and population of the desert with the figure of the mythic and independent Everyman at its center. The figure of the Western loner (cowboy, settler, or renegade) grew out of Fenimore Cooper and continued in the U.S. imaginary through the popular dime novels during the nineteenth and twentieth centuries. Against this one myth stood the figure of the Indian, portrayed more often than not under opprobrious lights. Peter Cowie, for example, notes how the silent film *The Friendless Indian* (1913) contains a title that reads: "Condemned to walk alone, a Red Man saves a life and is given only a nod of thanks—after all, he is Indian."[25] Around the same time, however, the 1915 documentary film titled *History of the American Indian* (directed by

Rollin S. Dixon) comprised thirteen reels that recorded "rites and ceremo-
nies that were already forgotten by young Indians."[26]

A preeminent if not magisterial presence among western directors, John
Ford created works for cinema that recall the romantic-inflected paintings
of nineteenth-century artists such as Albert Bierstadt (1830–1902), Charles
M. Russell (1865–1926), and Frederic Remington (1861–1909), painters
of Western magnificence, or what has come to be called the "American
sublime." Ford's many films contextualize mythopoeic Western conflicts
amid the wild and overwhelming beauty of the desert landscape.[27] Repeatedly filming on location in Monument Valley, Ford's films create, according to Cowie, "his own mythical domain" of the Old West, often "at the
expense of strict geographical or historical authenticity." In the case of *My
Darling Clementine* (1946), for example, he sets the town of Tombstone
within Monument Valley (in northeast Arizona and southern Utah), when
in reality the real town is located "almost four hundred miles to the south,
near the Mexican border," and although Wyatt Earp's character (played
by Henry Fonda) refers to "Tucson" as a "nearby cow town," it was in fact
"more than three hundred miles due south of Ford's location" (56). We
begin to appreciate how the coherent symbol of the United States West
operates in Ford's oeuvre: Athough perhaps not geographically accurate,
the arbitrary use of historical place-names and locations from desert landscapes that span countless miles and U.S. states supports the director's
keen interest in representing the myth of national personality within an
imposing and picturesque natural stage.

This mythopoeia of the U.S. desert would withstand the detonation
of the bomb in the 1945 culmination of the Manhattan Project in White
Sands, New Mexico, as Westerns continued to be a popular genre well
into the 1960s. This decade's countercultural movements represent a moment where the myth is again regenerated through an approximation
of the chimerical landscape with updated utopias, as a group of writers
begin to look to the desert as an escape from the repression and warfare
of the cultures of empire rooted in urban centers. The now-classic *Desert Solitaire* (1968) by Edward Abbey (a writer Larry McMurtry calls the
"Thoreau of the American West") returns again to that complete desire
for escape from cities, and even small towns, in favor of "all that which
lies beyond the end of the roads," of the "red dust and the burnt cliffs and
the lonely sky" of the desert.[28] Over a decade later, Sam Shepard's *True
West* (1981) represents two tensely combative brothers (one a vagrant,
the other a successful screenwriter who lives with his family in Holly-
wood) playing out their history of real life–poetic antagonism when the
first is able to outsell his brother in the crafting of a plot for a Western. In the end, the scene advances to a "vast desert-like landscape" that

encompasses Lee and Austin, where they are "very still but watchful for the next move."[29]

The European mythification of the American desert, moving parallel to the North American cartographies of disenchantment and regeneration, cannot be overlooked.[30] In fact, it was Sam Shepard himself (along with Clare Peploe and antiwar activist Fred Gardner) who wrote the screenplay for Michelangelo Antonioni's imagination of the affective possibilities of the American desert in the modern age of materialism and its discontents in the unsuccessful *Zabriskie Point* (1970). The gentlest climax in *Zabriskie Point*, which followed his acclaimed *Blow-Up* (1967), presents the viewer with the possibility of odd renewal and multiplication that appears to emulate the fluctuations and sandy renewals of the desert. Two individuals making love on the dunes of a North American desert landscape roll around, the sand covering them up until they become almost unrecognizable from the ground in their impregnated golden brownness. This unrecognizability of the lovers is followed by an interesting effect: Out of nowhere, as if in a dream (a very late-1960s countercultural one at that), more and more couples and threesomes appear on the dunes, engaging in coitus as well, all of them brown with sand, having the time of their lives. The camera pans out, and we see just how many of these people there really are: so many of them, becoming "one" with nature, promiscuously rolling around together, turning into breathing sand dunes in the distant vistas of the desert.

This scene—a by-product of the Vietnam-era revolutionary zeitgeist searching for spaces in the national landscape that could offer a promise of an untarnished, pristine existence when every other place was tainted by disillusion—proposes the desert as an answer to the specific queries posed by Antonioni's film as a whole. In other words, *Zabriskie Point* is a film that asks where the idealism of the antiestablishment movements can reside and flourish. The desert and the orgy scene choreographed within it become sites of organic possibility as well as (more ominously, as we see in the film's denouement) the combustive organic sites where the evil empires of capitalism and corrupt government can be literally blown up. Arguably a rereading of the desert's reinvention as atomic test site, this last scene in the film, where the ultramodern house of an oil tycoon is blown up, reinvents the aftermath of an apocalypse by giving the desert back to the revolution and its proponents.

South of the border, the Chilean filmmaker Alejandro Jodorowsky creates a bizarre desert landscape that stands as a receptacle for the fusion and subversion of multiple film genres, philosophies (from Freud to Plato to the Far East), and cultural contacts. *El Topo* (*The Mole*) from 1970 was filmed in different areas of the northern Mexican desert. It begins with a man and a boy riding a horse over pristine desert dunes. What follows is the first page of Jodorowsky's screenplay, a document that combines many of the director's philosophical explications with the images that actually appear on screen.

> When a man buries a pole in the sand, he automatically creates a sundial and begins to mark time. To begin marking time is to begin creating a culture.
>
> A pole rises out of the desert sand. El Topo appears riding a black horse. He is dressed entirely in black. . . . He carries an open black umbrella. His seven-year-old son rides behind him, holding on to his back. Except for a hat and moccasins, the child is nude. . . .
>
> El Topo dismounts and lifts his son down. . . . He removes a leather pouch from his saddle and takes out a toy bear and a picture of a woman. . . .
>
> EL TOPO: *Today you are seven years old. Now you are a man. Bury your first toy and your mother's picture.*
>
> The child sits beside the sundial. He digs a hole in the sand and buries the bear, although El Topo plays a flute. . . .[31]

This "culture" that begins to be marked with the pole in the scorching desert is, for Jodorowsky, a clustering of carnivalized images of desire that oscillate between cliché (two nude women in a desert oasis) and irreverent (three macho Mexican bandits kissing four bound, effeminate Franciscan monks). The narrative is told using structures commonly found in Chinese martial arts films and North American Westerns. El Topo wanders the deserts and adjacent towns (the latter which are pervasively sites of abusive perversion and homosexual desires) searching for the four "masters," with whom he is predestined to duel. After losing to the final master, he is taken underground into a cave by a community of "crippled, insane, retarded people" (53), where he remains in amnesiac slumber for years. He emerges from the cave looking like a desert ascetic, with shaved head and eyebrows. He travels into the "town" in the company of a woman from the cave, now his lover. After he attempts to reap vengeance on the townspeople, he dies through self-immolation, his tomb covered in swarming bees that have "created a river of honey over the grave" (93).

El Topo is in one way Jodorowsky's revision of the classic Western through a feverish internationalization of the desert landscape: He restores the "nobility" of "ancient Mexico" where the Western has insisted that the "Mexican is always the outlaw" (112), while the four masters pay homage to Chinese, Sufi, Mexican, and Japanese samurai stories, respectively. And yet, his aim is to empty his landscapes of historical or "normal time."

In the film there is no normal time sequence. There can be a thou-
sand years between one sequence and another. The film can start
with pre-historic time and end with the atomic bomb. When I burn
the village at the end of the film, I use the sound of the explosion of
an atomic bomb. (134)

In *El Topo* we discover a visual vortex of multiple transnational, trans-
ideological, and transtemporal representations of the desert myth to the
point that it becomes the site of a vertiginous amalgamation of folklores,
archetypes, and symbols. This entails an excess as well as an undoing
of signification. Jodorowsky takes John Ford's liberties with the de-his-
toricized desert to their logical end. However, whereas Ford privileges a
notion of interchangeable desert locations for the sake of a sublime national aesthetic, Jodorowsky's imagination seeks an understanding of this
landscape that is capable of undoing historical and national borders. The
latter's take on the Western constitutes a death or, better put, an implosion of the genre, as its privileged landscape becomes a repository for a
plurality of cosmogonies and fantasies. In other words, for Jodorowsky, the
desert landscape offers quite a mythological and even allegorical version
of simultaneity: He portrays the fantastical concurrence of desires, belief
systems, and styles within a space that has become recognizable to the
viewer as the canvas for a Western. In *El Topo*, he demonstrates how the
act of representing an American desert on film can be wildly haunted by
numerous other imaginations of the desert where mourning, desire, and
duels also play important roles.

Ghost Towns

Rather emblematically, the town used in *El Topo* was the abandoned
film set for the Western *The Law of Tombstone*.[32] "I needed a town, a
cowboy town. And when I was looking for locations, it was as if I were
dreaming," Jodorowsky recounts. "And then I saw a beautiful town in
the desert, and I said, 'It's impossible. A beautiful town in the desert.'"
He adds: "It was a cowboy town in the desert because an American
movie . . . had built sets there. They paid for the job, built it, shot the
picture, and left. . . . It was an abandoned town . . . a ghost town" (122).
Jodorowsky kept the movie ghost town intact, even retaining the building signs written in English. Quite remarkably, the ghost towns that
stipple deserts in the United States and Mexico (the focus of the rest of
this chapter) represent an intersection of the "indubitable" histories of
human movements across these landscapes, as well as the fictions that
were written over them.

Most of the historic North American ghost towns that are still standing date back to the mid- to late nineteenth century, a time when Easterners were being beckoned to the West with promises of employment in the mining and (earlier) railroad industries. Many of these settlements became societal vacuums rather quickly, with the coming of economic depressions that devastated the mining industry and the completion of the transcontinental railroad. Some ghost towns in the western United States existed as small, bustling hubs of life for as little as a decade.[33]

South of the border, in the aftermath of the Mexican Revolution of 1910, a period during which the industries in the urban center were disproportionately favored above the rural-agrarian economy, the Mexican capital witnessed a massive migration of peasants (*campesinos*) in search of employment. As Diane E. Davis points out,

> In theory, Mexico's Revolution could have taken several different paths after 1910. Given the involvement of *agraristas* like Emiliano Zapata and Pancho Villa, given the fact that rural populations with agrarian sentiments had struggled most actively in the armed struggle, and given the overwhelming anti-Americanism that prevailed at the time, it would have been perfectly logical for Mexico to have followed an ideological course not unlike that taken by Cubans in their revolution five decades later. That is, Mexico's revolutionary leaders could have built an anticapitalist social and political order structured around the objectives of rural development. But they did not.[34]

These abandoned sites beyond the peripheries of centralized urban populations are remnants of an existence hollowed out by the movements and migrations of human history across landscapes of conflict and shifting economies. Eerie and quiet, ghost towns exist today as museum pieces, as sites that reveal the winding down of human time. They are curious manifestations of places that continuously seem to bear witness to a long-departed past.[35]

Ghost towns appear on the landscape like immediate and modern ruins: They are traces of a past that is nevertheless not qualifiable as ancient, but that is instead marked by a trace of the dynamics of abandonment. In other words, the ghost town still bears the trace of the human act of desertion, of picking up and going away, that announces the mundane realities of dislocation. "In the ruin," writes Walter Benjamin, "history has physically merged into the setting. And in this guise history does not assume the form of the process of an eternal life so much as that of irresistible decay."[36] The ruin enacts the event of "becoming obsolete," which Benjamin attributes in the realm of language to the allegory (as in the example of

Baudelaire's poetry). This explains the now-famous assertion that "allegories are, in the realm of thoughts, what ruins are in the realm of things" (178).

The fusion of allegory and the ruin is simultaneously attractive and complicated when thinking about the ghost town in American history and the imagination that surrounds it. It becomes a difficult task to separate the material history from the symbolic order (and the entertainment industry, at least in the case of the United States) that has surrounded it. The ghost town is in many ways the architectural epitome of the desert myth: It is proof of the passing of time and of people within a certain site. The ghost town becomes as well the evidence of a human time that has been progressively emptied of the "active silence" of modernity's progress to the point of becoming hollow. As such, it is often inflected with new meanings (becoming, for example, reactivations of a "Wild West," or a saccharine muralization or indigenization of a bygone agrarian past in Mexico).[37] We could then say that allegory, a type of narrative that is encased within a much larger meaning, covers the structures of ghost towns like moss on a ruin.

Yet, allegory can result in a reductive way to address the iconic status and resonance of ghost towns. When reconstructing a location's genealogy in terms of a historical narrative, allegorical readings tend to centralize objects or figures that look to the past (reminding us of Benjamin's Angel of History), and in so doing remain prone to a fixation on emblematic yet static phenomena. In other words, allegorical readings of space forestall the possibility of reading places locally and materially. Geographical allegories run the risk of aestheticizing and distracting from the lived actuality of sites, whether real or imagined. Derek Attridge, in defending the act of reading literature as *"event"* against the temptation to allegorize, writes that "allegory, one might say, deals with the *already known*, whereas literature opens a space for the other. Allegory announces a moral code, literature invites an ethical response."[38] Attridge is here favoring an approach that, in avoiding allegorization, or what we could call a finalizing interpretive move, allows the reader to "repeat" the experience of reading, "though each repetition turns out to be a different experience and therefore a non-repetition, a new singularity, as well" (40). Choosing between the enclosed "moral code" and the open, multiple, and possible "ethical" outcomes of reading as event thus becomes an important decision in our perception of sites whose materiality has become so injected with a powerful representational life and afterlife.

Let us then return to Benjamin's example of the ruin. His conceptualization of its "decay" as "irresistible," it seems to me, not only points to an irreversible material process of deterioration but also signals the interpretive tendency to make something out of what is slowly dissipating. The challenge lies in the enclosure that develops around these suggestive tropes and myths. We should aspire to a reading of ghosts of the desert landscapes that perceives haunting in its eventuality rather than opt for this figure's tightening into archetype. Indeed, as Patricia Limerick has noted, the Western "cult of ruins" surrounding ghost towns has long been a "singularly unreflecting cult," for which a reading of the poetics and politics of "failure" is yet to be performed.[39] How do we construct a reading of haunting's architecture as event that can understand the representations of failure, as evidenced in depictions of ghost towns?

In his discussion of Rulfo's work, Carlos Monsiváis has written about the difficulty of reading through the "dense ideological mist that surrounds the rural world" in literature.[40] "The unknown," he writes, "becomes the stuff of legends or, preferentially, *myth*":

> . . . the time-without-time of small hamlets, cultural isolation, and the stifling morality of the parish, the poverty and endless migration, the irredeemable extinction of a culture due to the development of the nation, the voracious wearing away of belief and custom, the changes in and persistence of popular language. Everything is mythical, everything is incomprehensible, far off, self-enclosed. (58)

This "enclosure" of the rural within a tight regionalist archetype can thus be intensified by the "unreflecting" reading of ghost towns: Ciphers of the past, surrounded by tableaux veiled in myths, they can easily yield interpretations of what was simply *lost*. What we should look for, however, is the dramatization of the events that lead to the "irresistible decay" in order to populate the landscapes of failure. The towns I now move on to discuss— Juan Rulfo's Comala and Clint Eastwood's Lago—represent two ways of reading failure and community breakdown in desert landscapes. They encompass two versions of "irresistible decay" intercepted by the events of haunting, thus transforming a presumably paralyzed landscape that faces backward into the past, into a complicated dramatization of a continuous, reverberating present.

Jean Franco has pointed out the emphasis on the idea of "desvivirse" in Rulfo's *Pedro Páramo*.[41] The term comes up at the moment when Juan Preciado, the novel's first character who arrives in the town of Comala in search of the father he has never met and who finds a place full only of the echoes of the dead, meets a "married" couple who are, in fact, brother and sister. They have been in the now-abandoned town their whole lives, and describe themselves as living, while a multitude of souls ("el gentío de ánimas") wander through the streets at night.[42] The woman bemoans her isolation, and expresses to Juan her ignorance of places where many people

are to be found: "Figúrese usted. Y nosotros aquí tan solos. Desviviéndonos por conocer aunque sea tantito de la vida" ("Think of that. And us
all alone here. *Dying* to know even a little of life," 111; 50).[43] This concept
signifies not only "*un*living" (the translation in Franco's text), as the opposite of being alive, but entails also, more subtly, an excessive unraveling of
the acts of living. In life, "desvivirse" implies an active excess—a living *to
death*—or living to the point of the exhaustion of life itself. As it happens,
the same woman who participates in this "desvivir" disappears from Juan
Preciado's side through a process of crumbling: "El cuerpo de aquella mujer hecho de tierra, envuelto en costras de tierra, *se desbarataba* como si es-
tuviera derritiéndose en un charco de lodo" ("The woman's body was made
of earth, layered in crusts of earth; it was crumbling, melting into a pool of
mud") (116; 56). "Desvivir" and "desbaratarse"—both are processes whose
outcome is death, but they entail an observation of active unwinding. In
other words, their outcome entails something more complicated than a
disappearance, a cessation, or a switch to invisibility. Instead of seeing just
death, you see the ways in which death progressively arrives.

Comala and Lago are not ghost towns in the "unreflecting" sense of
lost pasts. They stand as fictitious landscapes that undergo the repetition
of life's unwinding through haunting, a repetition that in turn offers the
reader and viewer a look into the narrative making of ghost towns (which
is also, in effect, a town's unmaking). The events of haunting in turn inflict
the landscape with a sense of answerability. In other words, it is through
haunting that the ghost town is able to speak of its life, its failure, and the
unraveling of its living. Haunting, instead of representing the freezing of
landscape into archetype or mere symbol, can illuminate the human processes through which the desert can harbor and constitute a "desvivir." I
want to propose that these ghost-town narratives of "desvivir" render an
interesting play between the ideas of *desert* and *desertion* that intersect in
so many desert narratives. The connection between these two notions il-
luminates how, in turn, such stories hinge on explorations of the relations
between space and ethics, locations and agency. The "desvivir" action of
the desert is portrayed, in these fictions, as a chipping away, or a crumbling
of life in this landscape. Importantly, however, it still represents a life and
agency in a landscape so steeped in myth. These desert fictions, by challenging us with their haunted motivation, constantly ask us, as involved
readers and spectators, to scrutinize them for responsibility and answerability in a landscape that appears to be bent on silence and erasure.

"Todo parecía estar en espera de algo": Juan Rulfo's Comala

When everything in an abandoned town "appear[s] to be awaiting something" ["parec[e] estar como en espera de algo"],[44] the reader notes a paradox emerging from the observation of an isolated landscape. What is it that awaits, and who is the awaiting agent? What is that "something" that might or might not arrive? The character making this observation is Juan Preciado, who, following the wishes of his dying mother, returns to the town where he was born to settle accounts with the father who abandoned them. Rulfo's novel thus begins with the promise of a return, and the reader might suppose that that "something" the landscape is awaiting might have, in fact, arrived. "I came to Comala because I had been told that my father, a man named Pedro Páramo, lived there" ["Vine a Comala porque me dijeron que acá vivía mi padre, un tal Pedro Páramo"] (3; 65), are Juan Preciado's opening lines. His return is not merely confrontational; Juan confesses to be full of "dreams" and "imagination" in anticipation of this meeting. We thus (prematurely) begin to expect a narrative of filial fulfillment, of self-discovery through the encounter with the father, but almost immediately our narrator and the reader discover that the town is virtually abandoned and hollowed out, without a living soul, and, to make matters worse, Pedro Páramo, who owns all the land within sight, has long been dead, and instead exists as a "living bile," or "grudge" ["un rencor vivo"] (6; 68)—this, according to Abundio, the man who guides Juan to Comala. During this meeting at the opening of the novel, Abundio informs Juan Preciado that Páramo is also his father, thus revealing to Juan and the reader that Páramo is/was author of Comala in more ways than one. In the final fragments of the novel, Abundio reappears in the narrative as the man who, having arrived drunk in Páramo's house to ask for help in his wife's burial, inflicts a mortal wound on the landowner.

Pedro Páramo contains no numbered chapters and a chronological order can hardly be reconstructed for most of the characters' life narratives. Juan Preciado's return is just one story line that opens the novel and becomes entangled with numerous others, all with different narrators. These passages tell the story of how Pedro Páramo came to own everything (and everybody), while other fragments relate the story of a different subject. This voice tells his story from an impersonal, third-person point of view that uses only dialogue to develop the story. In addition, an unnamed dead tells of the ways he reached his end, not surprisingly, at the hands of the terrible Páramo. This entanglement of the deserted voices of Comala raises questions of how this space can be built up in narrative, if at all. Pieced together, these narrations weave a polyphonic story pattern relating how

Comala came to its demise, and how it achieved its present state of abject and haunted solitude.

The return or promise of a life coming full circle to its maker faces the worst deception with the discovery of the deserted landscape. Remarkably, Rulfo's novel curtails the expectation of a narrative of rebuilding a broken filial identity almost immediately. This is conveyed in an introduction to an eerie landscape where people seem to appear and disappear, and where sounds and echoes lead Juan to think he is surrounded by living people, when in actuality no one seems to exist in life. In place of a narrative of self-discovery, in which Juan will travel to the estranged father to get back the relationship he has been owed, the novel relates the crumbling or unwinding of these hopes. The promise of avenging his mother—before she dies, she tells Juan *"Make him pay, my son, for all those years he put us out of his mind"* [*"El abandono en que nos tuvo, mi hijo, cóbraselo caro"*] (19; 81)—also results in failure.

In *Pedro Páramo*, the wasteland Juan Preciado finds stands in stark contrast to the Comala his mother remembered. Her memories of the town, relayed to the son, were of a veritable Eden: *"The color of the earth, the smell of alfalfa and bread. A town that smelled like spilled honey"* [*"El color de la tierra, el olor de la alfalfa y del pan. Un pueblo que huele a miel derramada"*] (18; 80). What Rulfo offers us in this memory could in a way be described as a regionalization of the myth of a lost paradise, but interestingly, the desert space in the novel becomes so as the *effect* of a particular history. The author is not crafting a story of environmental or biblical determinism, but instead building a history of unbuilding, a writing of the "irresistible decay" of ruins: A history that, as I argued earlier, is nevertheless not lacking in human agency. In his reading of the mythifications of the rural, Monsiváis perceives Comala as an "eternal present" that counters those "ideologically coded" clichés that critics have too often used to explain Rulfo's work away. Conversely, Monsiváis understands *Pedro Páramo* as a negation of these clichés, because Rulfo provides "concrete causes and effects where others have offered only the prestigious terms of defenselessness" (58). These "causes and effects" lead us to an understanding of the novel not as a metaphysical morality tale where heaven and hell are simply Mexicanized, but as a text where a linear narrative is purposefully fragmented into scattered now-moments. Monsiváis notes how these "presents" textually embody a haunted zone whose image has itself dissipated through a history of violence. A place where the voices of the dead chime from above- and underground, Comala thus forever appears suspended in a web of alienation that its sometime inhabitants continue to experience indefinitely.

A reading of haunting as simply a *return* is complicated by the state in which Juan finds Comala: At first, it is actually Juan Preciado (whose vitality at the beginning of the novel is questionable) who comes to haunt the town after it has become deserted. His arrival, in this sense of haunting as return, *haunts* the abandoned Comala with the question of what has happened in that place. His mother's remembrance of Comala becomes dismembered immediately in the novel upon Juan's discovery of the desolate state of the town. More dishearteningly, however, it is a relayed memory that is doomed to hang suspended, without the possibility of a signified referent. This adds yet another layer to the discourse of haunting that Juan introduces to the town upon his arrival: a haunting of a relayed, and now emptied, memory. On a second level, we can say that Comala is haunted because its dead echoes and murmurs ("murmullos") reach Juan Preciado at every juncture. In this sense, Comala is haunted because the dead constitute the only society present in the town, a society that converses with Juan until he himself dies. Haunting entails a dialectical relationship between a point of view that perceives the state of desertion and implicitly poses the questions to the landscape, and the landscape that in turn answers back with its own narrative.

The same as Juan Preciado, readers are compelled to ask themselves what has happened for this place to become, and allow itself to be, haunted. Comala came to be a desert because it was deserted either by abandonment or by death. But which came first, the impoverishment or the dissolution of the community? The distinction between these two "causes" is not clear. This is because the narrators, speaking from death, multiply throughout the text, and vacillate between telling stories about how their souls were forgotten by the living, on one hand (pointing to a spiritual level), and anecdotes of how people packed up and left, on the other (citing a material level of history). This blending of the multiple forms that the forgetting of place and community can take is ambiguously perceived by Eduviges Dyada, the visitor's first contact in Comala, who explains to Juan: "Now, sad to say, times have changed, and since the town has fallen on bad times, no one brings us any news" ["Ahora, desventuradamente, los tiempos han cambiado, pues desde que esto está empobrecido ya nadie se comunica con nosotros"] (15; 78).

Eduviges represents the voice of juncture between the multiple narratives of desertion that run through the town. Through his meeting with her, Juan's narration begins to depend more heavily on the use of subjunctive clauses: When he sees her he says, "It was as if she had been waiting for me" ["Parecía que me hubiera estado esperando"] (9; 71). A continuous play with what "seems" and with the *if* clauses works toward a structural quaking of the lines separating the realms of the living and the dead. This play between indicative and subjunctive also stands opposed to the certainty of that first description of the father, who is, without doubt or hypothesizing, "a living bile." Further into his acquaintance with Eduviges, Juan perceives someone who must have gone through "hard times" ["Pensé que debía haber pasado por años difíciles"]: Her face "was transparent, as if the blood had drained from it, and her hands were all shriveled, nothing but wrinkled claws" ["Su cara se transparentaba como si no tuviera sangre, y sus manos estaban marchitas; marchitas y apretadas de arrugas"] (16; 79). In a later fragment that features Padre Rentería (Comala's priest during its living history, and who later leaves to fight in the *cristero* war in the late 1920s) as the main character, we discover that Eduviges had committed suicide, a form of death condemned by the Catholic faith. Rentería tells María, Eduviges's sister, that the only way to compensate for this act is to order "Gregorian masses" (which needed to be paid for with an offering), something María could not afford.

Eduviges's house, where Juan spends his first night, is full of "tiliches," furniture and objects left behind by those who had abandoned the town. "Tengo la casa toda entilichada," she says. "My house is chock full of other people's things. As people went away, they chose my house to store their belongings, but not one of them has ever come back to claim them" ["La escogieron para guardar sus muebles los que se fueron, y nadie ha regresado por ellos"] (9; 72). The abandoned "tiliches" thus stand as ciphers of a point in Comala's history during which the place began to unravel as a deserted site. Eduviges represents a first consciousness of the abandonment as a living reality of the town, a situation that Juan takes in without fully understanding, as his presumed contact with life is met with death at every angle.

Eduviges's point of view disappears in the novel, and is quickly replaced by that of Damiana Cisneros, who had taken care of Juan when he was born. She talks about Eduviges as a soul "in penance," making both reader and Juan believe Damiana stands apart from this world of the dead. She describes a town "filled with echoes" ["Este pueblo está lleno de ecos"], full of "laughter that sounds used up. And voices worn away by the years" ["unas risas ya muy viejas, como cansadas de reír. Y voces ya desgastadas por el uso"] (40; 101). In a remarkable passage, Damiana describes the sight of "wind sweeping the leaves of trees, when here, as you can see, there are no trees."

> Sí—volvió a decir Damiana Cisneros—. Este pueblo está llenos de ecos. Yo ya no me espanto. Oigo el aullido de perros, y dejo que aúllen. Y en días de aire se ve al viento arrastrando hojas de árboles, cuando aquí, como tú ves, no hay árboles. Los hubo en algún tiempo, porque si no, ¿de dónde saldrían esas hojas? (101–2)

> ["Yes," Damiana Cisneros repeated. "This town is filled with echoes. I'm not afraid anymore. I hear dogs howling, and I let them howl.

And on windy days I see the wind blowing leaves from the trees, when anyone can see that there aren't any trees. There must have been once. Otherwise, where do the leaves come from?"] (41)

The paradoxical sight of invisible movements of a natural world long dead and the sound of the exhausted echoes of expired voices come together to form an impression of a town where the lines separating life and death are strangely imperceptible. Although we are confronted with a confusion of sight and echo, we can only imagine the sweeping of leaves as mere re-membrances of a distant past. Like Eduviges, Damiana disappears in mid-conversation with Juan: He asks her if she is alive, and the only response he receives is the echo of his own voice.

In the persistent present of the novel that encases all the characters, the dead do not engage in dialogue with other vocal members of this necro-community: Though at times they hold dialogues with one another over- and underground, they are suspended in the re-dramatizations of their own deaths, and hear about others through the startled retellings of Juan Preciado before and after his death—a death that results, according to him, from the surrounding "murmurs" of the town. "Me mataron los murmul-los" ["The murmuring killed me"], he tells Dorotea, with whom he ends up buried (117; 57). Whatever hope we have of their voices connecting is undercut by the novel's fragmentary form. As readers we become increas-ingly aware of a terrible distance—of a place become unreachable and a time that is unrecoverable—through this scattering of voices that continu-ally haunt a present. Each utterance, however, joins the others in a retelling of events of a fracturing physical and spiritual violence. In this manner, the fragmented narrative dramatizes the fractured existences of the town's dead. Rulfo, through his narrators, works contesting temporalities in an astonishingly beautiful manner: He stretches and lets go of the lines that connect past and present (and, we imagine, a haunted future) in such a way that what may seem archaic is conjugated with a present and indissoluble urgency. Jean Franco perceives this fracture as symptomatic of a

> novel that reproduces not a coherent worldview but the actual frag-mentation and breakdown of a social and moral order, the survival within a new social order of remnants of previous codes and the con-flicts and confusions which arise from this mingling of the new and the old. (441)

The devastating isolation of each fragment and each subjectivity in the novel, however, represents something more nuanced than the "confu-sions" of a set of moral and social orders supplanted with the next. The voices, speaking in the novel's fragments, relate the diverse processes of rigor mortis for each subject represented, through an enunciation of the processes of decay. In other words, rather than simply representing the trauma of obsolescence, of the replacement of a worldview with another, Rulfo's novel dramatizes multiple events and perspectives of that "desvivir"—of a recognition of death's landscape, through the enunciation of each different character.

Returning to Franco's analysis, the enunciation of the different moral and social orders unravels more clearly in the fragments that tell the story of Pedro Páramo himself. We progressively learn of that past, when the cacique owned all of Comala's inhabitants in his acts of murder, rape, and disownment, in fragments that, together, form an ambiguous characterization of a man who was both a romantic and an opportunist. We also learn of the people's spiritual disillusionment in the fragments that recount the story of Padre Rentería, who was in charge of their souls and, demoralized by Páramo's stranglehold over Comala, lost all faith in his ability to save them.[45] As the wounds of this violence of communal dissolution continue to surface, historical time stabs the narration with the coming of the Mexican Revolution, which Rulfo represents as a disorganized scattering of loyalties that stir no significant action and even less fruitful results. Of all these intersections of loss, Monsiváis writes, "Rulfo is not in the least interested in idealization but, rather, in showing the village man as a concrete being, in his terrible subjection, living under the terrible rules of a game imposed and sustained by others" (61). In such a place and such a text, the return cannot and will not come full circle, and the son (Juan) will never meet even the ghost of the father.

Although the story of the rest of Comala is told in its "desvivir," Páramo's story (reconstructed from separate fragments) actually works more like a bildungsroman. His death is the only one isolated in its finality, while the rest of Comala (including his beloved, Susana San Juan) hangs suspended in the eternal disquiet of an echoing death. The first fragment in which he appears reveals an episode where Páramo, as a boy, daydreams about Susana. This fragment is one of pastoral distraction, as the boy addresses a distant lover.

> "Pensaba en ti, Susana. En las lomas verdes. Cuando volábamos papalotes en la época del aire. Oíamos allá abajo el rumor viviente del pueblo mientras estábamos encima de él, arriba de la loma, en tanto se nos iba el hilo de cáñamo arrastrado por el viento." (74)

> ["I was thinking of you, Susana. Of the green hills. Of when we used to fly kites in the windy season. We could hear the sounds of life from the town below; we were high above on the hill, playing out string to the wind."] (12)

This passage not only portrays Páramo as a romantic, nearly a poet, but also tells of a time when the town possessed a "living rumor" that was loud enough to rise up to the adjacent hills where the young people frolicked. Conversely, in the novel's first fragment narrating Juan Preciado's arrival, the voyage to Comala constitutes a descent from an elevated topography. In stark contrast to the interlude on the hill, however, this first perception of what lies below is described as "the very mouth of Hell" ["la mera boca del Infierno"] (6; 67) by Abundio, his first interlocutor. Thus, although the novel's fragments about Páramo represent him rather sequentially as he grows up from being a distracted boy in love to a tyrant, the rest of the fragments that tell the stories of those living under Páramo's domain are utterances of undoing instead.

Páramo's maturation into despot is revealed in episodes where, as the owner of the Media Luna (the hacienda at the center of Comala's economy), he enunciates the abolition of any laws and boundaries that might curtail his dominion: "¿Cuáles leyes, Fulgor?," he tells his employee. "La ley de ahora en adelante la vamos a hacer nosotros" ["What law, Fulgor? From now on, we're the law"] (100; 40). Páramo's opportunism reaches destructive levels with the arrival of the Mexican Revolution, when he provides funds to any faction, so long as they are on the "winning" side: "Ya te he dicho que hay que estar con el que vaya ganando" ["I've told you before we have to be on the side of whoever's winning"], he tells another one of his men (162; 106). His corrupt capitalization on any "winning" side works as perhaps the node of the town's evacuative forces. As the town empties after Páramo's refusal to continue the operations at the Media Luna, his sorrow for the loss of his beloved Susana becomes melancholic pastoral poetry again.

> Fue la última vez que te vi. Pasaste rozando con tu cuerpo las ramas del paraíso que está en la vereda y te llevaste con tu aire sus últimas hojas. Luego desapareciste. Te dije: '¡Regresa, Susana!' (172)
>
> [That was the last time I saw you. As you went by, you brushed the branches of the Paradise tree beside the path, sweeping away its last leaves with your passing. Then you disappeared. I called after you, "Come back, Susana!"] (116)

Páramo's descent into romantic musings in his old age is countered by the earlier narration of an anonymous dead buried near Juan Preciado's tomb underground. This voice retells how, after Susana's death, Páramo spent his days "staring down the road where they'd carried her to holy ground" ["mirando el camino por donde se la habían llevado al camposanto"] (79; 137). I quote this passage at length, as it unpacks the sequential history of how Comala became a town of ruins.

Le perdió interés a todo. Desalojó sus tierras y mandó quemar los enseres. Unos dicen que porque ya estaba cansado, otros que porque le agarró la desilusión; lo cierto es que echó fuera a la gente y se sentó en su equipal, cara al camino.

Desde entonces la tierra se quedó baldía y como en ruinas. Daba pena verla llenándose de achaques con tanta plaga que la invadió en cuanto la dejaron sola. De allá para acá se consumió la gente; se debandaron los hombres en busca de otros 'bebederos.' Recuerdo días en que Comala se llenó de 'adioses' y hasta nos parecía cosa alegre ir a despedir a los que se iban. Y es que se iban con intenciones de volver. Nos dejaban encargadas sus cosas y su familia. Luego algunos mandaban por la familia aunque no por sus cosas, y después parecieron olvidarse del pueblo y de nosotros, y hasta de sus cosas. Yo me quedé porque no tenía adonde ir. Otros se quedaron esperando que Pedro Páramo muriera, pues según decían les había prometido heredarles sus bienes, y con esa esperanza vivieron todavía algunos. Pero pasaron años y años y él seguía vivo, siempre allí, como un espantapájaros frente a las tierras de la Media Luna." (137)

[He lost interest in everything. He let his lands lie fallow, and gave orders for the tools that worked it to be destroyed. Some say it was because he was worn out; others said it was despair. The one sure thing is that he threw everyone off his land and sat himself down in his chair to stare down that road.

From that day on, the fields lay untended. Abandoned. It was a sad thing to see what happened to the land, how plagues took over as soon as it lay idle. For miles around, people fell on hard times. Men packed up and left in search of a better living. I remember days when the only sound in Comala was good-byes; it seemed like a celebration every time we sent someone on his way. They went, you know, with every intention of coming back. They asked us to keep an eye on their belongings and their families. Later, some sent for their family but not their things. And then they seemed to forget about the village, and about us—and even about their belongings. I stayed because I didn't have anywhere to go. Some stayed waiting for Pedro Páramo to die, because he'd promised to leave them his land and his goods and they were living on that hope. But the years went by and he lived on, propped up like a scarecrow gazing out across the lands of the Media Luna.] (79–80)

This anonymous voice that retells Comala's emigrations reconstructs the contingent histories of agency that only led to the town's demise and subsequent transformation into a desert. Although Páramo's narrative spells out a subjectivity forever cast away into a landscape's romanticized, distant, and increasingly irrecoverable past, this anonymous historian recounts the devastatingly real movements of desertion that began to crowd Comala's present. As Jean Franco describes his character in another context, Páramo stands as an "anachronism" (442), while the history of Comala's undoing moves forward. Thinking in terms of metanarrative, we could argue that a parallelism exists between Páramo's law and the "law of genre" (to use the title of Derrida's essay): Although the landowner endows Comala with one specific meaning and genre that he alone feels (the backward-looking and ultimately destructive mood of nostalgia and lost romance), Comala continues to exist in its multivocal disquiet.

This irredeemable disconnection between narratives—Páramo's and the anonymous storyteller who represents the remaining echoes and ghosts of the place—portrays an uneven haunting. As Páramo dies, looking at the emptied land in ruins ["La tierra en ruinas estaba frente a él, vacía"] (178), the narrator tells us he was afraid of the night: "Because he feared the nights that filled the darkness with phantoms. That locked him in with his ghosts. That was his fear" ["Porque tenía miedo de las noches que le llenaban de fantasmas la oscuridad. De encerrarse con sus fantasmas. De eso tenía miedo"] (122; 178). Rather remarkably, this confessional moment represents the first instance in which the word "fantasma" (ghost) is used in the novel—a word that is interestingly located between two mentions of the word "miedo" (fear), adding a dimension of fright within a narrative in which the ghostly becomes a de facto, everyday occurrence. Although we have been introduced to the town's haunting through a narrative architectonics of echoes, of visions that slip into the blurring of sight and sound, and of people who appear and then crumble into earth or just disappear (moments during which these subjects are never defined as "fantasmas"), Páramo is the first to name the dead as "ghosts." (The closest word is perhaps "ánimas" (souls), used in the fragment describing Juan's meeting with the incestuous couple.) As Comala's principal orchestrator of haunting and continuous disquiet—they are "his ghosts" ["sus fantasmas"], after all—Páramo's admission of being afraid of them comes too late in the novel. This act of naming Comala's future population, which transpires in the very last lines of the novel (though, of course, due to the fragmentary form of Pedro Páramo, chronologically precedes Juan Preciado's arrival) stands as a hollow signifier for the events of haunting that have already transpired throughout the text. That is to say, the narrative threads of the novel populate the deserted town with events (and effects of events) that transcend the mere fears of darkness and ghosts that haunt Páramo's melancholic mind. He remains disconnected from the eternal, yet material, disquietude he has left in his wake, leaving all the events of haunting to transcend his gesture of naming and fearing something that is altogether more abstract.

 Comala in *Pedro Páramo* elucidates that intersection of landscape and agency, and of the agents that can transform a landscape and its subjects into otherness. The fragments, intertwined, erect a story where the visible *desert* landscape is a product of multiple desertions, and where the sounds of dead echoes replace what was once a "living rumor" ["rumor viviente"]. Rulfo's novel, in its repetition and prolepsis of the dialectics of catastrophe and "desvivir," unpacks a landscape that, though abandoned, is still capable of enunciating its answerability. It dramatizes what Bakhtin, writing about the ethical dimensions of relating to an object through experience, describes as the "ongoing event" of such experiences—an event that unites what he calls the "what-is-given" and "what-is-to-be-achieved," as well as "what-ought-to-be."[46] Bakhtin's theory of narrating events of encounter and anticipation provides a valuable framework with which to understand the depiction of a haunted landscape like Comala. Rather than merely being a simple portrayal of an immediate landscape, one that we can easily come to understand—in other words, a topography that one can define theoretically or, using Bakhtin's terminology, as "pure givenness"—the narration of Comala begins to animate the landscape with its multivocal (dialogic) histories of desertion. We thus begin to see how the desert is not necessarily the quiet spectacle of nature in its twilight. It is instead a location that still vociferates about its participation in the ongoing history of Mexican modernity.[47] Understood in this capacity, the desert challenges us to address it as a living and inhabited realm whose representational and sociogeographic manifestations exceed its received image as a realm of emptiness, or as a quiet myth.

Spelling Out Hell: Clint Eastwood's Lago

One of the opening descriptions of the landscape surrounding Comala reads:

> En la reverberación del sol, la llanura parecía una laguna transparente, deshecha en vapores por donde se traslucía un horizonte gris. Y más allá, una línea de montañas. Y todavía más allá, la más remota lejanía. (67)

> [In the shimmering sunlight the plain was a transparent lake dissolving in mists that veiled a gray horizon. Farther in the distance, a range of mountains. And farther still, faint remoteness.] (5)

This "reverberating" or "shimmering" horizon of the desert landscape that will reveal the abandoned town to the novel's first narrator has a visual counterpart in the opening scene of Clint Eastwood's *High Plains Drifter*. A wavering horizon confusing different surface plains appears amid the piercing sound of what seems like a choir of synthesized moans.[48] The first shot dissolves to reveal the dark figure of a man riding on horseback forward from the horizon, while sun and sand continue to move and reverberate behind him. This cinematic trompe l'oeil represents the first instance of inexplicability in what will be a tale of a stranger's mysterious return to a town locked in among desert landscapes in the North American West. The following shot features a closer view of the Stranger (Clint Eastwood) descending from a hill, while the film score sheds its chiming edge to become a more conventional soundtrack for a Western. The descent among sandy hills is presented from different angles, while the man on horseback crosses different topographies of desert sand and brush, arriving finally in a valley harboring an empty saline lake. The camera pans down to reveal a minute, isolated town on its banks.

When he was asked about set selection for the film, Clint Eastwood explained:

> The town in the script was situated in the middle of the desert, like in most Westerns, but this convention bothered me because even in the West a city couldn't develop without water. I discovered Mono Lake by chance, while I was out driving around, and I was immediately taken with the strangeness of the site. The saline content is so high that no vessel can risk going out on the waters of the lake. I spent hours wandering around in the area. Not a boat, not a living soul, only the natural noises of the desert. . . . When [my art director] arrived, he blurted out, "You'd think you were on the moon!" I told him, "It's a weird place, but that's exactly what I want this story to be!"[49]

The deliberate decision to dislocate the town of Lago (Spanish for "lake"), to purposefully make it stray from the conventional setting for a film western, transforms the experience of visualizing the heroic sturdiness of the fictionalized West into something quite different. This sense of "weird" dislocation is compounded by the first scene of the Stranger's entrance into the town, where he is shown riding his horse through Lago's cemetery, a meager scattering of wooden crosses and tombstones displaying handwritten names of the dead. As he rides into the main street, Lago's buildings appear as strange as the barren lake: a stable without animals, houses and barns half-built, a sign over a painted building that reads "Lago Miners Hall" where there are no visible signs of anything like a mining industry. The only sound heard as the Stranger rides through Lago is that of his horse's hooves on the sand, as the town's scant population stares dumbfounded at the arrival. After the Stranger has ridden past the conventional

hotel, general store, and saloon, the last shot of this main-street reconnais-
sance shows Eastwood's stranger locking sights (in shot-countershot) with
Lago's undertaker, who has two open coffins propped over a fence.

The overall strangeness of Lago's population, like the set selection, is
intentional: In his interview with Richard Thompson and Tim Hunter,
Eastwood rather inelegantly explains that "the way the whole town was,
no children, kind of strange: it's a weird situation" (51). Interestingly, in
Pedro Páramo, Juan Preciado also remarks on this absence of children during his entrance to Comala, exacerbating his already intensified sense of
alienation.

> Era la hora en que los niños juegan en las calles de todos los
> pueblos, llenando con sus gritos la tarde. Cuando aún las paredes
> negras reflejan la luz amarilla del sol. Al menos eso había visto en
> Sayula, todavía ayer, a esta misma hora . . . Ahora estaba aquí, en este
> pueblo sin ruidos. (69)

> [It was the hour of day when in every little village children come out
> to play in the streets, filling the afternoon with their cries. The time
> when dark walls still reflect pale yellow sunlight. At least that was
> what I had seen in Sayula, just yesterday at this hour. . . . Now here I
> was in this hushed town.] (7)

Both texts thus immediately create an atmosphere of staleness and mor-
bidity through the elimination of any reference to a youth element. And
while Rulfo insists on representing this strangeness through a textual
description of silence in the "town without sounds," the first encounter
between the Stranger and Lago's townspeople is also devoid of any musical soundtrack, and all one hears is wind and the clopping of the horse's
hooves.

The eeriness that opens *High Plains Drifter* continues when we notice
that the townspeople's inspection of the Stranger is not like the zealously
protective stares exhibited in so many westerns: Strangely, there appears
to be an air of recognition in some of their looks. After he kills three trou-
blemakers in the saloon, this uncanniness is intensified when the unruly
Stranger's troubling nightmares are represented when he rests in his hotel
room. This dream sequence reveals a different trio of hoodlums whipping
Lago's (we infer previous) marshal to death in the middle of the main
street, while the darkened faces of the townspeople blankly look on, acting
as both witnesses and accomplices. Adding a dimension of uncanniness,
this marshal looks like a less stunning version of Clint Eastwood, a resem-
blance that is brought home in the film by the process of transposition and
dissolve: The close-up of the dying marshal on the ground half-dissolves

phantasmagorically into a shot of Eastwood's sleeping face. This marshal, named Duncan, comes up in conversation throughout the film, becoming a subject of interest for the laconic Stranger. The reason for his public execution is explained toward the film's denouement. In a scene portraying a marital argument between the couple that owns Lago's hotel, Mrs. Belding (Verna Bloom)—who has just spent the night with the Stranger—complains how the so-called "neighbors" of the town had "hidden a murder" behind words like "faith" and "trust." To this, Mr. Belding (Ted Hartley) confesses that Duncan had found out the "mine was on government property," and he was "determined" to turn the townsmen in.

It is here that questions of return and desertion emerge in our own inspection of the text as a whole. The Stranger is not a stranger at all, at least from his perspective, and the narrative of return is in fact one of retribution. This haunted motivation, however, is complicated when, in keeping with the formulaic story line, the townspeople now need help defending themselves against the same hoodlums who had done their dirty work for them, and they ask the Stranger for protection. He reluctantly helps, but in a twist to the classic western narrative, he punishes them for their perennial cowardice. After montage scenes show him on one hand teaching them to shoot from rooftops and, in others, taking whatever he pleases from the town merchants and other businesses (in one scene he gives a Native American family an inordinate amount of candy and blankets, after they had been verbally abused by the store owner), he orders the citizens of Lago to paint the town red. The Stranger is shown writing the word "Hell" over the signpost at the edge of the town, recalling Duncan's final "damn you all to hell" curse before his death. This act symbolically transforms Lago's existence into something that is quite "other" in spatiotemporal terms: On the one hand, it reveals a wound *literally re-opening* for the town's society. One the other, the promise of the town's survival thanks to the Stranger's defense is violently displaced and ultimately extinguished when he christens it with its new name.

The reexamination of Duncan's death is performed only through the points of view of the Stranger and Mordecai (Billy Curtis), the dwarf whom the Stranger names town sheriff when he sets out to subvert the town's property and propriety during the previous montage scenes. Although the Stranger's dream had revealed the darkened faces of the onlookers, Mordecai's recollection of the same event presents him hiding under the elevated floor of the hotel, as the rest of the townspeople watch above him, their faces now illuminated, some even betraying smiles of near-sadistic satisfaction. On the ground and visibly afraid, Mordecai represents the empathetic point of view that is level with that of the dying Duncan. When the marshal pronounces (for the second time in the film) the line "damn

you to hell," his eyes are facing upward to where one supposes the townspeople are standing. This repetition of the scene of the crime, told from
the point of view of the town's only innocent man reveals a Lago that has
become doomed to a repetition of its own undoing. Its only relevant history, contained in the barren air of complicity, is that of Duncan's murder.
The Stranger's haunting arrival thus becomes the dramatized excess of the
town's stagnation and ultimate failure: It marks the eternal return of the
moment in which the community began and continues to break down.
Away from the community against which the Stranger seeks retaliation,
the benign complicity between Mordecai and the Stranger reaches its denouement in the last dialogue scene of the film. The curious recognition
of the Stranger by the townspeople at the beginning of the film is left un-
spoken, yet insinuated, whereas, upon the Stranger's departure from Lago/
Hell, Mordecai asks the mystery man for a name a second time (the first
takes place toward the beginning of the film), while standing beside the
tomb of the murdered marshal—a cross that Mordecai is in the process of
marking with a name. The Stranger replies that he has always known. The
fact that the grave had not been named could imply that Duncan's death
was recent, or otherwise unobserved by the town until the moment of the
Stranger's arrival.

It is interesting to note how Eastwood, the director, reflects upon the
western genre itself by revisiting—or, even, "haunting"—two canonic examples with probing questions, namely George Stevens's *Shane* (1953) and
Fred Zinneman's *High Noon* (1952).[50] *High Plains Drifter* uses the mythic,
symbolic character of a stranger who enters the lives of common people
and becomes instrumental in their survival (à la *Shane*), but he turns out
to be an aftershock, or "apparition," of their former protector, who was
deserted by his own constituency (which is the main plotline of *High
Noon*): Eastwood says in a 1980 interview that he had played the part of the
Stranger "as if it could have been some apparition. You're not quite sure,
but you know that he has a strong interest in making this town suffer for
their sins and that it ties in with their complacency with the murder" (68).
In a 1984 interview with Michael Henry, Clint Eastwood relates the ques-
tion that inspired his film from the beginning: "The starting point was:
'What would have happened if the sheriff of *High Noon* had been killed?
What would have happened *afterwards*?'"[51]

Paul Smith writes that "westerns have chronically been a privileged site"
of the combination of "constituent elements of genre" and "a more general
set of cultural ideas of what is real, likely or possible."[52] Given Eastwood's
revisionist choices of plot and setting, *High Plains Drifter* can be read as
a conscious reappraisal of the western genre—it is a western that *haunts*
the genre itself—at a moment in film history when the cinematic genre

was in notable decline. However, this film announces the breakdown, or rather hollowing out, of what was once the consolidation of "genre" and other "cultural ideas" about the U.S. West. The director interestingly tries to give Lago a somewhat realistic (or *possible*) twist by locating it by a body of water rather than in the middle of the desert, but even this sign of life is immediately curtailed by the uselessness of the lake's water for any human living purposes. Moreover, Lago is portrayed half-built, absolutely frail: Seen in shots taken from a distance, it is conspicuously a film set that sits awkwardly on the deserted landscape. When it appears covered in red paint in the second half of the film, the spectacle of its undoing becomes an even greater farce.

At the level of plot, the film's haunting of western classics dramatizes its own self-differentiation from myths that now seem increasingly archaic. Eastwood even revisits these older films on a formal level, as evinced in his development of Mordecai's point of view, recalling Stevens's *Shane* directly. In the latter, the camera reproduces the point of view belonging to the young boy, Joey (Brandon De Wilde), to the point of making certain shots seem almost awkwardly distracted and misdirected. Mordecai thus stands as a strange reanimation of Joey's character: the child replaced by the dwarf in a town devoid of children. Thus, through its formal and emotional architectures of staleness, strangeness, and haunted return, *High Plains Drifter* strips down a genre that so often sought to tell American bildungsromans, and stories of expansion and industry.

Eastwood's film appears almost Brechtian: The characters are sketches and the actors never appear to fully assimilate their roles (something that can be attributed to a deficient screenplay), while half of the town's structures stand hopeless in their hollow theatricality. The powerful men of the town (like Mayor Hobart, played by Stefan Gierasch) are representatives of a mining company that we know has led to the town's complicity in a murder. And yet there is no mining or even a *reference* beyond words—the marquee that reads "Lago Miners Hall" or the brief conversations among the townsmen—to the labor or the place of mining in the film. Many of the ingredients of the western in its golden age are thus there—the dialogue that denotes mining as a historically recognized industry of western expansion, the mid-nineteenth-century period costumes, the on-site filming of a small society in the outreaches of the U.S. landscape. Yet, they appear more like signifiers floating over the landscape rather than references to any substantial point in reality.

"Repetition" acquires several meanings in *High Plains Drifter*. The hollowed structures of Lago give it the appearance of a ghost town, despite its population. In this sense, Lago is a representation of a site that is always and already abandoned: It is reflective of a larger historical retelling of landscapes in disuse. The narrative of the film rehearses an exhausted performance of boom-and-bust stories of the U.S. West in the nineteenth century. (This air of exhaustion is comparable to the description of the tired voices and laughter that Damiana describes in *Pedro Páramo*.) The film does this, however, from a point of view that is conscious of its location in the twentieth century, at a time when ghost towns have already become sites of spectacle in desert landscapes. *High Plains Drifter* thus takes the idea of the ghost town quite literally, and doubly signifies it: It stages the story of a ghost town before its demise—that is, of a ghost town in the making, within a set that already appears muted and vacant. At the same time, it introduces a literal ghost into its plot to haunt it, and therefore shock it back into a state of repetition. As I point out above, there is also a metatextual commentary on the western genre itself. *High Plains Drifter* is undoubtedly a western, but it is symptomatic of another era for the genre— one in which the idealization of a landscape and a certain heroic way of life have wound down and come to an end. The film casts a backward glance at the genre that precedes it and also highlights its spectrality within a film industry that has moved on.

Although Jodorowsky uses the discovered "ghost town" in the desert for *El Topo* in order to enliven it with his unique brand of eclecticism—as a backdrop for a performance of his radical mix of universal mythographies—Eastwood's own reflections on the ghost town have an altogether different effect. Lago stands as a portrayal of repetitive undoing, a dramatization of that "irresistible decay" of the ruin. *High Plains Drifter*'s narrative unveils a town that is ghostly from within as well as from the outside: Desperately obsolete and barren, its only visibly thriving industry is death itself. As representative of a poetics of failure, the film is a spectacle of a hollowing out of community as well as a foundering of the myths of restorative isolation. Plagued by the ghost of their crime, Lago's inhabitants make up a society ridden with their acts of communal desertion, events resulting in the literal resignification of the town's existence from western settlement to hell on earth. Rather than reading this renaming of Lago as simply a casting of the town into the realms of biblical allegory, however, we should attempt to read how the choreography of haunting, desert, and desertion fractures the historical allegorization of the history of the U.S. West. Instead of reading "Hell" as archetypalization of the landscape, it should be interpreted as a series of events that have resulted in the obsolescence of a town and community. In effect, Lago stands as a paradoxical evacuation of the meanings of community where a group of subjects still exists. By the same token, becoming "hell" should be understood as that process of failure in which sites are spiritually and physically emptied.

One of the most poignant moments related to the revenance of the dead in Rulfo's novel transpires in a fragment where Páramo begrudgingly pays his lawyer with a warning that he should take good care of those coins, because they do not "sprout" or "spring up." To this, the unsatisfied lawyer (who knows his employer all too well) begrudgingly replies, "Yes, just like dead men don't spring up from their graves" ["Sí, tampoco los muertos retoñan. . . . Desgraciadamente"] (103; 160). This correlation between natural wealth (a reference to Comala's agricultural economy) and the dead, recounts the different currencies that have existed in Comala during its mournful history. The paradisiacal wealth of the land has been cast into a past already too distant, but in its place a valuable currency of voices remains.

The ghost towns in Rulfo's and Eastwood's desert fictions introduce the troubling element of haunting as a reinvocation of the intersections of space and ethics in the narratives of desert landscapes. As spaces that exist, but are obscured or abandoned by the movements of modernity, ghost towns manifest the histories of failure that necessarily coexist with the successes of these movements. As dramatic accounts of how ghost towns come to be, the texts by Rulfo and Eastwood facilitate new readings of violent events that transform such sites forever and irredeemably. They achieve this without casting these locations into the realms of inassimilable symbolization, but by actually refuting and chipping away at the narrative formats often attached to the allegorization of wilderness landscapes—namely the pastoral and the classic western. (The refutation of these two genres is similar to what Raymond Williams terms the "counter-pastoral" narrative in British fiction.)[53] To read the desert as perpetually inhabited by the ghosts that desertion left behind—as a place deformed and afflicted by human movement, despite its emptiness—entails a modification, in turn, of our ideas of spatial modernity in the Americas. This conceptualization of the desert appeals to a productively haunted notion of the urgent, complicated simultaneities of both place and narrative. Thinking back to José Martí's contact with the birth of the spectacularized Wild West in the 1880s, we recognize in Rulfo's and Eastwood's narratives echoes of the anxieties that surround our attempts to see modernity as a univocal and thriving temporality, or in terms of singular spatialities. Instead, we are reminded of the importance to read modernity as multiply situated, and diversely traveled. In this sense, the places of American modernity are best understood according to how they are witnesses of events of living as well as of "desvivir."

3 / Urban Indiscretions

> *"But you told me the first time I had the pleasure of talking with you that it was not so terrible."*
> *"I don't say it's terrible—now. But it's damned disagreeable!"*
> —HENRY JAMES, "THE GHOSTLY RENTAL" (1876)

> *"Jaula es la villa de palomas muertas*
> *Y ávidos cazadores! Si los pechos*
> *Se rompen de los hombres, y las carnes*
> *Rotas por tierra ruedan, no han de verse*
> *Dentro más que frutillas estrujadas!*
> *[. . .]*
> *¡Me espanta la ciudad! ¡Toda está llena*
> *De copas por vaciar, o huecas copas!*
> *¡Tengo miedo! ¡ay de mí! de que este vino*
> *Tósigo sea, y en mis venas luego*
> *Cual duende vengador los dientes clave!*
> *¡Tengo sed,—más de un vino que en la tierra*
> *No se sabe beber! ¡No he padecido*
> *Bastante aún, para romper el muro*
> *Que me aparta! ¡oh dolor de mi viñedo!*
> *¡Tomad vosotros, catadores ruines*
> *De vinillos humanos, esos vasos*
> *Donde el jugo de lirio a grandes sorbos*
> *Sin compasión y sin temor se bebe!*
> *¡Tomad! ¡Yo soy honrado, y tengo miedo!*
> —JOSÉ MARTÍ, "AMOR DE CIUDAD GRANDE" (NEW YORK, 1882)[1]

Henry James cultivated and perfected the art of writing ghost stories throughout his career, and throughout this experiment with this particular narrative form, the issues of haunting became gradually more complicated, and, one could also say, progressively inscrutable. What at first seemed an interest in demystifying haunting turned, toward the end of his writing career, into the reflections of a man troubled by death, absence, and their consequences. Much like the author's migrations, the settings for his tales of haunting would shift from a U.S. setting to an English one—the most famous example of the latter being *The Turn of the Screw* (1898)—and would later return to New York, the city where he was born, in the stories of his late career. In "The Ghostly Rental," we have an early example of James's experimentation with the subject and forms of haunting in a story that takes place close to Cambridge, Massachusetts, where the author had attended Harvard College for a year.[2] In this rather humorous story, haunting is discovered to be a performance that nevertheless dupes the wretched character of Captain Diamond into believing that he is to be haunted throughout his lifetime by the ghost of his daughter, whom he had supposedly killed with his "foul and damnable words" (125). In a stroke that would recur later in James's career, haunting is not entirely disproved as a possible phenomenon when the real ghost of Captain Diamond haunts his trickster daughter toward the end of the story. This suspension of (dis)belief is artfully brought to its absolute climax in *The Turn of the Screw*, as the verdict on whether the ghosts of Mr. Quint and Miss Jessel actually exist is forever shrouded in doubt, as all evidence of haunting depends on the delicate narrative voice of the governess.

Three years after writing "The Ghostly Rental," on January 22, 1879, to be exact, Henry James began toying with the idea of writing a different kind of ghost story. In his notebook entry from this date, he wrote:

> Imagine a door—either walled-up, or that has been long locked—at which there is an occasional knocking—a knocking which—as the other side of the door is inaccessible—can only be ghostly. The occupant of the house or room, containing the door, has long been familiar with the sound; and, regarding it as ghostly, has ceased to heed it particularly—as the ghostly presence remains on the other side of the door, and never reveals itself in other ways.[3]

The first thing to note in James's "Subject for a Ghost Story," which, according to Leon Edel and Lyall Powers, is the germ for what would three decades later become "The Jolly Corner," is how the author builds his idea of a haunted tale with a premise that is fabulously basic in its everydayness and ubiquity: the locked door. This obstruction renders a portion of the house impossible to visualize because of its condition of being inaccessible, so that it haunts the experience of habitability throughout the rest of the dwelling. When James writes that the mysterious knocking "can only be ghostly," he seems to be creating a parallelism between the visually inaccessible and the inevitability of hauntedness. In this formulation for a ghost story, what we cannot see yet nevertheless remains so close to our everyday experience, is unsettling. On a different level James points to how haunting achieves a level of normalization within everyday life. The knocking on the door turns out to be such a commonplace event that it ceases to scare and becomes something else—a cohabitation of, as well as a kind of truce between, haunting and the everyday.

It is this portrayal of everyday life occurring simultaneously with haunted events that is the most disquieting aspect of James's note and the short story that eventually would emerge in 1908. For James, haunting occurs when one is incapable of visualizing the entirety of a location in space and time: The house, which would supposedly hold all that is familiar, contains areas that are out of reach, unexplored and unmanaged. To recognize that one lives alongside a parallel everyday reality that exists outside of usual perception is therefore to acknowledge the incommensurability of our experience of lived space. James's 1879 note hints at a supremely modern take on the ghost story, one which would later be echoed by Julio Cortázar, whose story "Casa tomada" ("House Taken Over") from 1951 would take the idea of the uncomfortable cohabitation with an unnamed, possibly spectral, other (or others) to a different and extreme level: When the unnamed and unexplained occupants begin to take over a house, the named inhabitants of the house (the narrator/protagonist and his sister) progressively reduce their quarters to smaller and smaller spaces, until the house is fully taken over and they escape, throwing away the key. In these two texts, anonymity takes the form of spectrality. But anonymity here means something more profound than undisclosed names: It becomes a question of the limits of understanding the changes that lived space undergo, and the loss of the means of expressing one's perception in the face of this transformation.

In this chapter, I explore haunting as a representational development that has more to do with modern socialization than it has to do with a full explanation of something repressed and past. I define "modern socialization" in terms of the complex networks of modern spaces, affected as they are by the transformations of material and interpersonal relations, of nations and races, of the anxious relationships between the present and the future. In what follows, I argue that the depictions of haunting in the American texts I engage with here (mainly Henry James's "The Jolly Corner" from 1908 and Felisberto Hernández's "El acomodador" from 1946) rework our expectations of haunting through a textual process of urban (re)invention. In turn, this urban invention of haunting echoes anxieties about the constant adjustments that a subject needs to perform within a space that challenges the very idea and form of community, its history and possibility. James's and Hernández's inflections of the extraordinary over the urban mundane represent a stylization of the landscape through a textual exposition of wonder—put simply, particular and individual "*what ifs?*" that contemplate urban living as strings of experiments with spaces.

In these two stories, the characters' *"what ifs?"* become the motivations to manufacture, act out, and verbalize haunting as one such experimentation within the "normal" dimensions of city living. As we will see, for James's hero, inventing the haunted city entails a concatenation of misplaced narrative styles, although in Hernández's story the spectralization of the urbanscape manifests itself through questionable illuminations and an aesthetics of the miniature. How these experiments of urban invention come to be marked with what I address as the element of "indiscreet" urban explorations, and of performances in and through property and identity, will be the subject of my final discussion in this chapter.

Cities, North and South: Stories of Shrinking and Expansion

Both "The Jolly Corner" and "El acomodador" are fictions that, to use James's own theorization of the ideal "ghost-story," contain a "critical challenge" that "may take a hundred forms."[4] This has definitely been the case with my attempt to read these two stories from opposite sides and languages of the hemisphere alongside one another. One early line of questioning has to do with the city as an American space. On a cultural level, can we think of these spaces as distinct from European urban spaces? Along similar lines, can we think of American ghost stories as any different from European ones? Consequently, how do we think of ghost stories through and within the different historical processes encountered in the Americas, north and south? As Ángel Rama notes, ever since Baudelaire penned the explication *"la forme d'une ville change plus vite, hélas! que le coeur d'un mortel"* ["the form of a city changes more quickly—alas!—than a mortal's heart"] to describe the feelings of a Parisian swan covered in Haussmann's dust, global writing on cities has in varying degrees been synonymous with the issue of the palimpsestic landscapes of unplaceable pasts. Put another way, Western literature has imagined cities on which a multiplicity of presents supplant the previous ones, transforming architectures and individuals alike. Toward the end of the nineteenth century, the changing city becomes a reality that afflicts subjects in all corners of the American hemisphere. The Mexican author Federico Gamboa's diary entry from April 12, 1894, for example, echoes Baudelaire's angst when he writes, "My Mexico City is disappearing!"[5] Inhabiting a city becomes, then, a negotiation between material realities of restructured landscapes and active imaginations and sentimentalizations of nostalgic subjects. In the case of Latin American writers crafting the art of urban description, as Rama chronicles in *La ciudad letrada* (*The Lettered City*), the writing of both past and future cityscapes constitutes an act of dreaming—a rehearsal of invention rather than archival rigor.

Cities of the past and future were equally constructions of the imagination, fueled by desire, induced by the disintegration of familiar urban surroundings around the turn of the century. Unlike the cities of the future, the cities of the past could be embellished with the discourse of nineteenth-century realism, but it would be imprudent to read the description of old Montevideo, Rio de Janeiro, or Mexico City as historical fact. . . . It is well to remember that the representations of the past city were not subject to verification and could not be compared with the external realities that they professed to document, because they had already disappeared. Indeed, it was precisely the disintegration of the material past that had cleared the ground for its literary reinvention. These reinventions could be judged only as texts, validated by their internal coherence rather than their historical rigor. A dream of the past, a dream of the future—and only words and images to steer the dreaming.[6]

Intending to look at cities through a double lens of reality and invention, I will first approach this question from a historical-material perspective and then move on to the issue of the imagination of urban space in the Americas. Rama suggests that modernization in the Americas differs from its European counterparts in that an appreciation of the urban histories of the Americas in the nineteenth century (to a greater extent in some countries than others) must take into account parallel histories of immigration and expansion into the countryside (54). Conversely, in Europe, as Raymond Williams has noted about England, the countryside of the second half of the nineteenth century was in many ways shrinking, though certainly not disappearing, "while the urban population continued to grow dramatically, in a general population increase, and while emigration to other lands notably increased."[7]

The lives of the city and the countryside in nineteenth-century American countries, most importantly, were tainted by the violent histories of the enslavement of blacks and Native Americans and the brutal appropriation of Indian lands. In the United States, the doctrine of Manifest Destiny—the Jacksonian institutionalization of "land-hunger," as Richard Slotkin describes it—paralleled the expansion of an industrialized urban society, which moved at a staggering pace after the Civil War. The year 1869 marked the culmination of the construction of the transcontinental railroad (a process on which Ralph Waldo Emerson reflected as early as 1842 when he wrote "I hear the whistle of the locomotive in the woods"), and when the western frontier was officially closed in the last decade of the century, the United States was already the world's leader in industry. There are no more spectacular summaries of the extent to which the postcolonial

American nations adapted to the feverish pace of modernity than the world's fairs and other exhibitions that took place in the late nineteenth century. Mauricio Tenorio-Trillo notes that to understand the phenomena of the world's fairs is "to grasp the internal composition of the awareness of modernity."[8] As one of the displays of this "compositions," the Centennial Exhibition of 1876 in Philadelphia, according to Richard Ruland and Malcolm Bradbury,

> put [North] American mechanical achievement on display, a mass of technological wonders like Thomas A. Edison's telegraph and Alexander Graham Bell's telephone. The spread of new land was matched by industrial innovation, the migration of national population by a massive increase in the scale of immigration, the emergence of new states and territories by the bursting upward energy of high-rise shock cities like Chicago. Industry, technology, capital investment and the growth of trusts led to the amassing of great personal fortunes, a new kind of wealth and power. . . . In 1893 came the World's Columbian Exposition in Chicago, the dynamic city that tied West and East into a single, interlinked, modern economic and social system. . . . The old order of Jeffersonian agrarianism had turned into an advanced industrial society, a unified process—but also a multiverse running beyond intellectual comprehension and control.[9]

In the southern hemisphere, half a century after the wars of independence in Latin America culminated in the 1820s, capitalist systems begin to take a stronger hold of the countries' economies, in what Jorge Larrain describes as a "very slow process."[10] Ruland and Bradbury describe the U.S. government's support for a surge in westward movement by immigrant populations, and, in contrast, Rama explains the difference in the position of the immigrant populations during the similar campaigns of the "*conquista del desierto*" in Argentina.

> Immigrants were a part of the frontier experience in the United States, where many of them were rewarded with land. Although the expansion of the Argentine frontier ("the conquest of the desert") closely paralleled the westward advance of the frontier in the United States, it was carried out by the landed oligarchy and the army, restricting access to newly incorporated land and paralyzing the democratic function of spontaneous pioneer migrations that occurred on the North American frontier. ("Lettered City," 54)

Moreover, the modernization of the countries of Latin America needs to be explored in terms of the discrete social and historical factors that tempered it. One of these was the cessation, or continuation, of slave economies in the various countries. Although slavery was abolished in nations that achieved independence from Spain, it continued to thrive in Cuba, Brazil, and Puerto Rico, which were still dependent on colonial plantation economies.[11] The countries that had gained independence from Europe in the early nineteenth century were nevertheless dependent on Europe for the export of their raw products. This resulted in a relationship that Jennifer L. French, among others, has described as a new-fangled form of colonialism.[12] The expansion of this export economy resulted in an influx of immigration by European and Asian workers into Latin America, coupled with an increased assault on Indian lands, as Larrain explains (79). And, with the implementation of this reformed economic relationship with Europe, the last quarter of the nineteenth century saw the creation of an "urban-industrial society" and the confluent diversification of social classes in these societies, namely the "middle class, the industrial bourgeoisie and the working class" (80). Larrain notes how, in the Rio de la Plata countries of Argentina and Uruguay, the bourgeoisie and the middle classes were more autonomous due to the condition of national control of export production (80).

However different, or uneven, these two stories of industrialization and change in the North and the South may be, Latin American countries were not free of the dark underside of expansion experienced in the United States. Argentina, for example, underwent a similar violent expansion of the frontier, as Rama notes (54). In this country, Governor Juan Manuel de Rosas began in 1831 a campaign to expel the Indians off the lands "as far south as the Rio Negro," an undertaking that continued in varying degrees of military "success" for decades until General Roca's "scorched earth" *conquista del desierto* campaign (1879–82).[13] By 1879, according to James Dunkerley, "all the fighters of the Ranquel people had been eliminated and the entire population uprooted."[14]

Rama's incomplete materialist-historical study of the emergent structures of modernity in Latin America (the critic tragically died while he was composing *The Lettered City*) is propelled by a thesis that describes the complicity between literature and the state's structures of power. This is something that he traces from the period of colonization straight through to the twentieth century. Thus, to Rama, the devastating struggles that sought to suppress cultural others within the spaces of Latin American nations were symbolically supported by the "ordering impulse" and ideologies of the written word. His theorization of the *ciudad letrada* [lettered city] sets out to describe the precedence of the written word and its centurions—the *letrados*, or men of letters—ever since the European colonialist "urban dream of a new age" (2). The model of the *letrado*'s ideologies that travels unaltered across the centuries has come under fire for how it entraps the figure of the writer in what Julio Ramos calls a "historical bloc" that "obscures the radical changes that doubtless occurred at the turn of the [twentieth] century, if not earlier."[15] Ramos traces the nuanced attachments between literature, ideology, and nation building to construct a nuanced (and at times splintered) correlation between cities and letters in the nineteenth century. His critique is informed by what he calls the "different subjects" and "different modes of authorization" and autonomy evidenced in the various writers of the national condition throughout the nineteenth century (60). Working on this diverse spectrum, Ramos (unlike Rama) identifies a will to aestheticization, especially in the work of fin-de-siècle writers, rather than a continuous relationship between literature and the state in Latin American letters since the colonial period. (Ramos also recognizes a form of chaos and fragmentation in urban literature of the late nineteenth century that contradicts the model of order and power in Rama's lettered city.) Moving a bit backward in time, however, both Rama and Ramos see in Domingo Sarmiento (who would become president of the Argentine republic in 1868) an interesting case study of how the city functions as ordering and modernizing logos: For Sarmiento, the city is the ultimate and unquestionable symbol of the utopia of progress and modernity. As Ramos explains, there is an evident etymological relation between the urban and the concept of civilization in Sarmiento's thought. At a time when the narratives of Latin America's participation in urban modernity were yet to be written, Sarmiento offered a blueprint for the modern Latin American country in which the ordering nucleus of culture and therefore of civilization lay within the city. As we will continue to explore in the next section as in Chapter 4, his was an exclusive and exclusionary interpretation of the spaces that can be made to represent the nation as it tries to incorporate itself within a history of progress and modernity.

Traveling Imaginations and the Chronicling of American Landscapes

Sarmiento's "shadow" (a term that I insert to forecast the analysis that follows in Chapter 4) is of critical importance because it directs our attention to how the city and the *othered* landscapes of a nation coexist in literature. Moreover, Sarmiento's writing displays a multifariously comparative sensibility that vindicates and buttresses his vision of Argentina (and we could say all of Spanish America) as a land divided between a "civilized" tendency to industriousness and prosperity, and its stark opposite, the pampas and those who inhabit this region. Importantly, in his writings from the 1840s and beyond, Sarmiento insists on a comparison between Argentina to his utopian model of civilization, the United States.[16] One of his reflections during his travels in the United States in 1847 pins the blame for the differences of the American North and South on the European countries that happened to colonize them.

> ¿Por qué la raza sajona tropezó con este pedazo de mundo que tan bien cuadraba con sus instintos industriales; por qué a la raza española le cupo en suerte la América del sur donde habia minas de plata, de oro, e indios mansos i abyectos, que venian de perlas a su pereza de amo, a su atraso e ineptitud industrial? No hai órden i premeditacion en todos estos acasos? No hai Providencia? Oh! amigo, Dios es la mas fácil solucion de todas estas dificultades!

> [Why was it the Anglo-Saxon race that discovered this piece of the world which is so well suited to its industrial instincts, whilst South America, a land of gold and silver mines and gentle and submissive Indians, has fallen to the Spanish race—a region aptly suited to its proud laziness, its backwardness, and its industrial ineptitude? Is there not order and premeditation in all of these cases? Is there not Providence? Oh, my friend, God must be the explanation for these things!][17]

This divine "order" (which culminates in the author's quite blatant call for Argentina to "be the United States of Latin America")[18] that Sarmiento claims has overlooked the countries of South America is, as Rama and Ramos demonstrate, to be compensated for with writing and literacy. To attain "order" in the land of the forsaken, writing (which Ramos argues is synonymous with modernizing in Sarmiento's thought) becomes an invaluable vehicle for taming the unruly *barbarie* through a process of scriptural submission, molding the countryside's orality into written discourse for the first time.[19]

Interestingly, this act of writing, with the civilized city as its urgent symbol, is considered necessary for the purpose of putting time in order as well. To Sarmiento, the barbarous element in South America is incapable of remembering, of possessing a cultural and historical memory. He writes in *Facundo*:

> Los pueblos en masa no son capaces de comparar distintamente unas épocas con otras; el momento presente es para ellos el único sobre el cual se extienden sus miradas: así es como nadie ha observado hasta ahora la destrucción de las ciudades y su decadencia; lo mismo que no preven la barbarie total a que marchan visiblemente los pueblos del interior.[20]

[The masses aren't capable of distinguishing some eras from others; for them, the present moment is the only one over which they cast their gaze. This is why no one has observed, until now, the destruction of the cities and their decadence, in the same way that the peoples of the Argentine interior do not foresee the total barbarity toward which they visibly are marching.][21]

This absence of the past in collective memory dangerously ignores the actual violence of erasure of the past by those in power. Sarmiento reads the barbarous "mass of men" that has achieved the ruination of cities through a parallel act of demolition of *history* itself, which, as he states in 1847, represents a "*jeolojía moral*" ("moral geology," or "geography," in Rockland's translation).[22] From this passage, we may gather that to only be able to observe the present—in the dual Latin American theaters of the decaying city and the primitive interior—is in itself a manifestation of barbarism. The insistence on the "present" that Sarmiento condemns in the man of the "mass" should be distinguished from the educated and technocratic cult to the present that was becoming increasingly evident in the United States and European societies that he so admired. His is a selective take on history, in the sense that it is the province of those who can manipulate it according to a specific, positive model. As we will see in Chapter 4, the Sarmiento of *Facundo* represents himself as the one capable of documenting a past while keeping his sights on the present conditions and the future possibilities of his nation. He thus sets himself the task of writing the biography of the barbarous Facundo Quiroga even if it entails a return to the "romantic tenets of inspiration and improvisation," as Sylvia Molloy observes.[23]

In what follows, I focus on how Sarmiento's travels to the United States represent a contradiction in terms of these absent temporalities and crumbling cities, so that we may reflect on the imagination of American cities in the late nineteenth and early twentieth centuries. William H. Katra points out that Sarmiento had never seen Buenos Aires before marking the rigid delineations of city/interior and civilization/barbarous on the pages of *Facundo* (92). When he traveled to the United States in 1847, two years after publishing his magnum opus, he came face to face with the spaces of industry that had populated his utopian dreams. He had, however, also been to Europe, and a shift in thought ensued, as Katra explains:

After his trip to the United States, this image of the urban experience suffers a change of emphasis in his writings. . . . Engraved in his mind was a contradictory image of Europe's urban centers; they were the site of both greatness and abjection, where humanity's most sublime and miserable attributes existed side by side. . . . From now on, he would alter the content of his famous duality . . . he would defend the town or the village, and not the city, as the source and the center of progress. (89–90)

Indeed, in his *Viajes*, Sarmiento—almost bewilderedly, perhaps a bit apologetically—creates an image of city living as a "wild" existence that is, ironically, tamed by the "colonizing spirit" [*espíritu colonizador*] of expansion: "En medio de las ciudades el hombre se cria salvaje, si es posible decirlo" ["In the middle of the cities men are reared in a 'savage state,' if you will"] (319; 161). He continues qualifying this idea by reflecting on an image of the United States subject as "imprisoned" in the cities. This reflection leads him to dream the North American as a lover, and colonizer, of nature.

> El espíritu yankee se siente aprisionado en las ciudades; necesita ver desde la puerta de su casa la dilatada i sombría columnata que forman las encinas seculares de los bosques . . . . Por qué se ha muerto el espíritu colonizador entre nosotros, los descendientes de la colonización oficial? (323)

> [The Yankee spirit feels imprisoned in the cities. It needs to see from the door of its house the vast and shady colonnade formed by ancient oaks in the forest. . . . Why has the colonizing spirit died among ourselves, the descendants of the greatest colonizers?] (168)

The image of the forest-gazing North American thus becomes the true model for Sarmiento's ideal of a forward-moving society. This is an idea of a man not merely enraptured with the sights of nature, but driven by a proprietary spirit as well. Sarmiento writes:

> El yankee ha nacido irrevocablemente propietario; si nada posee ni poseyó jamas, no dice que es pobre, sino que está pobre; los negocios van mal; el pais va en decadencia; i entónces los bosques primitivos se presentan a su imajinacion oscuros, solitarios, apartados, i en el centro de ellos, a la orilla de algun rio desconocido, ve su futura mansion, el humo de las chimeneas, los bueyes que vuelven con tardo paso al caer de la tarde el redil, la dicha en fin, la propiedad que le pertenece. (321–22)

> [The Yankee is a born proprietor. If he does not have anything and never has had anything he does not say that he *is* poor but that he is poor right now, or that he has been unlucky, or that times are bad. And then, in his imagination he sees the primitive, dark, solitary, isolated forests and in the midst of them the mansion he means to have on the bank of some unknown river, with smoke rising from the

chimney and oxen returning home with slow step to his property as
the sun goes down.] (166)[24]

It is impossible to deny the romantic influence of a James Fenimore Cooper over this particular act of imagination.[25] Yet, differently from Cooper's
myths of a perennial (inhabitant of) nature, Sarmiento's admiring vision
of the U.S. wilderness moves with a speed that Henry David Thoreau describes as "railroad fashion."[26] It reminds us of that sweeping description
of westward migration that Ambrose Bierce describes in "The Boarded
Window": The image of the solitary house in the deep forests quickly
flashes forward to the waves of migration that continue with the *"pioners"*
("pioneers"), quickly followed by the *"empresarios capitalistas"* ("capitalist
empresarios"), who also bring with them the immigrant laborers (342–43).
What Sarmiento documents, albeit in an embellished style, is the swift
movement outside of the cities and into these preferred spaces of the fertile
forest where the North American will to own is cultivated.

And yet, how is the divergence of cities and barbarous nature delineated
in *Facundo* adapted in his imagination during his journey to the United
States? In *Viajes*, Sarmiento's dream of progress is hampered by visions
of human destitution and is quickly replaced by the series of emptied-out
tableaux of the forest. The openness of the United States West (which he
calls the *"Farwest"* in the original Spanish)—whose "declining civilization" is quickly glossed over in *Viajes*—provides the space for his utopia to
spread unhampered:[27]

> Hácia el Oeste, donde la civilizacion declina, i en el *Farwest*, donde
> casi se estingue, por el desparramo de la población en las campañas,
> el aspecto cambia sin duda, el bienestar se reduce a lo estrictamente
> necesario, i la casa se convierte en el *log-house*. (300)

> [Westward, where civilization diminishes, and in the FAR WEST,
> where it is almost nonexistent because of the sparseness of the popu-
> lation, things are of course different. Comfort is reduced to what is
> strictly necessary, and houses are LOG HOUSES.] (131)

Here, the ideal man ("not sent by anyone") will follow his wanderlust and
desire to populate (*"de ir a poblar"*). This liberty constitutes one of the
more disturbing moments in Sarmiento's pictorial tale of population and
civilization: Ahead of the *"pioners"* and the "misanthropic *squatters*," goes
the *"indian hatter"* ("hater"), "que tiene por único dogma perseguir al
salvaje, por único apetito el esterminio de las razas indíjenas" ["persecut-
ing the savage is his only creed, exterminating the indigenous people his
only desire"]. He continues: "Nadie lo ha mandado; él va solo al bosque
con su rifle i sus perros a dar caza a los salvajes, ahuyentarlos i hacerles

abandonar las cacerías de sus padres" ["No one has commanded it. He goes to the forest with only his rifle and his dogs to hunt the savages, putting them to flight and making them abandon the hunting grounds of their fathers]" (342; 190). Soon after, Sarmiento complains that what happens almost organically in the United States would take "half a century" in his Argentina. (When he develops his Argentine "characters" or types in *Facundo*, he defines the Argentine "gaucho malo" as an *"outlaw"* and a "squatter.") The solitary figure that liberally kills indigenous people without being sent by any government, but out of sheer hatred, does not meet with criticism from Sarmiento, who, according to Katra, buys into many of the "mythic components" of expansionist politics in the Age of Jackson (90).

Three decades later in the century, José Martí (who lived in exile in New York throughout the 1880s and until the mid-1890s) would bring a different perspective to the Spanish American observation of the urban United States.[28] As Gerard Aching explains, Martí's vision of a Spanish America whose "cultural identity is inextricably related to knowledge about the other America," undoes the "epistemological and ideological comfort of purportedly autonomous, unilateral imagined cultural definitions in favor of a dialectics of identity construction that is more reminiscent of some contemporary approaches to the issue."[29] Contemplating the state of the American lands, Martí looks upon the ever-expanding United States as *"gigantes con botas de siete leguas,"* or "giants in seven-league boots," a monstrosity that stood against the plight of the Spanish American "natural man" [*"hombre natural"*]—the *mestizo,* from whom, Martí argues, springs an organic and autochthonous form of government that understands the continent from within, and who stands opposed to those who can envision politics only in terms of transplanted European or North American models. Denouncing this vision of Spanish American imitation of Europe and the United States, personified in the "artificial men of letters" [*"letrados artificiales"*], he writes:

> Cree el soberbio que la tierra fue hecha para servirle de pedestal, porque tiene pluma fácil o la palabra de colores, y acusa de incapaz e irremediable a su república nativa porque no le dan sus selvas nuevas modo continuo de ir por el mundo de gamonal famoso, guiando jacas de Persia y derramando champaña. La incapacidad no está en el país naciente, que pide formas que se le acomoden y grandeza útil, sino en los que quieren regir pueblos originales, de composición singular y violenta, con leyes heredadas de cuatro siglos de práctica libre en los Estados Unidos, de diecinueve siglos de monarquía en Francia.

[The haughty man believes that the land was made to serve as his pedestal, because he has a quill or colorful words at his disposal; and he attacks his native republic as helpless or hopeless because its forests offer him no new way of gallivanting around the world, steering Persian ponies and spilling champagne. The fault does not lie with the newborn country, but with those who try to rule originary peoples, composed of a singular and violent nature, with laws inherited from four centuries of freedom in the United States and nineteen centuries of monarchy in France.][30]

Aching describes the ways of these "artificial men of letters" in Martí's "Our America" as "fetishized" or "overdetermined cosmopolitans" who cannot be wholly separated from the literary productions of Martí's *modernista* contemporaries (most famously Rubén Darío).[31]

Just as the [*modernistas*] drew from a multiplicity of sources in order to create their literature, so [Martí], as one of the most traveled *modernista* thinkers of his day, assessed the validity of the ways in which cultural fragments (objects, gestures, referents, and allusions) were being combined to produce a modern literary and cultural expression. (157)

This "overdetermined cosmopolitanism," which contains within it the "unilateral cultural definitions" that Martí ultimately renounces, is in many ways reminiscent of the vastly idealized images championed by Sarmiento's touristic imagination of a country that was expanding westward and southward into Mexico in his time, and about to engage in overseas imperialism during the time of Martí. The latter's historical situation in the last decade of the nineteenth century, however, would produce something markedly different: a residential-documentarian narrative of the American hemisphere in what Ramos addresses as the fragmented *"rhetoric of strolling"* [*"retórica del paseo"*], or the exile's *flânerie*, in the form of the urban chronicle (126). Martí's *crónicas* of the United States are a record of his constant traveling along the East Coast of the country, documenting political and cultural events for a Latin American audience, exercising his keen eye for comparative observation of the development of the country. Arguing that, in Martí's experience, "modernism and exile are synonymous," Susana Rotker describes Martí's chronicle writing as "the way to shape that experience of being a witness, of trying to produce for the Latin American reader a sort of revelation and re-creation of the native land."[32] On a formal level, Ramos argues that the chronicle represents a "minor literature" that, "generically imprecise" (141), is an "area of confluence for competing discourses" (183): It "enabled the representation of diverse experiences linked to a capitalist field of daily existence that remained excluded from more stable forms of literary (or artistic) representation" (141). In what follows, I will add to Rotker's and Ramos's definition of this form of literature by proposing that, in dramatic and interpretive respects, the chronicle proves to be a haunting and haunted narrative.

One of Martí's *crónicas* documents the Charleston, South Carolina, earthquake of 1886. The atmosphere of the stricken town is discussed in detail, as Martí pronounces that "to say it is to see it" ["decirlo es verlo"].

> Un terremoto ha destrozado la ciudad de Charleston. Ruina es hoy lo que ayer era flor, y por un lado se miraba en el agua arenosa de sus ríos, surgiendo entre ellos como un cesto de frutas, y por el otro se extendía a lo interior en pueblos lindos, rodeados de bosques de magnolias, y de naranjos y jardines.

> [Charleston has been destroyed by an earthquake. There is nothing but ruins where once stood a city spreading like a basket of fruit between the sandy waters of two rivers, merging inland into beautiful villages surrounded by magnolia trees, orange trees, and gardens.][33]

The Charleston *crónica* is of particular interest in its representation of the intercalated landscapes of the city and the forest. We have already seen how Sarmiento's representation of North American cities included a reflection of the "wild existence" of these urban landscapes, leading his utopian imagination to travel westward to the settlement of the forest. Sarmiento's eventual preference for the small North American town surrounded by an enclosing natural landscape appears to be echoed by Martí's description of Charleston standing like a "basket of fruit" surrounded by the pretty towns that seem to blend in with a cornucopia of picturesque nature.

Yet Martí's *crónica* begins with the reportage of a disaster, and his second sentence opens quite markedly with the inserted images of "ruins" that not only deface the visible landscape but also seem to insinuate themselves into the bucolic register he would continue to employ. Julio Ramos has read this episode of catastrophe as a representation of the destruction of "all signs of modernity" that also make possible, "by means of the destruction of the city, the return to an origin that progress had earlier obliterated" (120). Indeed, one could say that, in Martí's *crónica* of the earthquake, there is a (re)birth motif: Two twins are born "under a blue tent" at the essay's midpoint, and the author closes his reflections with the same two newborns, who effect the powers of a double deus ex machina that bring hope into the devastated landscape. The earthquake also marks the rebirth of the "melancholy barbarous" element in the black population, who do not fail to strike the narrator as possessing in their reactions of fright and happiness something of the "supernatural and marvelous which cannot be found in other primitive races" ["algo de sobrenatural y maravilloso que no existe en las demás razas primitivas"] (278; 85).

In the midst of the brute reality of a city in ruins, the people take to the forests, seeking "shelter in the trees" and "singing" together, in what Ramos describes as a "reencounter with the community" and a "reconstruction of the *chorus*," both of which in his opinion imply "the restitution of the power of myth and the imagination (proper to literature) that was cut short in the city by the rationalization and its *disenchantment*."

> To *invent* tradition, an origin—to "remember" the past of the city, and mediate between modernity and areas that modernity has excluded or run over: this will be one of the great strategies of legitimation instituted by modern Latin American literature beginning with Martí. For in literature, as Martí suggests in "Nuestra América," the "mute Indio," the "victimized Black," *speaks*. Literature is, in effect, legitimized as the site of rationalization's *others*. (120)

Ramos reads in Martí's urban chronicles a description of the "fragmentation" of city life. He aligns the *crónica's* fragmentary form with precisely the material and metaphorical features of rupture and catastrophe that abound in the urban sphere. Ramos writes that the city, in Martí, "*spatializes* the fragmentation of the original order of discourse" (118), so that through literature the Cuban writer creates (invents) a point of mediation between these fragmenting spaces and those other locations that modernity obliterates and forgets.

If one reads just one paragraph further in the Charleston *crónica*, one notices that the momentary migrations to the forest are followed by Martí's scenes of diverse shock: of a Freemason who was "being initiated in a loggia," and ran terrified to the street "wearing a rope around his waist," as well as a Cherokee Indian who, having just put his "savage hand to his woman," fell to his knees upon feeling the earth shake under his feet (84). This is immediately followed by a caesura in the text.[34] We find here a divergence between the image/ideal of the "speaking" Indio that Ramos alludes to in the passage above, as the vision of this Cherokee who, enframed as though in a tableau vivant, performs violence at the time of the earthquake. The homology between human violence and an anthropomorphized savage, natural world that begins to shake it, cut short by a caesura, leaves the reader to deal with this projection of the image's afterlife—an image that Martí does not revisit later in the chronicle.[35]

In a *crónica* from October 25, 1885, Martí wrote of the problems that afflicted Native Americans in the United States. He writes that the Indian, sin propiedad que mejorar, ni viaje que emprender, ni necesidad material que no esté satisfecha, gasta en frusilerías de colores, que halagan su gusto artístico rudimentario, o en el licor y el juego que le excitan y aumentan los placeres brutales a que vive condenado. El indio es muerto.

[without property to make improvements to, nor a voyage to embark upon, nor any material necessity that isn't (immediately) satisfied, spends his money on colorful knickknacks . . . or on the drink and gambling that excite him and which augment the brutal pleasures to which he has been condemned. The Indian is [made] dead.][36]

"El indio es muerto": The Indian is (*made*) dead, as if freeze-framed, because he has been ensnared by a systematic order of dispossession and remuneration, leaving him a "beast that the system has itself developed." What does one make of Martí's portrayal in "The Charleston Earthquake" of the Native American who, shocked, is left hanging in the midst of a fit of rage? The effect of disharmony in this section of the Charleston *crónica*, where the Native American is left suspended, sits uncomfortably with the multiracial chorus in the forest that Ramos addresses. Such a portrait of frozen violence (and its afterlife), which Martí displays and then immediately abandons, diffuses a progressive model of the alternatives to a chronological modernity, and presents a volatile, and more ominous, idea of modernity's abiding movements and narratives.

"Restless Analysis" and Adventure Stories: On Modern Haunting

As we continue reading past the passage that Ramos quotes from the Charleston *crónica*, we are thus left with a cipher and its uncomfortable afterlife. The resolution met by most of the figures in the Charleston earthquake *crónica* stands on uneasy ground with this figure of the Cherokee: The abandonment of this subject on the page, more than fracturing our scope of modernity and modernization into separate and distinct landscapes and spheres, represents a rather complicated notion of a page haunted by an unassimilable figure that cannot easily be reduced to an originary narrative line. In other words, Martí's suspension of the Cherokee figure in the *crónica* leads to a refusal of resolution that cannot be explained as a reinvention of modernity's origin, or a fantasy about premodern solidarity, because the Cherokee is already, and continues to be, an unmythical, open, and present part of this modernity. Jeffrey Belnap has argued,

while Anglo-Americans blinded themselves to the multiethnic com-
plexities of their own nation by conceptualizing the natural landscape as an essentially empty space waiting to be taken up with
history, Martí's version of naturalistic nationalism is based on a principle of inclusion rather than one of exclusion. Instead of some concept that renders the natural landscape prehistorical and precultural,
American Nature for Martí is always already shot through with the
history of Native American peoples whose descendants pertain to
postimperial wealth.[37]

We could argue that Martí's literary act of framing this figure does not
simply constitute a rupture with a now-moment and its (better) past, but
that it is a creation of a scene of a present that is proleptically geared to a
disconcerting "savagery" that modernity has yet to suffer.

It is this image's afterlife—how it remains in the mind of the reader that
has been processing successive scenes of catastrophe—and how its presence complicates the portrayal of the diverse landscapes of the American
"scene," that alerts us to a new form of ghost-writing. The *crónica*'s purpose
is to convey news of recent occurrences to a Latin American reading public
and to offer a dynamic portrait of the events that transpire in the unseen
elsewhere of the American hemisphere. In this journalistic format, Martí
repeatedly leaves his readers with indissoluble figures of unresolution and
suspension, caught in the crevices of a narrative about urban modernity.
These are instances in which the author is asking his readers to watch for
the present ghosts of the society he is describing. Although Martí's is not
a witness account of the Charleston earthquake (his *crónicas* were largely
interpretations, or creative translations of what he was reading in daily
newspapers), this literary form allows him to visually scan the affected
landscape, to hover over it, infusing it with a diversity of scenes unavail-
able in the original reports of the disaster: "Estas desdichas que arrancan
desde las entrañas de la tierra hay que verlas desde lo alto de los cielos"
["Calamities such as this coming from the bowels of the earth must be
envisioned by the high heavens"], he writes (79; 274). In his desire to say
(*decir*) in order to see the event (*verlo*), Martí introduces the reader to a
haunted landscape, and a haunted U.S. nation, where the ghosts are alive
and visible if one watches out for them.

Let us recall how Ramos perceives in Martí's chronicle writing a kind
of restitution of an originary whole amid the threat of fragmentation that
urban modernity opens. This is indeed a compelling way of reading how
space can be reinvented by and assimilated through literary creation. And
yet, as I have been signaling in this section, there is another dimension
that we should also address in our readings of Martí's narratives that does

not necessarily conform to models of fragmentation or wholeness. Instead, it has to do with the way in which Martí includes certain hovering, suspended, and suspenseful features in his writing that call for a different interpretation by the reader. I want to propose a reading of Martí's chronicles as haunted (and haunting) literary sites, where instead of a palliative assimilation of different national landscapes, we find discrete, yet poignant moments of disquiet emerging throughout the different landscapes he describes. The figures he leaves suspended in the chronicles, I want to suggest, constitute an original call to ghost-watch—that is, to look out for the many unanswered problems and figures that exist on the page, and to ask what they have to say about the changing landscapes they emerge from— within a particular literary form that in itself reflects how a writer works through his complex impressions of modern landscapes. In what follows, I will read Martí alongside Henry James to elucidate how this different form of haunting (a haunting that is *present* and *progressive*) is evident in their perceptions of the United States.

As I note in my Introduction, it has not been customary to read James alongside Martí.[38] Unlike Martí, James was not an ardent political activist. Although we can call them both *transnational* writers, given that a great part of their careers were spent outside of their native lands, their reasons for their respective exiles were entirely different. In terms of hemispheric politics and as Philip Horne has recently shown, James maintained a poised, if critical, stance toward Assistant Secretary of the Navy and later President Theodore Roosevelt's political ideology of expansion following the Spanish-American War of 1898. (It was William, James's older brother, who was openly critical of Roosevelt and belonged to the Anti-Imperialist League.)[39] Martí died three years before the war that would place Cuba, Puerto Rico, and the Philippines out of the hands of Spain and into varying degrees of subjection to the United States, but his essays proleptically warn of the dangers of falling into relationships of submission with the northern country. I have found one mention by Martí of Henry James that does little to flatter the New York–born writer: In a letter from December 19, 1882 to Bartolomé Mitre y Vedia, who then headed *La Nación* newspaper in Buenos Aires, Martí surveys the state of U.S. writing. "De prosistas, hay muchedumbre, pero ninguno hereda a Motley. Hay un joven novelista que se afrancesa, Henry James" ["There are a multitude of prose writers, but none of them can claim to be [John Lothrop] Morley's heir. There is a young novelist who is becoming Frenchified, Henry James"].[40] One need only return to Martí's discussions of the "hombre artificial" in "Nuestra América" to see how James's Europeanization was not an admirable trait in the Cuban's eyes.

And yet, the two writers had much in common in terms of what they admired about other writers, and particularly how these other writers worked to conceive complex descriptions of space. The problems of representing the overwhelming landscape in U.S. literature are already evident in the early nineteenth-century work of the American "renaissance" writers, as Robert E. Abrams has persuasively argued. Although earlier practitioners resorted to a duality of a civilized *here* and a wild *elsewhere*, Abrams argues, the literature of Nathaniel Hawthorne, Henry David Thoreau, and Herman Melville proposes a more unsettling option. These writers, he argues, "begin to develop an alternative, less escapist aesthetic whose liberating power lies immediately *within* rather than *beyond* culture and history."[41] Thus, rather than re-create the romantic parity of represented open landscape and absolute freedom from the restraints of civilization, Hawthorne, Thoreau, and Melville produce what Abrams terms an "abidingly *negative* geography."

> The tendency of writers like Thoreau and Hawthorne is to redirect a conceived point of crisis—where known, settled space collides with a residually "unsettled" dimension—from the receding threshold of western wilderness into the vulnerable depth of all culturally accredited presence, where textures and features of everyday life remain as latently frail as the lost legibility of once decipherable hieroglyphics. (10)

Henry James was of course no stranger to the way that a writer such as Hawthorne crafted literary landscapes while manifesting a sense of perceptive uneasiness. In his 1879 essay "Nathaniel Hawthorne," James commends his predecessor's portrayal of "a life of the spirit more complex than anything that met the mere eye of sense," aligned with the "great complication" in expressing "the restless individual conscience."[42] In this analysis of the makeup of Hawthorne's tales of "complicated" morality, James picks up on the question of how a "restless" narrative voice can emulate the acts of seeing and sense-making, of both "emulat[ing]" and "enhanc[ing]" an impression of both places and characters in a state of analytical restlessness (13).

Along similar lines, Martí pays tribute to Hawthorne by reading him as a novelist not so much preoccupied with verisimilitude as he was with the mysteries of the "spirit." In a May 1884 article written for *La América*, he read the New Englander as "aquel descriptor leal, veedor privilegiado" ["that loyal describer, privileged seer"],

> artista extremo y sentidor sutil de la Naturaleza y de su espíritu; porque Hawthorne no veía, como Balzac y los noveladores de ahora, las líneas, minuciosidades y ladrillos y tejas de los lugares que copiaba; sino su alma, y lo que inspiran; y tenía una peculiar y

dichosísima manera de ir acordando sus criaturas y los paisajes en que las movía, lo cual daba a todas sus novelas aquella rica vida espiritual, caliente luz y perfecto conjunto que las avalora. Que otros pintan actos, y combates de la voluntad, y dramas de pasiones; pero Hawthorne pintaba lo que en sí mismo lleva el espíritu del hombre, y nadie supo como él descubrirlo y revelarlo. Le fue dado asomarse a lo invisible. (353)

[extreme artist and subtle feeler of Nature and its spirit; because Hawthorne didn't see, like Balzac and the novelists of today, the lines, minutiae and bricks and tiles of the places he rendered; he saw their soul and what they inspire; and he had a peculiar and most fortunate way of harmonizing his creatures and the landscapes in which he made them move, which gave all of his novels that rich spiritual life, that warm light and perfect ensemble that gives them weight. Others paint actions, and battles of the will and passionate dramas; but Hawthorne painted what man himself carries in his spirit, and no one else knew how to discover and reveal it like him. He was given the gift of peeking into the invisible.]

Describing Hawthorne as a "painter" of the spirit, Martí focuses on the way in which the North American author built a dynamic alignment between his imagined characters and the surrounding imagined landscape, all within his larger (paradoxical) project of revealing the "invisible." Both Martí and James thus activate an analysis of the earlier writer as gifted in his development of the shifting, movable art of representing something that is not quite *there* for one to see.[43] Dynamic invisibility, invisible movement of the spirit—though looking at Hawthorne on the level of literary critique, both James and Martí pierce the sphere of analysis with the admittance of that other, mysterious realm of the invisible, yet present, in representation. This particular consonance between the two writers—their interest in the complications inherent in describing a modern landscape, and their doubts about how one's perception can claim to cast a full light over that place—is my main interest here.

Writing about Charleston as an actual, as opposed to literary, visitor in 1904, James describes the episode of his arrival in the city: On the train to the South Carolina city, he declares that the "social scenes" at the "small stations" on the way to the city "might be sufficiently penetrated, no doubt, from the car window."[44] Yet, the arrival at the Charleston station brings a change of attitude to the "freshly repatriated," "restless analyst" of the American scene, and a play between *wondering*, and *wandering* about the southern city and its relation to the difficult "whole" ensues.

It couldn't have happened without one's beginning to wander; but the lively interest was that the further one wandered the more the suggestion spoke. The sense of the size of the Margin, that was the name of it—the Margin by which the total of American life, huge as it already appears, is still so surrounded as to represent, for the mind's eye on a general view, but a scant central flotilla huddled as for very fear of the fathomless depth of water, the too formidable future, on the so much vaster lake of the materially possible. Once that torch is at all vividly lighted it flares, for any pair of open eyes, over every scene, and with a presence that helps to explain their owner's veritable failure to conclude. (401)

In a 1906 letter to H. G. Wells, James refers to the United States (after his brief "repatriation") as "the vast uncomfortable subject."[45] His return to the native country after over two decades of absence, which he recounts in *The American Scene* (1907), constitutes a moment of absolute representational difficulty for James. His ideas, formulated in a restlessness of context, content, and form, suggest images and metaphors that offer no finality but illustrate his "failure to conclude" instead. James's inability to finish a complete idea about the subject signals his preoccupation with both a topographical immensity and a future gaping open: The possibilities of this "Margin" eventually signifying a "greater good" and/or a "greater evil," he writes, "lurk confused, disengaged, in the mere looming mass of the *more*, the more and more to come" (401).

One of the key aporias of the "Margin" of the American scene is consistently, for James, "the great problem of persons of color,"[46] one that resounds everywhere for him in the journey to Charleston. He arrives looking for the past—the signs of the "monomaniacal" antebellum period (418)—and first sees it intimated in the figure of "an elderly mulattress in an improvised wrapper." He writes, "The past, that of the vanished order, was hanging out there behind her" (*American Scene*, 403). Weaving through his observations, James arrives at an impression of the present South as "feminized"— a "sort of sick lioness who has so visibly parted with her teeth and claws that we may patronizingly walk all around her" (417)—while, analogously, the "effect" of Charleston was that of a "vacant cage which used in the other time to emit sounds, even to those of the portentous shaking of bars, audible as far away as in the listening North" (418).[47] This "cage," haunted by sounds of the past, makes the "restless analyst" *almost* arrive at the "very cruel and very perverse" conclusion that "the South is in the predicament of having to be tragic . . . in order to beguile," as there might not be any "use" for his genre of active analysis to find a "lively and oblivious type" (420). Yet he consciously stops short before arriving at this conclusion.

At different points in *The American Scene*, James extends his preoccupa-tion with the "great problem" of the multiracial United States to the Native American population in strokes that I would argue are similar to Martí's suspension of the question of U.S. national and racial answerability in the 1880s. One of the most unsettling moments in the whole work, James's Washington, DC, episode puts him in direct analytical contact with what could produce itself as the central conundrum of the "vast uncomfortable subject." At the end of the Washington scene, the "reinstated absentee" stands on the steps of the Capitol building waiting for the possibility of a "recovery of native privilege" (362). Gazing at the building from the out-side, James writes that the "great Federal future seems, under vague bright forms, to hover and to stalk." He finds that the great exteriors "are ide-ally constructed for 'raking,' and for this suggestion of their dominating the American scene in playhouse gallery fashion" (363). This imagination of the "raking" State that seems to blindingly illuminate and sweep the masses into the uncertain future, is quickly followed in James's episode, by the appearance of "a trio of Indian braves" (363) on the steps of the build-ing that appears to stand for an impression of a "huge flourishing Family" (362). Ironically, the "vast democratic lap" of the "marble embrace" of the Capitol steps is set into a tense scene with the arrival of the Native Ameri-cans. James's description of these men concludes his Washington essay.

> Though I had [the steps] in general, for contemplation, quite to my-self, I met one morning a trio of Indian braves, braves dispossessed of forest and prairie, but as free of the builded labyrinth as they had ever been of these; also arrayed in neat pot-hats, shoddy suits and light overcoats, with their pockets, I am sure, full of photographs and cigarettes: circumstances all that quickened their resemblance, on the much bigger scale, to Japanese celebrities, or to specimens, on show, of what the Government can do with people with whom it is supposed able to do nothing. They seemed just then and there, for a mind fed betimes on the Leatherstocking Tales, to project as in a flash an image in itself immense, but foreshortened and simplified— reducing to a single smooth stride the bloody footsteps of time. One rubbed one's eyes, but there, at its highest polish, shining in the beau-tiful day, was the brazen face of history, and there, all about one, im-maculate, the printless pavements of the state. (363–64)

James's reflexive narration confronts the sight of these three men, which at first seems like a hallucinatory apparition of history itself. Grand patriotic architecture and marginalized human subjects thus appear uncomfort-ably together in a scene that James imagines as a perverse display in an imagined exposition of, ironically, the feigned powerlessness of the most powerful nation. This "criminal continuity" of the United States takes up James's last thoughts in *The American Scene*, where he impersonates a Native American talking to his white counterpart: "Beauty and charm," he says, "would be for me in the solitude you have ravaged, and I should owe you my grudge for every disfigurement and every violence, for every wound which you have caused the face of the land to bleed" (463).[48]

James's impersonation of the "furious redman," according to Beverly Haviland, represents a "critical resource by means of which he creates a bond of solidarity with all those who [like James himself] have been dispossessed of their heritage."[49] Paul Giles has criticized this reading as an effort to "engage in a forcible act of intellectual repatriation, whereby James is conscripted to serve under the American national flags of pragmatism and romanticism." Conversely, Giles favors a reading of *The American Scene* as a treatment of "the hollowing out of national identity rather than its replenishment," precisely as the view of a "scene, a performative landscape within which national identity has taken on the characteristics of a charade."[50] Similarly, Sara Blair argues that the play of the "racial figures" in James's piece "hover[s] between metaphor and historical fact."[51] As in Martí's rhetoric of caesural inconclusiveness, so in James's chronicle the tensions between direct reportage and discursive embellishment become an operative principle. Proximities of this kind between scenic replication and symbolic fabulation call attention to the ethically problematic extent to which these writers respond to spatial modernity as an aesthetic exercise.

A comparative look at the ways in which the tensions of the United States's "racial theater" (Blair's term) are exhibited through the cosmopolitan imaginations of both James and Martí reveals the possibility of a nuanced middle ground between such opposing views of James's racial considerations. By means of this corrective exercise, I am not flattening out the differences between James and Martí, given the separate and distinct aspirations of their careers as writers. One blatant difference between the two is that, whereas for the "father of Cuban independence" the discussion of how the U.S. government treated the country's racially diverse population represented a laboratory in which to imagine and plan the political future of an integrated and "raceless" Spanish America, we cannot speak of a similar project in James's career. Curiously, however, the impetus to identify with the problem of the Native American populations of the Americas as a way to arrive at the actual *heart* of the problem is present in Martí's chronicle writing (and, one could say, goes even further than James). As Jeffrey Belnap has effectively pointed out, in a review of Daniel Brinton's historical text "Aboriginal American Authors" from April 1884, Martí arrives at the following remarks about an American literary and quite literal identification with indigenous warriors during the conquest, through landscape.

> ¿Qué importa que vengamos de padres de sangre mora y cutis blanco? El espíritu de los hombres flota sobre la tierra en que vivieron, y se le respira. Se viene de padres de Valencia y madres de Canarias, y se siente correr por las venas la sangre enardecida de Tamanaco y Paracamoni, y se ve como propia la que vertieron . . . pecho a pecho con los gonzalos de férrea armadura, los desnudos y heroicos caracas.[52]

> [What does it matter if we come from parents with Moorish blood and white skin? The spirit of men floats over the land in which they lived, and one can breathe it. With fathers who come from Valencia and mothers from the Canary Islands, one can nevertheless feel running through one's veins the flaming blood of Tamanaco and Paracamoni, and one can feel as one's own the blood of those . . . naked and heroic *caracas*, who squared up with the soldiers in steely armor.]

Indeed, Belnap remarks that this review "suggests that, by reading the historical literatures of Native America, the *criollo* class should learn to construct for itself a fictive-kinship relationship in which they learn to 'regard as their own'" the history and blood of the Indian warriors (204). The emphasis on identification through landscape rather than blood becomes in Martí a conduit toward a notion of historical continuity between separate races. In James, the apparent ventriloquy represents more a severance of identification between races through the concept of the perennially bloodied American landscape.

It would be fruitful to consider the ways in which these two authors arrive at a portrayal of a culture in which they are both uneasy participants, admitted outsiders, or (for the sake of giving it a Jamesian spin) "restless analysts." One of the major difficulties in writing critical work about *The American Scene*, it seems to me, is discovering ways out of discussions of genre.[53] Giles finds a way out of a reading of James as a "romance" writer through an interpretation of the novelist's early manifestations of what would later become a "surrealist aesthetics," which the critic in part defines as "the debilitating collapse of a larger metanarrative referent [that] leaves everything dependent on an iconoclastic, often highly idiosyncratic point of view" (112). Never arriving at a "metanarrative referent" encapsulates James's self-conscious refusal to offer a "conclusion" to any of his varied observations about a U.S. character. This opens the question, however, of whether the "iconoclasm" of a travelogue without a concluding or conclusive *idea* of national character is comparable to the interiorized experiments of the practitioners of surrealism later in the twentieth century.

Furthermore, there is again the question, raised by Sara Blair, of the suspension of "metaphor" and "historical fact" in James's discussion of race. It is important to stress that what James offers in *The American Scene* is a narrative of perambulatory reception of a culture he had become increasingly distanced from during a pivotal time in the country's meteoric, post–Civil War, modernization. James's main concern, I argue, is that unfathomable and mostly inexpressible process of taking in the "more and more to come," which cannot be compartmentalized into simple metaphor or fact. This is where the comparison with Martí's *crónicas* proves a fruitful endeavor. What Martí finds in chronicle writing is, according to Susana Rotker, a space for the "re-creation of the native land . . . by means of memory and writing," through the construction of "associative chains" formed "by means of symbol and analogy," weaving thus "a system of correspondences between the writer's internal states and objective reality."[54] Martí's "native land" is of course an untenable space because of the "objective reality" of his exile. Cuba thus becomes an unassimilable space that opens the floodgates of a desire for representation that is achievable only through an exercise of the mingled projections of imagination and memory.[55] The open *scene* of perception—open to experience, analysis, to a certain futurity—incapable of withstanding any set preconceptions, thus becomes a catalyst for self-scrutiny.

Chronicle writing, as Rotker and Ramos have explained, becomes something quite "heterogeneous" in the case of Martí: It represents that intersection of an interiorized poetry with the emergence of capitalist modes of mass communication, as well as with the writer's quest for a professional autonomy.[56] Ramos describes it as the confluence of an "act of informing" with a stylized "overwriting," so that Martí "writes *over* the newspaper in a kind of palimpsest," thus exposing the mediation between an external world and the poetic interior:

> If poetry ideally represented the interior of fin de siècle literature par excellence, in the sense that it constituted a field of immanence, purified or purifiable against external interpellations, then the chronicle in its (always contested) formal nature represents the struggle of authorities, a discursive competition, presupposed by the poetic interior. The interior, the field of identity for a subject . . . would therefore only acquire meaning in opposition to the exteriors that limit it, besiege it, but which also are the conditions of the subject's possibility as they demarcate the outer limits of his domain. (107)

This idea of the "discursive competition" of the chronicle echoes, for me, Blair's discussion of the problem of James's discursive "suspension" of the poetic figure and objective "fact." Both Martí and James, as writers of the "interior," are confronted with an onslaught of scenes in a cultural space that leaves James's restless analyst gaping in "magnanimous wonder" (80) at the "bignesses" and "newnesses" of a place he can only neologize as *abracadabrant* (120–21), and Martí in shock at the "annihilating and incomparable expansiveness, solid and frenetic."[57] Setting scenes, for both writers, implies a dual process of working out their shock as well as the dynamics of particular objects under observation, themselves in constant motion. In other words, in Martí's chronicle writing and James's process of "restless analysis" we find a meeting of discourses of personal observation that overcomes simple reportage or historic summarization.

Through this intimate reportage—neither case which can be described as thoroughly "romantic" in its depictive stylization—James and Martí engage in the difficulty of handling powerful impressions. In a discussion of the nature of impressions and artistic Impressionism specifically, Jesse Matz argues that from the moment of this movement's inception, the word itself "connoted, reflected, and even forced dynamic mediations" as well as a kind of "aesthetic delay": "Subjectively felt, impressions were nevertheless also true to life; momentary, they also lingered, and they were in a host of other ways essentially mediatory."[58] To look at a scene and then connect it to what James calls the "'big' impression" (which for James is ultimately an unachievable project) is what both writers must wrestle with in their depiction of the U.S. scene. Put differently, through a process of "aesthetic delay," they are both seeking the answerability of a landscape, of the whole that can only be intimated in incomplete scenes.

In an episode that finds James traveling on a train along the Hudson River on his return from the western United States (a "boisterous hoyden" compared to the East, also feminized, but instead a "seated, placid, rich-voiced gentlewoman"), he contemplates the constrained right to observe the American scene in the present moment of mass transport, and emerges with a critique of the "banishment" of the rights of the Native Americans.

> Thus it was, possibly, that I saw the River shine, from that moment
> on, as a great romantic stream, such as could throw not a little of
> its glamour, for the mood of that particular hour, over the city at its
> mouth. . . . That ordeal [of the railway journey from Chicago] was in
> any case at its best here, and the perpetually interesting river kept
> its course, by my right elbow, with such splendid consistency that, as
> I recall the impression, I repent a little of having just now reflected
> with acrimony on the cost of the obtrusion of track and stations to

the Riverside view. . . . A decent respect for the Hudson would confine us to the use of the boat—all the more that American river-
steamers have had, from the earliest time, for the true *raffiné*, their
peculiar note of romance. A possible commerce, on the other hand,
with one's time—which is always also the time of so many other busy
people—has long since made mincemeat of the rights of contemplation; *rights are reduced, in the United States, to-day, and by quite the
same argument, as those of the noble savage whom we have banished
to his narrowing reservation. Letting that pass, at all events, I still remember that I was able to put, from the car-window, as many questions to the scene as it could have answered in the time even had its
face been clearer to read.* (148–49, emphasis added)

In this passage, James defines the performative analysis of impressions as
an exercise of posing questions to a landscape. This exercise connotes the
lingering of an observation that may want to wrap itself around an idea of
a "whole" through associative thinking, but that nevertheless remains an
incomplete conversation between observer and scene, as well as between
changing landscapes. As Ross Posnock argues, "By refusing to resolve
paradoxes or dissolve difference into identity, Henry James avoids submit-
ting to an ideology of harmonious totality, be it organic form or what he
calls progressivism's 'American identity.'"[59] In this narration of the experience of observation during the train ride along the Hudson, James is able
to bring together, through delayed associations, impressions and mainly
questions of the landscape beyond the scope of his experience. This amalgamation brings about the larger question about the Native American's
progress of banishment beyond the limits of his ability to see.

In the first of Martí's *crónicas* about Buffalo Bill's Wild West show in
New York ("Búfalo Bill, William F. Cody," from June 1884), Martí ends on
a similar note of wonder about the immense North American landscape
that spreads from the confines of cities to an unplaceable "Nature" almost
morbidly out of place in the context of a circus tent in an urban center.
Much like the passage from the "Charleston Earthquake" discussed above,
Martí's chronicle emits an afterlife image that hovers over separate national landscapes and its narrations.

Y la fiesta se acaba entre millares de balazos con que hábiles tiradores
rompen en el aire palomas de barro, y coros de hurras, que se van
extinguiendo lentamente, a medida que la gran concurrencia entra,
de vuelta a sus hogares, en los ferrocarriles, y las luces eléctricas, de-
rramando su claridad por el circo vacío, remedan una de esas escenas
magníficas que deben acontecer en las entrañas de la Naturaleza.[60]

[And so the party ends among a million gunshots of the agile gun-
men firing at clay pigeons, among slowly dissipating choirs of *hur-
rays*, while the great crowds enter, back into their homes, into the
railroads, and the electrical lights, spilling their iridescence throughout the empty circus, recreate one of those magnificent scenes that
must transpire in the depths of Nature.]

Martí's almost compulsive use of the comma to separate the different pictures portrays a writer who appears to be pausing to take things in, viewing the scene in short flashes, almost like a film reel that is slowing down
to a halt and begins to show the blinking separations of the frames.[61] The
comma seems to signal the end of a poetic line of verse that is nevertheless stretched out on the page into the prose format of the chronicle. This
effect of continuous pause after the writer's imagination has been bom-
barded with rowdy scenes (supposedly) transposed from the U.S. West,
constitutes a critical and aesthetic delay in the sense of the impression that
Matz proposes: The reader becomes a witness to the mediation between
sights and analysis, spectacle and reality, city and the imagination of "the
depths of Nature." Differently from James, whose thoughts are elaborated
in sweeping, magisterial sentences, Martí's sense of delay leaves the reader
with an uncomfortable configuration of pictures that need to be pieced together in the chronicle's afterlife. James, in contrast, constructs a massive
sentence to finesse a complex thought, but the aftereffect is nevertheless
similar to Martí's in that the reader has been confronted with the critical
challenge of deciphering a difficult and charged impression.

Martí's remarkable portrait of the illuminated, yet deserted circus ring
that continues to reverberate the scenes that "must" happen in the elsewhere
of "Nature" even after the show and the *crónica* are over, represents the
haunting reminder of the multifarious modernity stippled with obscured
landscapes and silenced geographies. The writer's gaze continues to linger
on the emptiness of the scene of performance and reenactment although
his thoughts wander and wonder about the many simultaneous images of
U.S. modernity that the spectacle elicits. Here we have another instance
in which the writer asks his readers to be vigilant of a coexistent reality
and space that are inaccessible to plain perception, but that nevertheless
haunt the now-moment of his watchfulness. Furthermore, we see how these
unshakeable residual elements of the *crónicas* as well as of James's questions to the landscape in *The American Scene* unearth an idea of answerable landscapes and answerable modernity. Although James's rhetoric of
apprehension is borne out by a mass of spiraling questions, Martí concludes
his "Buffalo Bill" *crónica* by *amassing* images, piling them up paratactically
one by one, as though leaving them open to future reconfiguration.

In Mikhail Bakhtin's essays about answerability (which would later evolve into his theories of dialogism in fiction), he builds a model for looking at the dynamic "architectonics" of a scene, a multidimensional conglomerate of moment, tone, emotion, and form that also necessarily involves an ethical intonation. His description of what he terms the creation of the "emotional-volitional tone" of a scene of being and event ("Being-as-event") is useful for my discussion of nonconclusions and lingering afterlives. Bakhtin sees this "tone" as engaging both moment ("once-occurrent being-as-event") and an active "ought-to-be attitude of consciousness," comprising thus an "answerably conscious *movement* of consciousness."[62] This "movement" never seeks to arrive at a universal, "theoretical unity" about experience, but entails instead a theory of now-moments that are dual inflections of "what *is* and what *ought* to be" (41). Answerability is thus an open-ended play of questions about present moments and their contingent, multiple possibilities. Seeking the answerability of a landscape, as James directly does in *American Scene*, is of course beyond the bounds of Bakhtin's model, which describes localized interpersonal moments of exchange. We can imagine Martí still sitting alone on the stands of the Buffalo Bill circus after the show is over, mulling over a similar immensity that will only reply back in endless multiple and dissonant tones. Yet, what Bakhtin does in his description of answerable scenes is strip down the philosophical, theoretical, and *totalizing* elements of the fictional imagination in order to expose the mediations between lived experience and artistic expression. These links between life and art are accompanied by a sense of momentous doubt, which Bakhtin perceives as the very fabric of our relationships with others. Doubt, for Bakhtin, is the opposite of "the absolute past," what he calls "the past of meaning," in that it describes our participation in the present moment and the open future.[63] Martí and James, as I have been arguing, incorporate moments of suspension and ultimately doubt into their chronicles of U.S. life. Their combinations of wondering and wandering serve to propel their narratives forward—making them progressive assimilations of different scenes and present events— but they nevertheless stop short of conveying a sense of completeness to their impressions. Both writers shape their prose in specific ways to impress upon their readers that their perceptions are necessarily unfinished and ongoing. This quality makes for a haunted and haunting reading, as we are invited to also contemplate this openness and wonder about the present scenes that we cannot fully perceive, let alone understand.

How can the writer formulate an answerable landscape? The fictions of haunting, as I have been arguing, are fantasies in which an individual is able to openly converse with his perceptions of modernity's landscapes. It is through fiction, in the case of James's "The Jolly Corner" and, as we will see, in Felisberto Hernández's story "El acomodador" that (to varying manners and degrees) these authors of American cities are able to find ways to address spaces of geographical and sociological immensity head on. As we will see in the remainder of this chapter, they are able to do this through the projection of a spectral element that actively poses questions to the national imaginary. James's story presents the reader with a man who, incapable of coming to terms with a city that he had left behind, constructs his own self-haunting. Meanwhile, in Hernández's story, after confessing to his reader that he takes pleasure in wondering about the unknown that lurks about the unnamed city in which he lives, a theater usher reveals he has the power of illuminating all things around him with a strange light that emanates from his eyes. Aside from being representations of the indiscreet (and indiscrete) lengths to which imaginations of haunting can go, these two fictions are also meditations on the liberties and frustrations that surround the limits of knowing.

Urban Writing and the Pursuit of Haunting

The challenge of crafting a ghost story is, for James, not simply a matter of producing "the dear old familiar bugaboo."[64] In the preface to "The Altar of the Dead," where he explains the production of "The Jolly Corner," the author writes that

> the moving accident, the rare conjunction, whatever it be, doesn't make the story—in the sense that the story is our excitement, our amusement, our thrill and our suspense; the human emotion and the human attestation, the clustering human conditions we expect presented, only make it. The extraordinary is most extraordinary in that it happens to you and me, and it's of value (of value for others) but so far as visibly brought home to us. At any rate, odd though it may sound to pretend that one feels on safer ground in tracing such an adventure as that of the hero of "The Jolly Corner" than in pursuing a bright career among pirates or detectives, I allow that composition to pass as the measure or limit, on my own part, of any achievable comfort in the "adventure story." [65]

As many critics have argued, Spencer Brydon's "adventure" in "The Jolly Corner" is similar to James's adventure of 1904—that of the "so strangely belated return" of a native New Yorker who has spent "thirty-three years" living abroad.[66] Brydon's return has to do with his "property," which had subsidized his lifestyle in Europe: two buildings in New York City; the first is being remodeled into an apartment building, and the second, on the "jolly corner," is his now-vacant childhood home. The story opens with the following complaint from the main character:

"Every one asks me what I 'think' of everything," said Spencer Brydon; "and I make answer as I can—begging or dodging the question, putting them off with any nonsense. It wouldn't matter to any of them really," he went on, "for, even were it possible to meet in that stand-and-deliver way so silly a demand on so big a subject, my 'thoughts' would still be almost altogether about something that concerns only myself." (463)

This confessional opening—a confession Brydon makes to his friend Alice Staverton—echoes James's own mentality of self-disclosure upon arriving in New York. Spencer Brydon, like James, discovers that the repatriation is inextricably attached to a question on "so big a subject." In *The American Scene*, we find the overwhelmed "restless analyst" who is confronted with questions on his hometown and on the state of the "'American' character" (121). It becomes a matter of a "big subject" that nevertheless provides the author with the prospect of "waiting to see" what can become of the whole (122). James writes in his chronicle that "you find your relief not in the least in any direct satisfaction or solution, but absolutely in that blest general drop of the immediate need of conclusions," or in the "general feeling for the impossibility of them, to which the philosophy of any really fine observation of the American spectacle must reduce itself " (121). The following passage from *The American Scene* delivers an explanation of the complexity of this anxiety of definition.

It is more than a comfort to him, truly, in all the conditions, this accepted vision of the too-defiant scale of numerosity and quantity—the effect of which is so to multiply the possibilities, so to open, by the million, contingent doors and windows: he rests in it at last as an absolute luxury, converting it even into a substitute, into *the* constant substitute, for many luxuries that are absent. He doesn't *know*, he can't *say*, before the facts, and he doesn't even want to know or to say; the facts themselves loom, before the understanding, in too large a mass for a mere mouthful: it is as if the syllables were too numerous to make a legible word. The *il*legible word, accordingly, the great inscrutable answer to questions, hangs in the vast American sky, to his imagination, as something fantastic and *abracadabrant*, belonging to no known language, and it is under this convenient ensign that he travels and considers and contemplates, and, to the best of his ability, enjoys. (121–22)

In "The Jolly Corner," where Spencer Brydon finds himself at a similar loss for words when asked to describe his impressions of his native land, we also discover the tension between the individual's ability to draw conclusions and a spectacle that at once elicits sublimity and fear. In James's own "restless analysis" (cited above), the inability and reluctance to say a final word about the endless possibilities of an answer are remarkably replied to with an appeal to the imagination of the "fantastic and *abracadabrant*" "something" that looms over the American scene.

In "The Jolly Corner," that "*il*legible word" becomes for Spencer Brydon the *what if?* of his life had he remained in his city of birth. As James himself points out in the "Altar of the Dead" preface cited above, it is the *story itself* that, from beginning to end, unravels the suspense of thinking this question. Indeed, "The Jolly Corner" describes in fiction what in *The American Scene* is the restless analyst's conjoined effort of "waiting to see," all the while producing an open-ended representation of the scene.[67] The result of this postponed representation is, in the case of Spencer Brydon, the construction and stalking of his own ghost. His arrival in New York is detailed through a dual process of astonishment at that "*abracadabrant*" element of the towering, changing city as well as the affirmation of a certain "compromising" imagination to counter the "unattenuated surprises attending" his return (463).[68] This tension between the felt astonishment of observation within the changing landscape as well as a certain sense of anticipation, manifests itself in the first pages of James's story in terms of delay and belatedness. This expression in turn amasses impressions geared toward the ever-open, still bewildering, question.

> It would have taken a century, he repeatedly said to himself, and said also to Alice Staverton, it would have taken a longer absence and a more averted mind than those even of which he had been guilty, to pile up the differences, the newnesses, the queernesses, above all the bignesses, for the better or the worse, that at present assaulted his vision wherever he looked. (464)

This curious wish of temporal extension—an incongruous, suspended belatedness to catch up with the present New York (a present that will undoubtedly keep changing and impressing him with more surprise)—reveals Brydon's own sense of "aesthetic delay" as well as a certain historical inadequacy of his position in time. His journey is also one of a disjointed, almost hallucinatory discovery and occlusion: "he missed what he would have been sure of finding, he found what he would never have imagined" (464).

Running parallel to this belatedness is Spencer Brydon's discovered "sense for construction" (465). What first reveals itself as an ability to deal in hands-on fashion with the remodeling of his property becomes a discovery of a more general hidden talent.

> It had been not the least of his astonishments to find himself able, on the spot, and though without a previous ounce of such experience, to

participate with a certain intelligence, almost with a certain authority. He had lived his life with his back so turned to such concerns
and his face addressed to those of so different an order *that he scarce
knew what to make of this lively stir, in a compartment of his mind
never yet penetrated, of a capacity for business and a sense for construction.* (465, emphasis added)

This "sense for construction" that reveals itself in the first house (the one
being remodeled) in Brydon's ability to "work," "walk the plank," and
"climb ladders," becomes something quite different in the second house,
the old homestead on the "jolly corner," which vacant, served no particular
purpose in the real-estate market as yet:[69] "There were values other than
the beastly rent-values," he complains; to which his friend Alice Staverton
replies, "You're to make so good a thing of your sky-scraper that, living in
luxury on *those* ill-gotten gains, you can afford for a while to be sentimental here!" (470). It is at this point in the story that the "sense for construction" veers away from the first property of "rent-value" and focuses instead
on the eventual "sentimental" value and construction of the second house,
where the ghost will be produced.[70]

Interestingly, it is Alice's "having so much imagination" (470) that signals the conjugation of this "sense" and sentimentality: She announces
and will indeed turn out to be the accomplice in Brydon's haunting. As
with James's earlier *The Turn of the Screw* (1898), certain original takes on
haunting are made explicit in this later ghost story: The narrative of "The
Jolly Corner" describes haunting as imaginative practice, an active play
of a restless construction and the excitement of sentimental associations.

What will be the features of the constructed haunting of the "freshly
repatriated" cosmopolite? There is, first of all, the sentimental interrogation—the "impotence" of the "native appeal"—that begins to burrow
in Brydon's mind, and which he shares with his accomplice: "He found
all things come back to the question of what he personally might have
been, how he might have led his life and 'turned out,' if he had not so,
at the outset, given it up" (473). The establishment of this conversation
of wonder between the two friends results in a concoction of the figure
of the ghost: Whereas Alice imagines that "possible" development of the
what if as "quite splendid, quite huge and monstrous," Brydon thinks up
something "quite hideous and offensive" (474). This tête-à-tête of what
James describes as the main character's "'unnatural' anxiety" gains resolve in Brydon's mind when he tauntingly pronounces, "*He* isn't myself.
He's the just so totally other person. But I do want to see him. . . . And I
can. And I shall" (475). Where before, Brydon did not "want to know"
or "say" anything about the hovering questions of change in immensity,

this invitation of spectral creation remedies his fear of unknowing and difficulty of expression.

The haunting in "The Jolly Corner" appears at first a self-reflexive staging of an elaborate séance or phantasmagoria show, even down to the glass-harmonica musical detail: Brydon's life, upon the pronouncement of his purpose of haunting, lives between the "projection" of his "dim" social life—a game of "extravagant shadows"—and the "other, the real, the waiting life" that lurks every night in the house on the jolly corner (477). He imagines this house as "some great glass bowl, all precious concave crystal, set delicately humming by the play of a moist finger round its edge" (478). Brydon thus orchestrates a haunted cosmopolitan response to that "native appeal": Through the construction and elaboration of the ghost of his North American possibility, he is able to conjure up his own solution to belated and disjointed repatriation.[71]

The entrance into the second house every night also represents an entry of one form of romanticized national discourse of landscape into this other, urban space where the house on the jolly corner stands. In other words, the story of the pursuit of haunting portrays, through "the tremendous force of analogy" (479) a certain *invagination* of the urban narrative actually haunted with an anterior narration of untamed landscape.

> He had tasted of no pleasure so fine as his actual tension, had been introduced to no sport that demanded at once the patience and the nerve of this stalking of a creature more subtle, yet at bay perhaps more formidable, than any beast of the forest. *The terms, the comparisons, the very practices of the chase positively came again into play; there were even moments when passages of his occasional experience as a sportsman, stirred memories, from his younger time, of moor and mountain and desert, revived for him—and to the increase of his keenness—by the tremendous force of analogy.* (479, emphasis added)

What we encounter in the "practices of the chase" is Brydon's act of writing over a narrative of urban living with the dislocated structures of feeling of those narrative "passages" of life elsewhere, in "moor and mountain and desert." He imagines his prey "roam[ing], slowly, warily" (478), and he questions the degree of his fear as he "believed gentlemen . . . in close quarters with the great bear of the Rockies had been known to confess to having put it" (479). Outside, under the "white electric lustre," lies the "human actual social" (480), while the house's interior provides an open socialization with an imagination that folds over narrative landscapes through a "practice" (481) of haunting, hunting, and taunting his own ghost: "People enough . . . had been in terror of apparitions, but who had ever so turned the tables and become himself, in the apparitional world, an incalculable terror?" (480)

Where other critics have found the psychodramatic, or what John Carlos Rowe addresses as the "psychopoetic" appeal of this story the most interesting feature of analysis,[72] its emphasis on the ghost that finally "turns" and whose "bared identity was too hideous as *his*" (494), what I find most appealing is Brydon's reflexively narrative response to his anxieties of repatriation. My key point of interest is how the arrival among the "bignesses," "newnesses," and "queernesses" of the massive city yields an opening of the imagination and performative creation of the architectonics of a wider, more primeval and romantic, expansive landscape. Brydon's return to New York is of course implicit in a larger return to the United States, and a more expansive digestion of an immense geography. Yet, the imagination of haunting (and of seeking out haunting) in James's story projects an "afterlife" that is entangled in simultaneous now-life—that "human actual social" sphere of the return—as well as a sentimentalized past. In other words, Spencer Brydon's pursuit of haunting represents the imagination of an answerable landscape of simultaneity. On one level, an interior and interiorized urban life seeks to converse with the life outside of the city. On another, actual life is set against a disjointed, anachronistic "afterlife" whose existence is narrated through an imagined style of bucolic Americana. Importantly, Brydon is not necessarily seeking a ghost of the past, or a ghost cast away into indefinite futures, but instead a fifty-six-year-old ghost who has grown up amid New York's immensity—"another agent," as he calls him when the tables begin to turn and Brydon starts to become frightened of his own creation (486)—whose life runs and has run parallel to his, and the *waiting* of whom is concocted in a story of invaginated narrative landscapes.

We should consider how to interpret this architecture of narrative invaginations in a tale of urban haunting. Brydon's quest is essentially a quest for the "Form": His lifetime "over there" now taunts him with the thought that "some variation from *that* . . . must have produced some different effect for my life and for my 'form'" (475). Contrapuntally, James's narrative journey in *The American Scene* is marked by the observation of the native country's absence of forms: "The ugliness—one pounced, indeed, on this as on a talisman for the future—was the so complete abolition of *forms*; if, with so little reference to their past, present or future possibility, they could be said to have been even so much honoured as to be abolished" (25). The formlessness here is connected to an idea of temporal suspension, intimated in that absence of past, present, and future possibilities.

"The Jolly Corner," as I argue above, portrays the fictionalization of this formal and temporal discontinuity: It discloses the struggle for legibility (that confrontation with the "*il*legible word") and retains it within an arena of debate about the possibilities and limits of comprehending the present. Within the coordinates of the ghost story, Brydon seeks to summon and form his "compromising" possibilities of the *over-here* existence by forming a sentimental narrative of romantic lore. I quote the following passage at length to show the progression through which Brydon compensates for the formlessness produced by his absence from the native city by concocting the sentimental narrative of his haunted "crystal bowl" in the jolly corner.

> The concave crystal held, as it were, this mystical other world, and the indescribably fine murmur of its rim was the sigh there, the scarce audible pathetic wail to his strained ear, *of all the old baffled forsworn possibilities*. What he did therefore by this appeal of his hushed presence was to wake them into such measure of ghostly life as they might still enjoy. They were shy, all but unappeasably shy, but they weren't really sinister; *at least they weren't as he had hitherto felt them—before they had taken the Form he so yearned to make them take, the Form he at moments saw himself in the light of fairly hunting on tiptoe, the points of his evening-shoes, from room to room and from storey to storey.* (478, emphasis added)

The stealthy chase of "all the old baffled forsworn possibilities"—Spencer Brydon's fantasy of an adventure—ultimately shapes the absent "Form" and transforms the space of the urban dwelling into a hallucination of a mythologized wilderness.

In his discussion of the literature of myths of American wilderness at the turn of the nineteenth century, Richard Slotkin sets two practitioners of the romance of the frontier against one another: one, Chateaubriand's European evolution of the poetry of the West in the 1790s, and the other Charles Brockden Brown's gothic novel *Edgar Huntly* (1799).[73] In the first case, the myth of the frontier is a continuation of a Rousseauian tradition of the search for the "Indian" as an aesthetic device to represent the quest of solitude of the "poet-hero."[74] In the North American case of Brown, as Slotkin argues, the proximity to the realities of the frontier and the Indian wars yielded a constant renewal of stories where the "man of action is as much the poet and hero" as Nature's sulky émigré in Chateaubriand's *Les Natchez* (1802). Thus, where the European romantic imagination sees the wilderness as "an escape from the reality of society, where riddles lie waiting for solution and where their real responsibility as heroes lies," for North American heroes like Edgar Huntly, "the path into the wilderness is the path . . . that leads them into greater involvement in reality in all of its moral ambiguity and psychological complexity" (393).

At the close of the nineteenth century, the frontier myth becomes amplified and complicated with the imperial expansion of the U.S. frontier and the confluent resurgence of the narrative of rugged individualism. Theodore Roosevelt's concept of the "strenuous life" and the then-popular phrase "national muscle-flexing" reopened the spectacle of the frontier (already closed by the 1890s) through a revival of romance. Indeed, as Amy Kaplan explains, the sickly Roosevelt's search for physical restitution out West as well as his later swashbuckling adventures as a fighter in Cuba and a hunter in Africa were theatrical spectacles. Kaplan notes how the events of the Spanish-American War of 1898 also resulted in a proliferation of a "double discourse of American imperialism" of embodied and disembodied national power: The United States's imperial expansion "defined itself ideologically against the territorially based colonialism of the old European empires" thanks to the more intangible material webs of international commerce that resulted from the annexations of the Philippines and Puerto Rico, while a parallel discourse of "robust" and "reincarnated" American masculinity took hold of the literary imagination in a series of (often fantastical) historical romances.[75]

Spencer Brydon's narrative of haunting, with its stealthy, progressive hunting of the "Form" of his ghost, appears like a curious compressed journey of several sections in the history of frontier mythologies. One of these would be a Chateaubriand, who uses the myth of romantic wilderness to arrive at an urban, and more cosmopolitan, explanation of the self. Another could be likened to Brown, who explores the idea of the frontier as a projection of a national "field of investigation" of the moral ambiguities of the wider question of the "condition" and "wonderful diseases or affections" imbibed in the U.S. national landscape.[76] Finally, and, contemporaneously with his fictitious arrival in the native country, Brydon's hunt appears to echo the romances of reincarnation of the "strenuous life." The spatial and temporal complexity of Brydon's belated return, caught between the "native appeal" and a perspective that has long been in the position of the *over there*," renders a weirdly misplaced commentary on the frontier myth in the context of the urban home in the early twentieth century, a twisted architectonics of misplaced emotions and tones.

Furthermore, Brydon's fiction of the wilderness inside the home ends up trapped between the two opposing poles of the "thinking" and the "acting" hero of the spectacles of the artificial frontier: When the tables turn and his ghost, finally formed and "*done*," haunts *him* (the ironic "embodiment" of what had until then been "disembodied"), Brydon is faced with the conundrum of doubt and fear.[77]

> Oh to have this consciousness was to *think*—and to think, Brydon
> knew, as he stood there, was, with the lapsing moments, not to have
> acted! Not to have acted—that was the misery and the pang—was
> even still not to act; was in fact *all* to feel the thing in another, in a
> new and terrible way. How long did he pause and how long did he de-
> bate? There was presently nothing to measure it; for his vibration had
> already changed—as just by the effect of its intensity. Shut up there,
> at bay, defiant, and with the prodigy of the thing palpably provably
> *done*, thus giving notice like some stark signboard—under that ac-
> cession of accent the situation itself had turned; and Brydon at last
> remarkably made up his mind on what it had turned to. (486–87)

The "thing palpably provably *done*," the finished climax of Brydon's tale
of haunting, thus collapses on itself when the mixed narratives run the
course of their invagination, and the appearance of the so-desired ghost
puts an end to Brydon's injudicious thrill of sentimentally *writing* over the
reality of his cosmopolitan return.

From this point on, James's story quickly turns from the architectural
invagination of sentimental landscapes to an appraisal of "Discretion," and
Brydon's appeal to the reality of the property in New York: "It had turned
altogether to a different admonition; to a supreme hint, for him, of the
value of Discretion!" (487) His "spell" broken, he turns his attention to the
"great lamplit vacancy" of the street outside, watching out for "some vulgar
human note, the passage of a scavenger or a thief, some night-bird however
base" (488). The sentimental imagination is supplanted with the "thought
of recording his Discretion," a measurement so powerful "that the importance of this loomed large and something had overtaken all ironically his
sense of proportion" (488). His internal "Discretion," searching for the
"base" or "vulgar" elements outside, in turn performs the clashes of urban
fantasy and reality that result in a loss of Brydon's "sense of proportion."

What do we make of the turn to this search for measure and discretion
in the present and "vulgar" humanity outside the urban house? The development of the legibility of the "Form" that can encapsulate all of Spencer
Brydon's possibilities turns into an excess of confident contemplation, that
is in turn coupled with an overflowing practice of appropriating mythopoeia in his search for an adequate stylistic medium capable of addressing
both personal uncertainties and the wider public anxieties of the present.
In other words, the turn to "Discretion" signals a limit to the "tremendous
force of analogy" that had led to Brydon's initial confidence in deciphering
"so big a subject"—that big, new, and queer world outside—through the
recourse to a sentimental and mythic narration. The fantasy of an answerable landscape that yields the construction of the "spectral yet human"

figure of Brydon's ghost of simultaneity "ironically" stunts the legibility of the contemporary American scene that the story's hero so desired. The return of the native in the ghost story thus constitutes a pulling and stretching of the limits of the legible, which only manifests itself in impressions that are themselves engaged in a complicated interplay between interiors and exteriors, self-portrayals as well as attempts to portray the scene at large.[78] The scene becomes answerable in a "life larger than his own, a rage of personality," an "evil, odious," and most interestingly, "blatant" figure (494).

One needs to question what is so indiscreet, indiscrete, or so indecent about blatant legibility. Spencer Brydon's brand of "restless analysis" insists on spectralizing his "'unnatural anxiety" of belated repatriation as a way to force the absent landscapes and bygone decades to form a poetic, yet somehow material "human actual social" figure of an afterlife (for, ghosts hail from this afterworld). His appeal to his "sense for construction" to build a legible past, present, and future of the "big subject" through "analogy" represents a failure of conclusion—a "mistake of insistence," to use one of James's headings from *The American Scene*. Brydon's becomes an indecent desire to read the city and to intimate the value and possibilities of the American scene after his repatriation. All the while, however, the "great lamplit vacancy" of the street outside yields no particular answers, no deciphering specters, and no straightforward legibility.

Elegies of Illumination

Images of urban iridescence, of solitary landscapes accompanied only by the enveloping electrical light, contain within themselves captivating afterlives. They involve vacancies onto which a passing observer might project any particular meaning to any particular question. In "The Jolly Corner," the street under the electrical lights becomes the solace for the overactive imagination run amok of a cosmopolite seeking answers inside the ancestral home he had left thirty-three years earlier. Out of the realm of fiction and inside the world of Martí's *crónicas*, the illuminated empty circus ring after the Buffalo Bill show signals for the writer the paratactic accumulation of hovering images of simultaneity of an immense national landscape that is transposed, made spectacle, yet also disquietingly obscured.

The illumination of this dialectical potential within images arising from the nation's landscapes of modernity becomes, in these passages from James and Martí, anxieties of legibility about what has been transgressed as well as of that "more and more to come." Such spaces of epochal simultaneity surround the delicate interdependency of lived history and unnerving prophecy. Their complicated modernity readily exceeds the sweeping allegorization of proliferating bigness, industrialization, immigration, and invisible expansionism. "The operation of the immense machine, identical after all with the total of American life, trembles away into mysteries that are beyond our present notation and that reduce us in many a mood to renouncing analysis," writes James in the pages addressing the entrance of immigrant aliens into the United States (*American Scene*, 124). How can one read the directions of the millions of entrances and dispossessions in the "vast uncomfortable subject"? What does it mean for those entering their homes and the railroad cars to have seen "the magnificent scenes that must happen" in a distant Nature uprooted by the forces of spectacle? How can one shed light on these questions that "tremble away into mysteries" to address the idea of an "American" subject, after all?

Illumination and enlightenment in the Americas have stood as symbols for rationalization and the inscription of the unknown elements of national societies through the doctrines of modernization and progress. The theories of nineteenth-century thinkers in Latin America such as the Cuban José Antonio Saco and the Argentine Domingo Sarmiento, as Julio Ramos has shown, saw "enlightenment" as "concomitant with the imperative to work" as well as "a means for counteracting vagrancy, a way of incorporating the *other* into the territory of rationality" (33). In the first half of the twentieth century, as discussed in Chapter 1, positivist and post-Enlightenment ideas of the literature of the nineteenth century were countered by an introduction into narration of what multiple practitioners and critics term "magic." On this counterattack of "reenchantment," Jean Franco has noted that the "magic" of literature "secures belief even as it goes against common sense."[79] As I expressed in my first chapter, however, the argument for literary transformations in Latin America needs to welcome a more nuanced critical approach than the one offered by the advocates of magical realism, who use the term as a receptacle for myriad readings of sanguine multiculturalisms, elastic pasts, and easy utopias, as well as problematic superpositions of discordant literary and cultural theorizations. The strange and fantastic, in my readings of ghosts and afterlives in the American imaginary, signal an anxiety over the elements of disquiet rather than the magical, "irreducible" qualities of simple literary reenchantments.

The problems posed by illumination serve as a case in point for this need of a more nuanced reading of the strange in literature of the Americas. When Felisberto Hernández published his short-story collection *Nadie encendía las lámparas* (*No One Turned On the Lamps*) in 1947, the critic Carlos Ramela argued in the Uruguayan weekly *Marcha* that Hernández's "invertebrate" work was marked by a "distillation" of memories and a "new

element" (for the author) of an "appellation to the supernatural, an im-
plication of the absurd that irremediably suggests the memory of Kafka"
["El elemento nuevo que aparece en los cuentos . . . es una apelación ahora
directa a lo sobrenatural, una implicancia del absurdo que sugiere irre-
mediablemente el recuerdo de Kafka"].[80] Although Ramela sees Kafka's
supernatural-absurd as having "metaphysical repercussions," in the case of
Hernández's stories this appears to be just a "mere recurrence" ["mero re-
curso"] of the Kafka model. Of the story "El acomodador" specifically, the
critic writes that it "laxly relates a long and repetitive nightmare," lacking
a "convincing" structure (14). In a way signaling what was to come later in
the critique of Hernández's work, Ramela's dismissal of the writer's stories
as a pseudo-Kafkaesque "recourse" to formless, nightmarish landscapes
cuts short the possibilities of reading him against the grain. Ramela was
not alone in his criticism. Rosario Ferré notes how the figures that made up
Uruguay's "Generación Crítica" in the mid-twentieth century were split on
the subject of Feliberto Hernández: Juan Carlos Onetti and Ángel Rama
considered him one of the country's most important writers, but others,
such as Emir Rodríguez Monegal, criticized the fiction writer's sexual, artistic, and emotional immaturity.[81] More recent critical work on Hernández often reveals a turn to psychoanalytic readings of his characters' many
neuroses. These often result in suspended exercises of content analysis that
appear disengaged from the author's location in the imagination of Latin
American spaces.[82] For her part, Ferré champions an interpretation of
Hernández's stories using Todorov's theories of the fantastic. Away from
the psychoanalytical and genre readings, Rama locates Hernández specifically within the material context of the Uruguayan middle class in the first
half of the twentieth century. He perceives in Hernández an imagination
of the "extravagance of existence" within a society that often tries to define
itself only statistically.[83] A considerable amount of critical attention has
been paid to Hernández's peculiar writing style, which appears truncated,
incomplete, and "distracted," although at other moments it displays an
almost excessive description.[84] Taking the term from the title of Hernández's short story ("acomodador," which literally refers to an individual who
places subjects or objects in a given location), Ferré describes the author as
an "acomodador" of reality in a particular way (25). Although Ferré uses
this description of Hernández as a launching pad for her reading of the
author's fantastical inclination, this interpretation of Hernández could
also inspire a different take on his idiosyncratic arrangements of words
and images. We can use it to contend that Hernández represents an extreme example of a literature that has doubt and unknowing as its shaping
principle. Spencer Brydon's anxiety of not knowing what to think is tem-
porarily supplanted with the indiscrete and haunted fantasy of too much

knowingness. Hernández's characters, in contrast, already and always exist within this troubled nexus of cognition. This perennial dilemma in turn shapes the form of Hernández's way of telling.

Hernández's unique imagination of the material realities of this society reveals a different fictionalization of the issues of legibility in American cities. I want to focus specifically on the ways in which he crafts a discourse of illumination in the context of a city that is legible only through minuscule objects, other people's property, and foreign street wanderers. Hernández is a writer of objects, of the minute details of the bric-a-brac of domestic interiors that can become immensely fetishized in a high-capitalist society (what Rama calls "cosificación"). Julio Prieto reads the author's turn to the miniature as a symptom of the vanguard movements of the early century, a theme that concerns Hernández from his early career, specifically his 1928 work *Libro sin tapas* (*Book without Covers*).

> En este libro se perfila ya un cambio de "escala" en cuanto al espectro imaginario de la vanguardia, al sugerir una transición desde la 'amplitud' de la Historia—el ámbito grandilocuente del "progreso," de la acción en un espacio público—a otro modo de "amplitud"—el territorio infinito del deseo, la extensión inexplorada de lo minúsculo, lo cotidiano: la extrañeza de los "interiores," de un espacio y tiempo privados.

> [This text already features a change in "scale" as to the imaginary specter of vanguard movements, as it suggests a transition from the "amplitude" of History—the grandiloquent sphere of "progress," of action in a public space—to another type of "amplitude"—the infinite territory of desire, the unexplored expanse of the minuscule, the quotidian: the strangeness of "interiors," of private space and time.][85]

Indeed, many of Hernández's fictions rework an idea of desire in the observation of mysterious humanity latent in objects (recalling Marx's theorization of the fetish in *Das Kapital*), as in the beautiful example of the erotics of two window shutters in his 1928 story "El vestido blanco" ["The White Dress"], where he describes "esa violenta necesidad física que tenían las ventanas de estar juntas ya" ["that violent physical need the window shutters felt of being close together, once and for all"].[86]

Outside of these domesticities, the later stories of *Nadie encendía las lámparas* (which have been translated by Luis Harss under the title *Piano Stories*, although the literal translation is *Nobody Turned On the Lamps*) do not allude to a specific Montevideo, a feature similar to Borges's practice of locating his later stories somewhere that is not quite Argentina.[87] "El acomodador," the tale in first-person narration of a theater usher who develops the power to illuminate objects with light emanating from his own eyes, is set in a "ciudad grande" ("big city"): "Su centro—donde todo el mundo se movía apurado entre casas muy altas—quedaba cerca de un río" ["Its center, where everybody moved hurriedly between very tall houses, was close to a river"].[88] The usher's modest existence is improved by his supernatural *flânerie*, his pleasure in finding "unexpected connections" ["conexiones inesperadas"], in imagining the city's multiple unknowns: "me daba placer imaginar todo lo que no conocía de aquella ciudad" ["it gave me pleasure to imagine all that I didn't know about that city"] (37). As explained above, the links between desire, the imagination, and the unknown are some of the most unique features to be found in Hernández's oeuvre. The usher's thrill about the mysteries of his urban environment are reflective of a wider concern in the author's novels and stories: to uphold the suspense of not knowing despite a main character's efforts to establish an intimacy with an other, whether animate or inanimate. To this end, Santiago Colás highlights the manifestation in Hernández's writing, of an "unknowing relating," an "endless chase after an elusive object of representation" that injects the latter's literary production "with a haunting and dim, repetitious strangeness."[89]

In "El acomodador," the usher's narration vacillates between his insistent excitement in the face of undisclosed mystery lurking in the city, and the drive to know, *see*, and possess more. His "imagination" of the urban unknown is aided later in the story by the development of the usher's extraordinary ability to illuminate objects with a light emanating from his own eyes.

> Había estado insinuándose poco a poco. Una noche me desperté en el silencio oscuro de mi pieza y vi, en la pared empapelada de flores violetas, una luz. Desde el primer instante tuve la idea de que me ocurría algo extraordinario, y no me asusté . . . Bajé los ojos hasta la mesa y *vi las botellas y los objetos míos*. No me quedaba la menor duda; aquella luz salía de mis propios ojos, y se había estado desarrollando desde hacía mucho tiempo . . . Miré la bombita de luz eléctrica y vi que ella brillaba *con luz mía*. Me volví a convencer y tuve una sonrisa. ¿Quién, en el mundo, veía con sus propios ojos en la oscuridad? (41–42, emphasis added)

> [It had been insinuating itself little by little. One night I woke up in the dark silence of my room and saw, on the wall papered in purple flowers, a light. From the first moment I had the thought that something extraordinary was happening to me, and I was not afraid. . . . I lowered my eyes to the table, and *saw my bottles and objects*. There was not a doubt left in me; that light was emerging from my own

eyes, and had been developing for a long time. . . . I looked at the electric bulb and saw that it was shining with my own light. I again convinced myself and smiled. Who in the world could see with his own eyes in the dark?]

As with Spencer Brydon's slow development of his narration of self-haunting, the usher's power to illuminate arrives at first by slow "insinuation." What in the beginning is a discreet talent that appeases the usher's ennui in his small room above a butcher shop, progressively becomes throughout the story a narrative of the fantasies of control through illumination. In this passage, the insistence on the "mine," with the possessive adjective that is placed after every noun—"la luz *mía*," "los objetos *míos*"—gestures toward the increasingly consuming desire of ownership of the spaces and objects that surround the usher. The imagination of the unknown details of the city turns, in this fantastic and felicitous turn of events, into the direct possibility of illuminating these details.

The urban secrets the usher chooses to reveal at the beginning of his practice of illumination move from the whimsical and minute to the spectral and horrific. He first practices his light on teacups and bottles hung by threads in his room. These objects had been kept in an armoire that had been carved with his initials, although he makes the point of saying that he had not carved them himself ["donde estaban grabadas mis iniciales pero no las había grabado yo]" (42). This curious detail points to an uncanny, dreamlike dimension in the story, although it may also represent the anonymity, dispossession, and alienation that describe this urban landscape. (This coincidence echoes Hernández's philosophy of literature, which was evident throughout his career. In his work, he advocated for the permeability and thus continuous reinvention of the text, as the differences between author and reader dissolve to create a text containing multiple inscriptions, by multiple authors and multiple readers.) After seeing his objects in this literally new light, the usher suffers the terror of seeing his own image in the mirror, his otherworldly eyes ["aquellos ojos de otro mundo"], and a face torn into fragments, "dividida en pedazos que nadie podría juntar ni comprender" ["split into pieces that no one would be able to put together, let alone understand"] (43). Interestingly, the sentence following this revelation, which makes up a full paragraph, returns to the scene of benign everyday violence outside the usher's fantastic room: "Me quedé despierto hasta que subió el ruido de los huesos serruchados y cortados con el hacha" ["I stayed awake until I heard the noise of sawed bones, cut by the cleaver, coming from below"] (43). The solitary experience of seeing his face fragmented into incomprehensible pieces moves into the realm of shock when followed by the anonymous bangs of the butcher downstairs.

Hernández's amassed images of ornamental illumination of interiors, horrid self-revelation, and jolting quotidian sonority represent for the reader a strange exposition of the interiors and exteriors of a peculiar urban life that seeks to define itself between the private world and what lies outside.

The usher's "luz mía" continues to seek objects to illuminate throughout the story. His viewing "lust"—"lujuria de ver" ["lust of seeing"] (46)—takes him to the house of a rich man who has promised to host open dinners as a form of gratitude for the survival of his daughter from drowning in the river: "una promesa hecha por haberse salvado su hija de las aguas del río" ["a promise made after his daughter was saved from drowning in the river"] (39). In this house, the usher spots a room of display windows "bursting with objects" ["cargadas de objetos"] (43) that he will infiltrate to continue his practice of possession through illumination. With dazzling descriptions of ornamental curios, the usher's light loses "stability" when it encounters the reflection of sequins ["mi luz perdió un poco de estabilidad al pasar sobre algunos (objetos) que tenían lentejuelas"] (48), and finds that it can otherwise have complete control over another object portraying a "Chinese man with pearly face and silk dress" whom the usher describes as being the only figure capable of being "isolated in that immensity," and whose stillness makes him think of "the mystery of stupidity."

> Sólo aquel chino podía estar aislado en aquella inmensidad; tenía una manera de estar fijo que hacía pensar en el misterio de la estupidez. Sin embargo, él fue lo único que yo pude hacer mío esa noche. (48)

> [Only that Chinese man could be isolated in that immensity; his way of staying still made one think of the mystery of stupidity. And yet, he was the only thing I could make mine that night.][90]

This odd sequence of associations that emerge from the observation of the Chinese figure begins to portray the indecency of the usher's desire for legibility and possession through illumination: Stealing into the space of staged bibelots, the usher's lust of seeing insinuates the desire to possess what to him is both foreign and illegible. His reference to "that immensity" connects the spaces of the large domestic interior and the even larger space outside. The cosmopolitan space of the secret city that the light-less usher originally sought to imagine becomes miniaturized and trapped by the process of his illumination. This becomes a microcosm of the abolition of the strength of impressions, where the character ironically cites "mysteries" he immediately reduces to the nevertheless impermeable sphere of stupidity. This echoes an earlier idea expressed in one of Hernández's fictions of the early 1930s: that of "strange simultaneities," of the connection of things that appear to be irrelevant to one another, but

that are felt together like a "musical chord" ["un acorde"], where "a medida que pasaba el tiempo unas quedaban tendidas y otras se movían" ["as
time passed, some remained suspended while others moved"].[91] Shifting
between permanence and precarious movement, the desire of possession
of these mysteries is played out in a simultaneous conceptualization of
immensities and miniatures.

But objects are not the only things the usher encounters in the gallery
room of the rich man's house. When the latter's sleepwalking daughter begins to enter the room he has trespassed, the usher allows her to walk over
him, letting the train of her nightgown "erase dirty memories" ["la cola del
peinador borraba memorias sucias"]. On the nights she does not walk over
him, the usher feels the angst of being "cut off from communication," as
well as the "threat of an unknown present" ["entonces yo sentía la angustia
de que me cortaran la comunicación y la amenaza de un presente descono-
cido"] (50). As with the passage where the usher first discovers his light, the
reader is struck by how the character makes obscure connections between
his infatuation for the woman, the erasure of "dirty memories," and the
larger anxiety over lost communications and a mysterious present. This
strange synthesis of desires and fears reverberates later in the story, when
the usher spots a woman whom he thinks is the sleepwalker on the street,
in a scene of concentrated cosmopolitanism. The diversity of cultural elements in this episode of "El acomodador" allows us to liken Hernández's
city to a place like Montevideo (or Buenos Aires), where immigrants made
up nearly half of the population.[92]

> Al pararme en una casucha de libros viejos vi pasar una pareja de ex-
> tranjeros; él iba vestido de negro y con una gorra de apache; ella lle-
> vaba en la cabeza una mantilla española y hablaba en alemán. (52)

> [As I stopped in a used-book stand I saw a foreign couple walking by;
> he was dressed in black and wore an apache cap; she wore a Spanish
> shawl on her head and spoke German.]

In the space of the city street, the usher, still possessed of his power of illumination, is unable to stalk and decipher the alien mysteries of the couple.
He remains locked out of their communication and intimacy—a communication that is indecipherable due to its foreignness. The result is a fear for
the loss of the "world" he had imagined as "closed out" to others, in that
other "immensity" of the room of bibelots and sleepwalking women. The
usher in fact attempts to metonymize the foreign man by singling out his
hat, and in his next and final foray into the room in the rich man's house,
he brings a cap to show to the sleepwalking woman in what seems like a
Pavlovian game of adult sexual attraction.

It is during this meeting that the usher's illumination arrives at its spectralizing denouement, when he tries to possess the body of the woman with his eyes' iridescence.

Mi luz no sólo iluminaba a aquella mujer, sino que tomaba algo de ella. Yo miraba complacido la gorra y pensaba que era mía y no de ningún otro; pero de pronto mis ojos empezaron a ver en los pies de ella un color amarillo verdoso parecido al de mi cara aquella noche que la vi en el espejo de mi ropero . . . Al instante aparecieron pedacitos blancos que me hicieron pensar en los huesos de los dedos . . . Empecé a hacer de nuevo el recorrido de aquel cuerpo; ya no era el mismo, y yo no reconocía su forma; a la altura del vientre encontré, perdida, una de sus manos, y no veía de ella nada más que los huesos. No quería mirar más . . . Pero mis ojos, como dos gusanos que se movieran por su cuenta dentro de mis órbitas, siguieron revolviéndose hasta que la luz que proyectaban llegó hasta la cabeza de ella. Carecía por completo de pelo, y los huesos de la cara tenían un brillo espectral como el de un astro visto con un telescopio. (55–6)

[My light not only illuminated that woman, it took something from her as well. I looked with satisfaction at the cap and thought that she was mine and no one else's; but suddenly my eyes began to see in her feet a yellowish-green color that resembled the color of my face that night I saw it in the mirror on my armoire. . . . Shortly after that I saw little white pieces that made me think of finger bones. . . . I began surveying the body again; it wasn't the same, and I couldn't recognize its form; at chest's height I found, as if lost, one of her arms, and I could only see her bones. I didn't want to see anymore. . . . But my eyes, like two worms that moved on their own within my orbits, continued twirling around until the light reached her head. It was missing all hair, and the bones on her face had a spectral glow like that of a star seen through a telescope.]

The usher's x-ray vision accomplishes the phantasmagoric effect of death's image superimposed on the previously beautiful—and alive—female figure. The effect of his desires of legibility becomes, as in the case of Spencer Brydon's "sense for construction" of his bygone possibilities, a "blatant" and morbidly finalizing reading of a completed cryptograph of desire. Here the possibilities of finding the "dynamic mediations" (to recall Jesse Matz) that impressions might offer in the ever-tenuous process of "knowing" the city are rendered impossible by the blatant unearthing of the spectral. To render spectral does not mean here to make mysterious, to deepen the questions raised by urban landscapes, or even facilitate a visionary cityscape reimagined in all its complexity, but actually its opposite.

We should ask what the significance of illumination is in this text. When the writers of *Marcha* did an end-of-year review of literature in 1948, they wrote that "encender las lámparas (en el sentido de Hernández, indiscernible aquí) no es en literatura el camino más conveniente" ["'to light the lamps'—in Hernández's sense, which is indiscernible here—is not the most convenient path to take in literature"].[93] More like a journalistic catchphrase to round off a poor review of Hernández's text, their designation of what is the "indiscernible" element of "lighting the lamps" is more provocative than they made out at the time. The act of illumination—whether it is with the power of electricity or the fantastic projections emanating from one's own eyes—can announce the possibility of extracting an object or subject from obscurity. When that object is a modern landscape (of a city, of a nation) with its webs of movements, migrations, entrances, and dispossessions, the temptation to miniaturize, to uncomplicate via illumination, renders the spaces even more illegible. Illumination thus contains the capacity to spectralize—to see something or someone *to death*—but by the same token it obscures the "mysterious present" that correlates seemingly distinct urban realms. In his essay "Tal vez un movimiento" ("Perhaps a Movement"), Hernández connects discourse with what he calls "talking with the known dead," and ponders the problem that exists "in letting an idea live, so that it doesn't stop . . . [or] become a conceptual thought, in other words, another corpse" ["la dificultad que existe en dejar vivir una idea, en que ésta no se pare, se termine, se asfixie, se muera, se haga pensamiento conceptual, es decir, otro muerto más"].[94] We could argue that, in lighting an object to enhance the perversity of understanding it away, life stops and we are left with the banality of the dead thing. The unlit lamps might then stand for a considerably nuanced notion of legibility and discourse—of the limits of representations that seek to encapsulate wholes, of the indecent sense of making specters in an immense and already mysteriously obscured present.

4 / Transnational Shadows

No limit, confine—not the Western sky alone—
the high meridian—North, South, all,
Pure luminous color fighting the silent shadows to the last.
> —WALT WHITMAN, "A PRAIRIE SUNSET" (1888)

Limitless nations, landscapes without confines: Such are the dreams defined and refined by the continuous reimagination of community space. The limit may be quantified—as Darwin does and as Borges recounts in "La pampa y el suburbio son dioses"—and contained to the positivist extent of the eyes' visual horizon. But in immeasurable ways, the creative reinscription of national frontiers continually finds itself negotiating the anticipation but also the immediate experience of unbounded movement. In 1887 Martí, in both praise and discomfort, describes Whitman in the following lines: "All things are contained in him; and all of him is in everything; . . . he is the tide, the ebb, and flow," a poet for whom "accumulation" is the "best sort of description," and whose "reasonings emerge from the mystery of insinuation, the fervor of certainty, and the fiery whirlwind of prophecy."[1] This description of the "whirlwind of prophecy" (el "giro ígneo de la profesía") that is achieved through a formal accumulative style, stretches out in poems where, without fail, subjects and landscapes (all of different colors, features, and races) move forth into an unspecified, limitless horizon. In "A Prairie Sunset," this movement also constitutes a banishing of the "silent shadows" that skulk in the way of the grand illumination of the setting Western sun. Here, the shadows are not necessarily ominous figures (one would be hard-pressed to find in Whitman's poetry something ominous not transformed at once into a force of benign energy), but they are nevertheless figures that are "fought." A shadow is the necessary negative of illumination, and it is also simultaneous with illumination: Every moment of iridescence entails and supposes a shadowing. To what extent is the shadow a metonym for that which stands in our way, something always and already there, yet surprising or disturbing? In Whitman's poem, the setting of the sun to the "West" is magnified and made immense by an illumination that encompasses "North, South, all" as well, so that the shadows are assailed from all possible directions. Whitman's dream of a multidirectional iridescence—an insurmountable accumulation of illumination—is a dream of extinct shadows, a luminescence that contains no negatives. What kind of stories, however, can shadows tell? How can we read the darkness of the illuminated?

The previous chapters contemplate how narrations of haunting interrogate and reframe spatial imaginations in literature and films of the Americas. The narratives imagined by the practitioners here studied, rather than summon those "familiar bugaboos," craft the figures of these phenomena as events of space and time, as ciphers of an ongoing and modern history of change. Rather than representing haunting as instances of retrogressive time, these texts include haunting within the enunciation of a progressive present—a present-progressive—that nevertheless opens into a questioning of how the modern Americas should be represented in their complexity. In this way, haunting interrogates the futures of spaces that evolve or unwind in the multiple movements of modernization: Its acts become the urgent questions of how one can address and pronounce an incommensurable web of change that alters everyday life across the American hemisphere.

Haunting, as I have argued in Chapters 2 and 3, is enmeshed in an idea of landscapes of modern simultaneity in the fictions of city and desert: These narratives dramatize the difficulty of telling the multiplicity of events invaginated in the fluctuations of the hemispheric present. In the realm of representation, haunting becomes a way of posing questions to an active landscape, and it is also a means of constructing answerable landscapes—those that can outline and speak for the locations of national elements that have been obscured. This chapter moves beyond the city and the desert to focus on what is a symbolic and diverse transnational topography. Specifically, I embark on an expansive reading of nations and the evolution of their cartographies in the nineteenth and twentieth centuries. I analyze the figure of the shadow as a locus of where a cartography—understood here as an imagined construction of place and national belonging—has become haunted.

"Nation" is a charged term, and so is the notion of the transnational. As I have been showing throughout *Ghost-Watching American Modernity*, the works of artists in different locations throughout the decolonized Americas defy the limits and limitations that the "national" imposes. Benedict Anderson notes how, in the nineteenth and twentieth centuries, nationalist projects in postcolonial nations were intercepted by what he calls capitalism's "remorseless, accelerating transformation of all human societies."[2] These changes range from a form of technological advancement that knew no boundaries to mass immigration, especially where the Americas are concerned. In terms of an American poetics, we have seen how aspirations toward an understanding of the local harbor a wider, haunting, questioning of modernity's transformative powers. In turn, these interrogations are lodged within a vast array of artistic formats that so often defy the standardizing notion of genre. In this analogy between porous literary form and belonging the idea of the transnational can gain momentum. Rather than charting patterns of decolonization, I have plotted a number of dialogues among writers across nations, and I have tried to include them within what I have been calling a haunted hemisperhic imagination. Far from saying that the figures I have analyzed are unconcerned with the idea of nation, I am suggesting that the ghostly, as an expression of unknowingness, stands in the way of any attempt to find an assuring notion of national cohesiveness. Writing about a different spectrum of postcolonial texts, Peter Hitchcock notes how an enunciation of concepts such as "*colonialism, nation*, and *postcolonialism*" carries the "weight of a ghostly afterlife in neocolonialism, postnation, and transnationalism."[3] As I intend to demonstrate in the readings that follow, even when demarcating the nation is the very purpose of a writer such as Sarmiento, a haunted dimension reveals itself in the text—one that opens up questions of the location of literature and invention in post-independence Latin America, in relation to the world. And although in *Souls of Black Folk* (1903) W. E. B. Du Bois describes the Black Belt, a discrete region within the confines of the United States, the text nevertheless opens the South to a larger, transnational theater of racial politics.[4]

Although the shadow in literature often needs to be read in metaphoric terms, a reading that I will not shy away from here, I want to propose the shadow as a *way of reading*. Put differently, I argue that the shadow should be perceived more importantly as a site where geopolitical maps of nations run into hermeneutic trouble, as they entail the negative movement of subjectivities that might not form part of a national sense of inclusiveness. Shadows are disquieting negative presences: Only a Whitmanesque dream of a sunset that comes from every cardinal position can implode the possibility of shadowing. In the readings of the shadows in Domingo Faustino Sarmiento's *Facundo* and W. E. B. Du Bois's *The Souls of Black Folk* that follow, I inspect how the location of shadows over national geographies represents a reframing of the map's most valuable stratagem: the line. How can we use the dynamically haunted form of the shadow to reconfigure how we organize our ideas and ideologies of what constitutes a nation, and what does not?

Topographies of the Future

"Only Hegel is fit for America," wrote Whitman in an unpublished lecture on the philosopher. Only the German philosopher "is large enough and free enough."[5] In his oft-cited 1830–31 lectures published in *The Philosophy of History*, Hegel's expansive World-Spirit is shown to be selective of its topographies and boundaries. The philosopher defines this process through a limited definition of the "continental," a concept lodged in cardinal specificities. "The true theater of History," he writes, "is . . . the temperate zone, or, rather, its northern half, because the earth there presents itself on a continental form, and has a broad breast, as the Greeks say. In the south, on the contrary, it divides itself and runs into many points."[6] These multiple "points" of the south, according to Hegel, constitute a multifarious problem of heterogeneity: Where Spirit reigns better over "animals and plants with common characteristics" in the northern hemisphere, in the south "natural forms" show "individual features contrasted with each other" (80). These features transcend topography in Hegel's theory that constitutes a Spiritual postponement of America as the "land of the future," where the "burden of the World's History shall reveal itself" (86): He predicts "perhaps a contest" between North and South America, due to his contemporary witnessing of "a prosperous state of things" in the "colonized" and centralized North (this is thirty years before the Civil War in the United States), although the "conquered," and multiple republics of the south, whose "history is a continued revolution," "depend only on military force" (note that the Latin American wars of independence had transpired in the previous decades).[7] To Hegel, the racial-cultural "vanishings" of the New World are superseded by a movement of the European Spirit (he claims that the "entirely national" cultures of Mexico and Peru necessarily "expire[d] as soon as Spirit approached it") (81). For the modern reader, this sense of inevitability, of a movement of the overdetermined Spirit into the future, is shaken by Hegel's amalgamation of the geographies of the "multiple points" that a continent can contain within it, points that fold in histories of cultural and racial contact, and their all-too-often violent outcomes.

When Marx and Engels were writing about the Mexican-American War of 1847, they appropriated the Hegelian sense of America as the "future" when they assimilate the U.S. extension into former Mexican lands as a confirmation of the progressive movement of the Spirit of History. Engels writes in a January 1848 article for the *Deutsche-Brusseler Zeitung* that "In America,"

> we have witnessed the conquest of Mexico and have rejoiced at it. It is also an advance when a country which has hitherto been exclusively

wrapped up in its own matters, perpetually rent by civil wars, and completely hindered in its development, a country whose best prospect has been to become industrially subject to Britain—when such a country is forcibly drawn into the historical process. It is to the interest of its own development that Mexico will in future be placed under the tutelage of the United States. The evolution of the whole of America will profit by the fact that the United States, by the possession of California, obtain command of the Pacific.[8]

The "historical progress" noted in this passage echoes Hegel's bifurcated summary of the primitive histories of the Americas, and Engels uses the Mexican-American War as a confirmation of the success of this movement. Indeed, as James Dunkerley points out, Marx himself, criticizing the antiwar sentiments of his *New York Tribune* editors, Horace Greeley and Charles Dana, saw this conflict as an auspicious indication that the U.S. forces, fighting "STUBBORNLY for their objective, SPONTANEOUSLY exploiting every incident," were making strides in their creation of a "measure of wholeness" for their society.[9] Yet, as Dunkerley also notes, by 1861 Marx adopts a more "anti-imperialist" position with regard to U.S.-Mexico relations,[10] one that nevertheless reveals Marx's "tense ambivalence between the merits of accepting capitalist expansion . . . and those of upholding independent republican politics," an indecisiveness that "was never to disappear from the Marxist assessment of Latin America" (240).

Whether through economic, political, or geographical prisms, thinkers such as Hegel, Marx, and Engels attempt to understand the territories of the Americas through a spread of the tidal wave of frameworks and developments that they see as having come to fruition in the European context. For Hegel, that future in which North America will "be comparable" with Europe hides behind the moment in which "that immeasurable space" of the continent has been occupied (86). It is fascinating to me that Hegel's understanding of history and progress should be so based on a topography, on the features of a landmass. For doesn't the southern hemisphere also harbor an "immeasurable space"? How do these "many points" of the southern continent's tangible topography compete or tamper with abstract ideas of political and economic advancement? Marx and Engels, in their adaptation of Hegelian philosophy to the economic realities of capitalism in mid-nineteenth-century Europe, were living in a crucial moment when the drives and desires of empire would become increasingly tangible. Their concept of the single completion of a predetermined economic process moving westward across an enormous ocean and into the mass of the American hemisphere would slowly come into focus as a new form of imperial constitution. To put it in topographic terms (à la Hegel perhaps), the expansion of capitalism and the development of its empire were two ideas that were still moving around like shifting tectonic plates that, as would become evident (for example) with the Spanish-American War of 1898, would progressively mount one another to become the new form of empire.

Interestingly, Marx's conception of the United States's movement toward this "future" and the fulfillment of the historical process, as Martin Harries (after Derrida) has noted, encloses a history of attention—and inattention—to ghosts as strategic metaphors. In the following passage from *The Eighteenth Brumaire of Louis Bonaparte* (1852), Marx relates the lessons of the June revolution of 1848 in France through a comparison of European revolutionary history with the "conservative" development of bourgeois society in the United States. The revolution

> had demonstrated . . . that in Europe the question of today is something other than "republic or monarchy." It had revealed that *bourgeois republic* means the unlimited despotism of one class over the others. It had proved that in long-civilised countries with a developed class structure, with modern conditions of production, and with an intellectual consciousness representing centuries of effort in dissolving traditional ideas, the *republic* signifies *in general only the revolutionary way to destroy bourgeois society* and not a *conservative way to develop* it, as for example in the United States, where there are already classes, to be sure, but they have not yet solidified, rather they are in constant flux, changing and switching their component parts; where modern means of production compensate for the relative paucity of heads and hands, instead of declining together with a stagnant surplus population; and where finally the feverish youth of material production, which has a new world to appropriate, left neither time nor opportunity for exorcising the spirits of the old.[11]

The "constant flux" of those "conservative" developments of the bourgeois republic (a concept that, as I mention above, does not yet spell out the threat of empire for Marx) simultaneously represents a postponement of haunting. What, however, does Marx see as "the old" in the Americas, from whence these spirits may emerge? If Marx assumes, like Hegel, a position that historical process is yet to be achieved in the New World, who or what is he addressing in his invocation of the "spirits of the old"? If we read this formulation of the nation in flux in *Eighteenth Brumaire* with Marx's remarks about the Mexican-American War made a few years earlier, we see through the "stubborn" and "spontaneous" achievement of "wholeness"—in a war of expansion as in economic (bourgeois) development—that haunting by the "spirits of the old" assumes an unassimilable form. But, which exactly is the economy that precedes the "feverish youth" of conservative capitalism in the United States for Marx? If Europe harbors a "stagnant surplus population," subject to haunting, and the United States does not, where do the ghosts come from? Furthermore, is the "specter that haunts Europe" (which opens the *Communist Manifesto*) also different from the American ghosts? Marx appears to be gesturing to something rather indescribable: a proleptic haunting of indeterminate past spirits. One wonders which point in North American history (before 1852) he is addressing when he describes the moment of "exorcism": Is it colonialism and conquest? Or perhaps, manifest destiny and the U.S. expansion into Mexico?

Through the invocation of these ghosts on "unsolid" grounds, Marx (moving on from Hegel) is casting the conflicts of the United States—conflicts that inevitably will engage a whole hemisphere, north and south—into future acts of national transformation, a prophecy of hauntings to come. What is remarkable about Marx's writing (something that Derrida eloquently discusses in *Specters of Marx* and which Harries localizes in Marx's use of the ghosts of Shakespeare) is his strategic use of the ghost as a necessary aporia in the progressive accumulation of history. It is important to note, however, that, although his theorization of the specter in Europe is well developed, the American ghost is still undergoing transformations, and possesses an indeterminate past. Like the class system in the United States, the ghosts are still "in flux."

I have included Hegel, Marx, and Engels in this discussion of American ghost-watching because, despite the fact that their eyes are set on Europe as the model of a completed historical process, their horizons are necessarily beginning to be in the west, across the Atlantic. Beginning to depart from Hegel's brief consideration of the Americas in *Philosophy of History*—this American section of his lecture comes to an end when he pronounces that "what *has* taken place in the New World up to the present time is only an echo of the Old World . . . and as a Land of the Future, it has no interest for us here" (87)—Marx and Engels invoke that "echo" and, both slowly and incompletely, fill it in with events and material histories that begin to re-map an American geography for Europe. It is important, I think, to understand Hegel, Marx, and Engels in their historical and European specificity, especially when they address the American scene directly. Reciprocally, we should look carefully at how these thinkers were being appropriated in the intellectual life of the Americas to tell narratives of exceptionalism or Old World reverberation in the unfolding histories of these "new" continents (I am reminded here of Roberto González Echevarría's assertion that, in his opinion, *Facundo* is Latin America's *Phenomenology of the Spirit*).[12] Hegel, Marx, and Engels represent a conception of America as different and, for the purposes of my own discussion, as a hemisphere that hosts different, future, and unquantifiable ghosts. The American hemisphere represents for them a future frontier in a historical process that needs to account for "many points" and heterogeneities that their theories might or might not have projected.

As we have seen with figures such as Martí, this status of the New World as "echo" is an entirely conscious reality for North and South American intellectuals, and it will be both reconceived and disavowed throughout the nineteenth century.[13] What is more, the constitution of the maps of the Americas will also change before the eyes of the continents' subjects and the world at large, as the intangible flux of U.S. empire begins to be felt within the hemisphere and abroad, dramatically beginning with the turn of the century. We should focus on how the histories of difference are told from within this realm of the "echo"—whether through adaptation or disavowal of the theorizations of the Americas from outside—and how they interpret the Americas' transformations of nationhood in terms of local differences and internal differentiations. This way we may begin to see a clearer picture of how the imagination of a nation constitutes itself both in terms of its local geography and its shadows.

Illustrating the Shadow

It has become a critical commonplace to consider that narrations of nationhood are inextricably linked to the histories of anxious enunciation inherent in the dynamics of storytelling itself.[14] In this section, I briefly focus on three hemispheric texts in order to provide a sketch of the ways in which the metaphor of the shadow has been used to complement the displacement of national self-identity. These brief considerations, far from exhaustive, outline three different ways in which the shadow is used in texts that seek to conjugate narrative style with the problems of national definition: They are distinct enunciations that include this figure in the process of developing a self-scrutinizing model of nationhood.

As we saw in Chapter 2, Martí creates, in his 1886 *crónica* of Buffalo Bill, an image of the Native American shadow that haunts the Wild West showgrounds after the crowds have gone home, a shadow play that acts like a counternarrative to the description of the U.S. West enveloped by Buffalo Bill's shadow, as detailed in the Wild West's program. This conflict of shadows of singular and metonymic figures across the immensity of the landscape that stretches from an Eastern cosmopolis into the unseen reaches of the continent mobilizes a dramatization of the racial and cultural conflicts in the United States through both mythification and the implosion of a myth. Although the shadow of the mythic white, rugged individual tells a story of heroic expansion and conquest from sea to sea, the unnamed Native American doctor in Martí's *crónica* is his immediate and urgent counterpart—a reluctant figure who stands outside the Wild West tents that demarcate what belongs to Cody and his expansionist imaginary, and whose shadow projects outward into a landscape marked by dispossession. Put together, these two narratives develop a portrait of the North American continent as enveloped in a contrapuntal narrative of shadows emanating from figures that represent a decisive conflict in the constitution of a history of expansion. More than allegorical (or, facing a past that is already known, to recall Derek Attridge's argument), these shadows stand as important dialectical ciphers: Contingent on an illumination that would elicit their legibility, they are evidence of the immediate presence of something awaiting understanding.

The shadow emerges through a tighter intersection of geographical metonymy and mythology in a novel such as the Argentine Ricardo Güiraldes's *Don Segundo Sombra* (1926). Written during a period when Latin American writers and artists were seeking elements of their native countries that would produce a new and autochthonous form of expression,[15] Güiraldes's novel tells the story of a young boy named Fabio who is indoctrinated in the ways of survival in the pampas by a reticent man called Don Segundo Sombra ("sombra" means "shadow" in Spanish). Güiraldes's bildungsroman uses the language of the pampas to represent that "totemic" and expansive natural life outside of the cities. These elements of the rural life are personified in the figure of Fabio's mentor and knowing shadow. Indeed, the Borges from *El tamaño de mi esperanza* (1926) describes Güiraldes as a writer who is "praying" to that "god" that is the Argentine plain (25).[16] Sombra stands as both the metonym and voice of a regional style of the pampas: He is region *and* man, a lifestyle encoded in a particular parlance. He is also the emblem of an ethics and a sentimental education under threat in the modern and increasingly cosmopolitan nation—the lone shadow of a man whom Güiraldes posits as that most endemic element of Argentine patrimony, now in danger of extinction. Fabio affirms in his retrospective narration about the "men of the pampas" ["hombres de la pampa"] that they "had the souls of cattle-drivers, which means to have a soul driven by the horizon" ["tenían alma de reseros, que es tener alma de horizonte"].[17] Here, in a deceptively short sentence, Güiraldes interlocks the idea of a man's "soul" with the topography of the pampas in what is a grand and sweeping manner. Likewise, and in a prose style that attempts to capture the oral particularity of these "hombres de la pampa," Don Segundo's final maxim to Fabio when the boy is about to return to the city after life among the men is: "Mirá . . . Si sos gaucho en de veras, no has de mudar, porque andequiera que vayas, irás con tu alma por delante como madrina'e tropilla" ["If you're a real gaucho, you never really change, because wherever you go, your soul leads the way like the lead mare of a herd"] (176). Güiraldes's reflexively iconic creation, as totem, freezes the man-shadow of Sombra amid a surrounding world that complicates the meanings of the regional and the autochthonous. In this manner, Sombra is an endless soul and shadow of a past that the writer seeks to project into a progressively amnesiac and urbanized present that is becoming forgetful of the natural wisdom of the plains.

The benevolent shadow of an increasingly invisible regional culture gains a different meaning in Ralph Ellison's *Invisible Man* (1952), a bildungsroman of racial consciousness—a parable of what Du Bois called in *Souls of Black Folk* that "strange meaning of being black" in the United States. In this tale of racial self-discovery in the twentieth century, a young black man travels from the rural South to the urban North. Through a series of experiences that reveal how racial categories and the theoretical narratives they spawn lose sight of the individual experience of being a black man, the narrator arrives at the conclusion (which opens the novel) that he is "an invisible man," invisible by virtue of his unanswerability, of the fact that "people refuse to see me": "Like the bodiless heads you see sometimes in circus sideshows, it is as though I have been surrounded by mirrors of hard, distorting glass" (3). This nameless "invisible" man decides to go underground, where he lives in a basement "hole" illuminated by "exactly 1,369 lights."[18] "Perhaps you'll think it strange that an invisible man should need light, desire light, love light," he pronounces in the novel's epilogue. "But maybe it is exactly because I *am* invisible. Light confirms my reality, gives birth to my form" (6).

Ellison's novel elicits the fascinating correspondence between absolute illumination and the casting away of shadows. In his "hole," he is not only consciously invisible to the world above, but he is also without a shadow: the 1,369 lights that cover ceiling and walls obliterate any possibility of his form projecting its negative. His existence as racial theory aboveground— the experience of false illumination, where flesh and blood have fallen prey to a narrative shadowing—is transcended by literal and material illumination of his actual and solitary life underground. In other words, the transformation of his living form into *projection* aboveground leads to his decision to live in a state of absolute and personal illumination underground, where he may not project a second, dark figure even to himself. Oscillating connotations of illumination spawn a further consideration of the different implications, actual and theoretical, of shadows and shadowing. For what does it mean to eliminate the possibility of one's form emanating a shadow?

In Ellison's novel, it seems to me, the shadow symbolizes residual personhood: the trace of an individual's humanity on which the rest of the world may overwrite a narrative of stifling generalizations of negative existence. The shadow in *Invisible Man* becomes the only part of a man that the world is willing to see. In other words, the form's negative is transformed into the individual's only usable shape, an outlining of that subject's humanity that erases the possibility of ethical exchange. In this process of shadowing, the subject's answerability is lost. Bakhtin makes the connection between theorization and rendering something complete or "finished," thus useless in the world of the living. "An object that is absolutely indifferent, totally finished," he writes, "cannot be something one becomes actually conscious of, something one experiences actually."[19] He observes:

> Any kind of *practical* orientation of my life within the theoretical world is impossible: it is impossible to live in it, impossible to perform answerable deeds. In that world, I am unnecessary; I am essentially and fundamentally non-existent in it. The theoretical world is obtained through an essential and fundamental abstraction from the fact of my unique being and from the moral sense of that fact—"as if I didn't exist." And this concept of Being is indifferent to the central fact—central for me—of my unique and actual communion with Being (I, too, exist), and it cannot in principle add anything to it or subtract anything from it, for it remains equal to itself and identical in its sense and significance, regardless of whether I exist or not; it cannot determine my life as an answerable performing of deeds, it cannot provide any criteria for the life of practice, the life of the deed, for it is *not* the Being *in which I live*, and, if it were the only Being, *I* would not exist. (9)

This "as if I didn't exist" becomes the realization that dawns on Ellison's invisible man in the society that claims to understand the meaning of experiencing life as a black man in the United States in the twentieth century. Cultures of strategic appropriation, such as the communist organizations that embrace him, become the "moral code" of racial allegorization that ultimately refuses the possibility of an ethical—eventual and living—exchange with his particularity.

This raises an important question: Can the shadow help us read beyond a moral encoding? Are there instances in which the shadow becomes an agent of something more than a morality tale? Throughout this book, I have been arguing for a reading of haunting as enunciative of answerable landscapes—of ghosts and haunting as narrative devices that set into motion a correspondence between simultaneous landscapes, which in turn tell stories of acknowledged and unacknowledged modernity. The shadow in narrative is a materialized ghost insofar as it satisfies our appetite for the empirical evidence of haunting. In this way, it becomes a teasing gesture toward the visible specter. In the following sections, which focus on Sarmiento's *Facundo* and Du Bois's *Souls of Black Folk*, I explore the ways in which these writers use the shadow to enunciate and trace national and regional geographies. I want to argue that, by placing the shadow over the national topographies of Argentina in 1845 and the United States in 1903, Sarmiento and Du Bois give a sense of topographical embeddedness to the ghosts that need to be made answerable. In this way, Sarmiento and Du Bois seek to illuminate shadows that cannot be made to disappear, because they already outline, and are embedded in, the (narrative) maps of these nations.

Ann Laura Stoler, in her introduction to *Haunted by Empire*, writes that "to haunt is 'to frequent, resort to, be familiar with,' to bear a threatening presence, to invisibly occupy, to take on changing form."[20] We have been seeing how these meanings of haunting are dramatized in the fictions of desert and city. That said, I want to focus on her definitions of haunting as "threatening presence," invisible occupation, and transformation. Sarmiento's and Du Bois's texts are haunted by shadows—shadows which in turn haunt a national geopolitics. The shadows are darkened forms cast upon these landscapes, and, in these two texts, they succeed in transforming what is presumably a given geography. What is intriguing about these two texts is that they embody a dual idea of *transformation*: On one level, the image of the shadow is used to represent a landscape's anxiety for an answerability that contains the possibility of reconstructing that landscape's structure. On a second level, the analysis of the shadow must take into account how these texts, on a constructional level, transcend any given *narrative or generic form*, and are thus what I will call here *transforms*. We are faced with the symbiotic relationship between ideas of landscape and narrative form, which in turn accomplish a *different* reading of national constitution. What follows is a consideration of the dramatization of this relationship in two texts that, by transcending genre, begin, in their particular ways, the work of untangling haunted geographies and their constitutive shadows.

Finding and Losing the "Terrible" Shadow

Domingo Faustino Sarmiento, self-taught man of letters and future president of the Argentine republic, wrote *Facundo* while in exile in Chile during the time of the despotic military government of Juan Manuel de Rosas. Originally titled *Civilización y barbarie. Vida de Juan Facundo Quiroga y aspecto físico, costumbres y hábitos de la República Argentina*—a title that, as González Echevarría notes, has taken on a number of forms throughout the years—Sarmiento's text seeks to tell the life of the caudillo general Facundo Quiroga (d. 1835) as a way to arrive at an explication of the terrorized nation under Rosas, who had been, like Quiroga, a ferocious caudillo before his presidency. Quiroga—an exemplar of what Sarmiento calls a *"gaucho malo"* in his sketches of Argentine "types" in the first part of the text—is a product of the savage provinces of the country, the threatening presence of desert landscapes outside of the civilized cities. Throughout its three sections, Sarmiento's text seeks to represent Argentina along a positivist vein through descriptions of the landscape and the people. This pseudoscientific description of the landscape spawns the larger-than-life, romantic figure of Facundo Quiroga (whose history is actually recounted in Sarmiento's second section). The "gaucho malo" first appears in the text in a now-legendary passage where he nearly falls prey to a tiger (jaguar) in the middle of the pampas.[21] "Entonces supe lo que era tener miedo" ["That was when I found out what being afraid means"], Quiroga tells a group of soldiers years later, or so Sarmiento asserts (130; 93).[22]

Indeed, much has been written on Sarmiento's embellishments, misquoting, and brazen inventions while crafting his masterpiece. In the prologue to the 1851 edition, a letter to his colleague Valentín Alsina (who had sent the author a letter with fifty-one errata from the first edition), Sarmiento apologizes for his oversights, claiming that, as an "essay and revelation" ["ensayo y revelación"] of ideas as they reveal themselves to the author, "el *Facundo* adoleció de los defectos de todo fruto de la inspiración del momento, sin el auxilio de documentos a la mano, y ejecutada no bien era concebida, lejos del teatro de los sucesos y con propósitos de acción inmediata y militante" ["*Facundo* suffered from the defects of the fruits of spontaneous inspiration, with no aid from documents at hand, carried out scarcely was it conceived, far from the theater of events, and with the purpose of immediate, militant action"].[23] The lines between anecdote, romanticization, and truth are thus in question at every turn. In the "Barranca-Yaco" chapter that relates Quiroga's death, for example, Sarmiento professes the need to avoid any omissions when recounting the caudillo's death, an assertion that refers to a footnote where the anecdotal source is revealed: The story of Facundo's demise was told to Sarmiento by a Dr. Piñero, a relative of Dr. Ortiz, who was Quiroga's travel companion during his last days. "Es triste necesidad, sin duda, no poder citar sino los muertos en apoyo de la verdad" ["It is without doubt a sad necessity to cite none but the dead in support of the truth"], writes Sarmiento to conclude his note (303; 202).

Sarmiento's misappropriations, which he attributes to the inevitability of death and its silencing effect in his 1851 note, are one of the many reasons why criticism of the author is at once inexhaustible and problematic. This has led critic Carlos Alonso to admit in an aptly titled chapter, "Reading Sarmiento: Once More, with Passion":

There is always, at least in me, the lingering apprehension that even after we have plied our critical tools on Sarmiento, so very much has been left unaccounted for—that there is an untameable, overwhelming quality to Sarmiento's writing that refuses to be reduced to any category, no matter how capacious or rigorous.[24]

Alonso's apprehension over the "untameable" in Sarmiento yields a reading that in many ways echoes the author's own apologia in the 1851 prologue: He chooses to understand Sarmiento's many volumes as performative of the event of writing. Thus, according to Alonso, Sarmiento's "stratagem" in the "rhetorical crisis," "consists of an attempt to found the authority of his writing in a conception of discourse as an act that is continuously being performed before the reader's eyes" (60). This way of reading Sarmiento allows for an apprehension of literary production as constitutive of the urgency of the present, of an understanding of writing as a "passionate" endeavor.

How does this urgency of "passion" conjugate with a reading of shadows? I want to focus on the specific aspect of *Facundo*'s introduction and prologue of the 1845 and 1851 editions, respectively, to see how Quiroga's "terrible shadow" appears and disappears as the opening figure of a text that would come to represent Argentina to the rest of the hemisphere. How does the shadow complicate a text that seeks to disseminate an idea of a country divided between barbarous desert and civilized city? Furthermore, how does the shadow enable a transformation of discourse itself?

The original 1845 introduction to *Facundo* opens:

¡Sombra terrible de Facundo, voy a evocarte, para que, sacudiendo el ensangrentado polvo que cubre tus cenizas, te levantes a explicarnos la vida secreta y las convulsiones internas que desgarran las entrañas de un noble pueblo! Tú posees el secreto, ¡revélanoslo! Diez años aún, después de tu trágica muerte, el hombre de las ciudades y el gaucho de los llanos argentinos, al tomar diversos senderos en el desierto, decían: "¡No!, ¡no ha muerto! ¡Vive aún! ¡Él vendrá!" ¡Cierto! Facundo no ha muerto; está vivo en las tradiciones populares, en la política y revoluciones argentinas; en Rosas, su heredero, su complemento: su alma ha pasado a este otro molde más acabado, más perfecto; y lo que en él era sólo instinto, iniciación, tendencia, convirtióse en Rosas un sistema, efecto y fin. La naturaleza campestre, colonial y bárbara, cambióse en esta metamorfosis en arte, en sistema y en política regular, capaz de presentar a la faz del mundo como el modo de ser de un pueblo encarnado en un hombre que ha aspirado a tomar los aires de un genio que domina los acontecimientos, los hombres y las cosas. (37–39)

[Terrible shadow of Facundo, I will evoke you, so that you may rise, shaking off the bloody dust covering your ashes, and explain the hidden life and the inner convulsions that tear at the bowels of a noble people! You possess the secret: reveal it to us! Even ten years after your tragic death, the men of the cities and the gauchos of the Argentine plains, following different paths in the desert, were saying: "No! he has not died! He still lives! He will return!" True! Facundo has not died. He lives on in popular traditions, in Argentine politics and revolutions, in Rosas, his heir, his complement; his soul has moved into that new mold, one more perfect and finished, and what in him was only instinct, impulse, and a tendency, in Rosas became a system, means, and end. Rural nature, colonial and barbarous, was changed through this metamorphosis into art, into a system, and into regular policy, able to present itself to the world as the way of being of a people, incarnated in one man who has aspired to take on the airs of a genius, dominating events, men, and things.] (31)

Facundo's shadow, in this first edition, is the haunting and messianic host of the narrative of political and geographic division that Sarmiento is about to unpack. The shadow is here synonymous with the ghost rising from death: It is the presence that haunts both city gentleman and rural gaucho into saying "He will come!" ["¡Él vendrá!"]. Interestingly, these two figures, which Sarmiento separates distinctly in the rest of *Facundo*, are haunted in the specific location of the desert pampas, a rhetorical move that locates the evils of the nation within a specific topography, outside of the city. The shadow's convulsion back into life yields the explication for the convulsions of a terrorized country: a country where that "instinct" of the barbarous pampas has been transformed into "art" and mode of governance. Julio Ramos reads this opening of the introduction as a rhetorical *way in* to the national question of "What are we?," which in Sarmiento takes "the form of an investigation (and an account) of an enigma."[25] Certainly, Sarmiento portrays the "enigma" of the shadow as an unriddling of the present "pueblo encarnado": It is the paradoxical disembodiment of what is embodied in the Argentine Republic of 1845. Instead of invoking Greek muses, however, Sarmiento chooses to invoke the native "terrible shadow" at the beginning to immediately signal the aporia that divides the country into its distinct and irreconcilable fragments.

In this introduction, Sarmiento sets out to describe Facundo Quiroga as a profoundly and necessarily autochthonous character. He describes the deceased caudillo as

el tipo más ingenuo del carácter de la guerra civil de la República Argentina, es la figura más americana que la revolución presenta.

Facundo Quiroga enlaza y eslabona todos los elementos de desorden que hasta antes de su aparición estaban agitándose aisladamente en cada provincia. (47)

[the simplest example of the character of civil war in the Argentine Republic; he is the most American figure the revolution offers. Facundo Quiroga links and ties together all the elements of disorder that were stirring up separately in every province, even before his appearance.] (37)

Sarmiento's evocation of the shadow is aligned with this understanding of Facundo as exemplar of a native way of life.[26] In this passage, the shadow is synonymous with those "elements of disorder" that slowly begin to take on the shape of Facundo, and are later "perfected" in Rosas. The gothic evocation becomes a way of arriving at a *localized inspiration*, or, to cite Sarmiento's own words in the 1851 prologue, to act as that immediate intuition that dramatizes both the events of the "essay" and its developing "revelation."

These localized inspirations manifest themselves in the rest of *Facundo* via a continuous appraisal of an Argentina divided—what multiple critics have read through the "and" in the title[27]—by two opposing forces of civilization and barbarism. The division is firmly localized: Civilization abides and is transmogrified in the cities, but is continuously threatened by the barbarism of the surrounding countryside: "La ciudad es el centro de la civilización argentina, española, europea; allí están los talleres de las artes, las tiendas del comercio, las escuelas y colegios, los juzgados, todo lo que caracteriza, en fin, a los pueblos cultos" ["The city is the center of Argentine, Spanish, European civilization; the artisans' workshops are there, the commercial stores, the schools and academies, the courthouses: in short, everything that characterizes cultured peoples"] (66; 52). It is in his comparison of large and more provincial cities, however, that Sarmiento unearths the topographical divisions that delineate the violent conflict in his title:

La elegancia en los modales, las comodidades del lujo, los vestidos europeos . . . tienen allí su teatro y su lugar conveniente. No sin objeto hago esta enumeración trivial. La ciudad capital de las provincias pastoras existe algunas veces ella sola sin ciudades menores y no falta alguna en que el terreno inculto llegue hasta ligarse con las calles. El desierto las circunda a más o menos distancia, las cerca, las oprime; la naturaleza salvaje las reduce a unos estrechos oasis de civilización enclavados en un llano inculto de centenares de millas cuadradas, apenas interrumpido por una que otra villa de consideración. (66)

[There, elegant manners, the convenience of luxury, European clothing, the tailcoat, and the frock coat have their theater and their appropriate place. Not without purpose do I make this trivial enu-
meration. The capital city of the pastoral provinces sometimes exists
by itself, without any smaller cities, and in more than one of them
the uncivilized region reaches right up to its streets. The desert surrounds the cities at a greater or lesser distance, hems them in, op-
presses them; savage nature reduces them to limited oases of civilization, buried deep into an uncivilized plain of hundreds of square
miles, scarcely interrupted by some little town or other of any conse-
quence.] (52)

The encroaching desert threatens the cities not only in a topographical way
but in a quite literal manner of speaking as well: The plains themselves
are described as "ignorant" ["*incultos*"]. When he portrays the inhabitant of these plains, he describes a person who repudiates the ways of the
city, its manners, and its dress: "ningún signo europeo puede presentarse
impunentemente en la campaña. Todo lo que hay de civilizado en la ciudad
está bloqueado por allí, proscrito afuera" ["All that is civilized in the city
is blockaded, banished outside with impunity"] (67; 53). Here, Sarmiento's
language combines "sign" with a physical and psychonatural "blockade":
The symbols that spell out European influence are attacked by that nearly
viral and impermeable landscape that haunts the city so menacingly. We
begin to see how the shadow of Facundo Quiroga becomes the menace of a
past that has become engrained in the landscape: His shadow is representative of the infiltration of pampas into the city, of uncouth rurality into
Europeanized cityscape.

I now want to move on to a discussion of how the shadow of Facundo
was lost in 1851. The prologue to the second edition of *Facundo* contains
the following claim: "He suprimido la introducción como inútil, y los dos
capítulos últimos como ociosos hoy, recordando una indicación de usted
[Valentín Alsina] en 1846 en Montevideo, en que me insinuaba que el libro
estaba terminado en la muerte de Quiroga" ["I have omitted the introduction as useless, and the last two chapters as superfluous today, recalling
something you indicated in Montevideo in 1846, when you insinuated to
me that the book was finished with the death of Quiroga"] (52; 40). The
elimination of the 1845 introduction means that the opening "evocative"
act is lost, and the dramatization of the author faced with the enigma disappears. But not quite.

"Tengo una ambición literaria" ["I have literary ambitions"], writes
Sarmiento in this second prologue, following the statement of self-edit-
ing above (52; 40). Immediately after this pronouncement, he makes the

following admission: "Facundo murió corporalmente en Barranca-Yaco; pero su nombre en la historia podía escaparse y sobrevivir algunos años" ["Facundo died in body in Barranca-Yaco, but his name in History was able to escape and survive for some years"]. What follows is a critique of the self-sufficiency of European cultures, who "prostrat[e] themselves" before a "phantom," and who have "accommodat[ed]" ["contemporizado"] an "impotent shadow" ["una sombra impotente"]. These other writers, according to Sarmiento, need to be instructed by a "poor American narrator" ["un pobre narrador americano"] who can show them a book—an "*Ecce Homo*"—that will tell the story of Argentina. "Hay una justicia ejemplar que hacer y una gloria que adquirir como escritor argentino" ["There is an exemplary justice to be done, and a glory to be attained, as an Argentine writer"] (54; 42), he concludes.

There are several notable things happening in this 1851 revision. The initial appellation is gone, but the shadow reappears here in a more nuanced form: It speaks for a particular literary necessity using a different rhetorical register—a necessity that appears in the form of a letter to someone who had tried to correct the author. Sarmiento is a firm believer in the civilizing power of European cultures (throughout his life he will be a passionate proponent of European immigration as a way of curing Argentina's ills, for example), but he has the "literary ambition" of crafting a distinct Argentine literature. This was already evident in the 1845 introduction, where Sarmiento laments the absence of an American biography of Simón Bolívar, until then only portrayed as a "less-colossal Napoleon," but "Bolívar, the true Bolívar, is still unknown to the world" ["a Bolívar, al verdadero Bolívar, no lo conoce aún el mundo"] (39; 50). His biography of Facundo—a native projection of a human and mythic figure emerging from a richly described landscape—becomes an antidote to this inaccuracy.

> Es que las preocupaciones clásicas europeas del escritor desfiguran al héroe, a quien quitan el "poncho," para presentarlo desde el primer día con el frac . . . Bien; han hecho un general, pero Facundo desaparece. (49)

> [Because the writer's classical, European prejudices distort the hero, from whom they remove the poncho to present him from the first wearing a tailcoat. . . . Very well: they have made a general, but Facundo disappears.] (39)

There is an interesting interplay here between the necessity for the appearance (one could say apparition) of an autochthonous literature, and the appearance (and disappearance) of Facundo, portrayed from within his cultural theater. This concern, it seems to me, is connected to Sarmiento's imagination of shadows: The "terrible," overbearing shadow of Facundo that opens the 1845 introduction in a way goes underground (reminding us of the ghost, or "old mole," under the stage boards in *Hamlet*) in the 1851 prologue, but only to emerge as a sort of negative image of the "impotent shadow" of a tale that, unlike Sarmiento's "ambitious" project, is obscured and weakened by its foreignness.

Although Sarmiento alleges to have eliminated the first introduction as being unusable, he subtly reintroduces the same ideas and the same figures, in order to reframe and in many ways transform the text into a direct reflection of his "literary ambition," the assertion of his authorship, as well as his privileged perspective on autochthony, which is informed by a transnational literary appreciation. The first introduction and the prologue to the second edition, in dialogue, create an opposition between powerful and meaningful shadows told from within, and the impotence of the others that are placeless in the currency of events in the Argentine nation. In both essays, one idea remains intractable: that only the *native* shadow, the one that rises from within the "torn entrails" of the nation's soil, can cast an "explanation" of the realities of that nation. In other words, the shadow in *Facundo* is the agent of an answerability that can be achieved only through a process of *native telling* of landscape and politics.

It is important to remember that this native form of narration nevertheless converses with a transnational constellation of literary styles and modes. Put differently, the event of the birth of Argentine literature is concurrent with an incipient transnationalism in strategies of narration. The shadow emerges throughout acts of generic implosion. One could argue that the agency of haunting, lost and found in these two essays, limits the veracity of a text about politics. But, then again, Sarmiento's enunciation of the shadow transpires at a moment of nation-formation when literature, fiction, and politics were not necessarily estranged from one another. The shadow is a literary strategy that hovers over the delineations of national literature, regional politics, and the desire to broadcast these formations to a transnational audience. Ricardo Piglia writes that Sarmiento marks the beginning of Argentine literature because "he finds a solution that attends both to the freedom of writing and the necessities of political efficacy." He argues that Sarmiento "uses genres as distinct modes to enunciate truth," where "each genre has its system of evidence, its legitimacy, its method of making credible." The genres are thus "stances of enunciation that guarantee the criteria of truth."[28] For Piglia, then, Sarmiento is a manipulator of genres, writing at a moment when Argentine literature was in many ways unbounded, and open to multiple (re)inventions. Sarmiento's freedom with generic appropriations (how he takes a European or North American

genre and adjusts it to his own needs and aspirations) constitutes a knowing naïveté about a text's power to convince, and its ability to shape an
understanding of civility and politics. Similarly to Piglia, Doris Sommer
describes Sarmiento's *Facundo* as a "*generically immoderate book* that obviously adds up to much more than one." She adds,

> He is writing inside what he might have called the American idiom,
> as well as against it, writing *in* conflict as well as about it. Sarmiento
> is founding a peculiarly American political rhetoric by resisting, si-
> multaneously, his anarchic environment and the unnatural con-
> straints of European genres that would distinguish between poetry
> and politics and that keep missing the specificity of American life.[29]

For Sommer, Sarmiento's is an organic style that replicates the improvisa-
tional necessity of American letters during the period in which he is writing. "Poetry" and "politics" thus need not be estranged from each other.
Sarmiento's project, according to Sommer, is to temper a landscape in
order to shape the political future of the Argentine nation, while tearing
down any form of expressive limits in the literary blueprint for his vision
of a political future.

To Piglia's and Sommer's claims about the intemperate nature of
Sarmiento's *Facundo*, I would add a further dimension of the shadow as
the author's way of maneuvering a connection between literary form(s) and
physical locations in the Argentine landscape. Sarmiento not only shadows
different genres as a way of transforming literature, of "exploiting" the lack
of solidity of literary forms of expression. He also uses the shadow as a
haunted vehicle to move even further beyond a bending of genre: It becomes a strategic tool that allows him to travel across both the written and
topographical form. As is evident from the apparition and disappearance
of the initial evocation of this figure, the shadow becomes an agent that
Sarmiento cannot do without in his multiple—and transgeneric—narrations of truth, and which he rediscovers through rhetorical indirection. It
announces the drama of national constitution to the world at a moment
when the very category of the national is a frail and unfinished business.
At the level of literary practice, the shadow reflects Sarmiento's "literary
ambition," his "passion" as feverish writer. At the geographical level, it allows him to represent a population in the midst of defining itself against
its past. In the pages of the different editions of *Facundo*, Sarmiento visualizes a developing Argentine topography that cannot be divorced from the
literary development of the country as a textualized nation. The shadow
becomes a defining feature of a country and a literature vis-à-vis the rest of
the world. Ultimately, it reveals the strategies that can overcome the forms
of genres in order to cross native terrains, both physical and symbolic.

"A Land of Rapid Contrasts": Du Bois's Shadows

Sarmiento's *Facundo* reached a public in the United States in 1868, three years after the conclusion of the Civil War, thanks to the friendship with his devout translator Mary Mann (wife of Massachusetts educator Horace Mann). The edition prepared for North American audiences, as Ilan Stavans explains, constitutes an "abridged" version that would reinvent *Facundo* as "no longer a biography but a travel book of sorts, an exotic vista of a foreign land refined for an English-speaking audience."[30] The 1868 edition eliminates the introduction (and the 1851 prologue), as well as the last two chapters of the original *Facundo* (XIV and XV), which discuss the future of Argentina, post 1845—something that seemed now irrelevant to the successful statesman. Instead of this conclusion, Mann decides to insert a new chapter on General Fray Félix Aldao, as well as an appendix "in the form of a letter on politics and education to a U.S. senator" from Sarmiento (xxix). Stavans remarks:

> This last ingredient . . . displays the Argentine's remarkable talent for a comparative if flawed political thinking: as the United States is just recovering from a bloody Civil War and mourning the death of Abraham Lincoln, Sarmiento takes the opportunity to recycle his concepts of barbarism and civilization to explain the struggle between the Union and the Confederacy. "The greatest antagonism between the Southern States and the Northern," he ventures to write, "has come, in my judgment, from the Southern following the same plan as that of ancient society in Europe and South America, and the Northern advancing in new and peculiar ways." (xxx)

This enunciation, which rehearses Sarmiento's admiration of the expansion experienced in the United States (as we have seen in Chapter 3), becomes a textual imposition of the narratives of particular hemispheric tensions: In what appears to be one fell swoop, his divisive line between civilization and barbarism in Argentina is used to explain the Mason-Dixon divide in the United States. Sarmiento's diagnosis is a flawed reading of postwar Reconstruction in the United States, but one that does not lose the impetus of the Argentine's native and localized inspiration, and which we can say becomes an obscuring narrative palimpsest over the particular issues and failures of this period in U.S. history.

Speaking from beyond the failures of Reconstruction in 1903, in *The Souls of Black Folk* W. E. B. Du Bois sets out to redraw the map of the United States according to the problem of what he calls the "color-line." (The second chapter of *Souls*, titled "Of the Dawn of Freedom," famously begins with the sentence: "The problem of the twentieth century is the problem of the color-line—the relation of the darker to the lighter races of men in Asia and Africa, in America and the islands of the sea," 17). Similar to Sarmiento's *Facundo*, Du Bois's text represents a *trans-form*: It adheres to no specific genre, as each chapter combines a poem, a pentagram with the melody of a sorrow song, followed by a text that combines autobiography and travelogue, with a political-historical register replete with allusions and cross-references.[31] Du Bois's story of the post-Reconstruction South is told, as Wald notes, "through indirection" and "an exuberant aesthetic of uncertainty," as a narrative hybrid that seeks to subvert the predominant discourse on race at the turn of the century.[32] Interestingly, Wald reads this narrative style as "incremental" rather than "progressive," calling "attention to an author's constructing, to an *authorship* stemming unabashedly from biases and in the service of a point of view" (192). Like Sarmiento's text, to recall Carlos Alonso's reading of the Argentine's discursive "passion," *Souls of Black Folk* works in the form of a nonlinear revelation of a problem both personal and cultural.

The formal and rhetorical similarities between the two projects, however, branch away into two opposing ethical directions. If we recall Sarmiento's 1847 plea, mourning the fact that North America had been blessed by both industry and providence, whereas the abject southern continent remained its opposite, we encounter a writer who appears paralyzed at the contemplation of this dichotomy. In Du Bois's conclusion to *Souls* (the chapter titled "The Sorrow Songs"), however, we find a completely different position—what Shamoon Zamir has addressed as the author's labor "against the grain of his own dichotomization of primitive and civilized" (176). Pushing against divisive binaries (which are, again, part of the popular racial discourse of the time), Du Bois breaks open the dichotomy by questioning the racial and cultural inertia implicit in questions like the one posed by Sarmiento. He writes:

> The silently growing assumption of this age is that the probation of races is past, and that the backward races of to-day are of proven inefficiency and not worth the saving. . . . So woefully unorganized is sociological knowledge that the meaning of progress, the meaning of "swift" and "slow" in human doing, and the limits of human perfectability, are veiled, unanswered sphinxes on the shores of science. . . . Why has civilization flourished in Europe and flickered, flamed, and died in Africa? So long as the world stands meekly dumb before such questions, shall this nation proclaim its ignorance and unhallowed prejudices by denying freedom of opportunity to those who brought the Sorrow Songs to the Seats of the Mighty? (162)

The world "meekly dumb before such questions" is precisely what Du Bois seeks to counteract through a temporal and spatial narrative that accounts not only for a southern landscape, but is an appraisal of black history throughout the generations. As Wald rightly argues, Du Bois aims to account for an idea of "blackness" that "changes meaning across generational lines" as well as topography (213).

I will now focus specifically on the seventh chapter of *Souls* ("Of the Black Belt") in order to analyze how the South is defined as a "land of shadows" through this historical and spatial network. It should be noted that the shadow works on a number of spectralizing levels throughout Du Bois's text. In "Of Our Spiritual Strivings" (the first chapter), the equation of racism and spectrality, as well as the haunting quality of the "Negro problem," is introduced within the historical progress of the United States after the Civil War: "Years have passed away since then,—ten, twenty, forty; forty years of national life, forty years of renewal and development, and yet the swarthy spectre sits in its accustomed seat at the Nation's feast." He aligns this "swarthy spectre" with the "shadow of a deep disappointment" that "rests upon the Negro people" (12). This use of "shadow" language might appear allegorical and rather static (facing the past), but I want to argue that, in the chapter on the "Black Belt," Du Bois makes a very explicit cartography over the landscape of the state of Georgia that includes a geography of shadows. This map of shadows in turn introduces an answerable sphere of events, personalities, and ruins that transform both our geographic and rhetorical understandings of the U.S. South as it has been artistically received.

When Henry James writes about Charleston in *The American Scene* he makes a note of the state of writing within the unnerving presence of the "vacant cage" of the postwar South.

> How, in an at all complex, a "great political," society, can *every-thing* so have gone?—assuming indeed that, under this aegis, very much ever had come. How can everything so have gone that the only "Southern" book of any distinction published for many a year is *The Souls of Black Folk*, by that most accomplished of members of the negro race, Mr. W. E. B. Du Bois? Had the *only* focus of life then been Slavery? . . . To say "yes" seems the only way to account for the degree of vacancy, and yet even as I form that word I meet as a reproach the face of the beautiful old house . . . , whose ample spaces had so unmistakably echoed to the higher amenities that one seemed to feel the accumulated traces and tokens gradually come out of their corners like blest objects taken one by one from a reliquary worn with much handling. (418)

The restless analyst is here confronted with the conflicting views of a landscape as an echo of "political" and ethical failure, and as "reliquary." James is here wondering, and unable to fully discern, *how* one can possibly look at the Southern scene in 1904, how one can even *begin* to read the impressions of absence that Charleston provides. In his restless analysis seeking to *read* the signs of the present as best as possible, James recognizes in Du Bois a singular voice emerging from a Southern scene that is now full of echoes of days past. Like James in *The American Scene*, in *Souls of Black Folk* Du Bois gives his readers a series of visualizations of a landscape and geography that have undergone dramatic transformations in less than half a century. Unlike James, Du Bois goes further in making each narrative impression of the explored sites an appellation for social reform.

Du Bois's text shares with *The American Scene* what he calls the "perspective of the car-window sociologist." Whereas James rides in all the luxury that the Pullman has to offer, Du Bois invites his reader to a different passenger situation.

> But we must hasten on our journey. . . . If you wish to ride with me you must come into the "Jim Crow Car." There will be no objection,—already four other white men, and a little white girl with her nurse, are in there. Usually the races are mixed in there; but the white coach is all white. Of course this car is not so good as the other, but it is fairly clean and comfortable. The discomfort lies chiefly in the hearts of those four black men yonder—and in mine. (76)

This direct address to the audience—simultaneously a persuasion to a reader of any race and a warning to his white readers—establishes the experience of this particular journey into Georgia's Black Belt as one in which *he* is the tour-guide whose audience will see specifically what he wants them to see, and listen to the story he wants to tell. For Du Bois's journey into the area around counties such as Albany and Dougherty in southern Georgia in July conjures up a geohistory of family names, old plantations, "luxuriant" locations as well as a land in ruin.

In *Souls*, after Du Bois has succinctly stated that the problem of the United States in 1903 is that of the "color-line," he also explicitly locates the "center of the Negro problem" within the specific radius of the land southwest of Atlanta: "And there, not far from where Sam Hose was crucified, you may stand on a spot which is to-day the center of the Negro problem,—the center of those nine million men who are America's dark heritage from slavery and the slave trade" (75). Here the meaning of "spot" as a conventional way to address a location is transformed into geopolitical burden: The "spot" becomes a site that remembers the specific lynching of Sam Hose in 1899, and beyond that, the immense history of the horror of slavery, where in 1800 there were "a million Negroes among its citizens" (75). The "rumbl[ing] south in quite a business-like way" (76) with Du Bois's narrator as a guide thus transforms the reader's idea of traveling and sightseeing into geohistorical scrutiny, where sites are indeed all too answerable if one only observes them the way in which he directs us.

"Of the Black Belt" travels from statistics, to personal histories, to landscape description rather seamlessly, but in a way in which the reader is never lulled into harmony with the scenery. In the passage where Du Bois specifically addresses this area as a "land of shadows," the reader is shocked into attentiveness after a rich description of the country as seen from the "Jim Crow car" window begins to make way for a view of the "darker" world of the Black Belt.

> The bare red clay and pines of Northern Georgia begin to disappear, and in their place appears a rich rolling land, luxuriant, and here and there well tilled. . . . Below Macon the world grows darker; for now we approach the Black Belt,—that strange land of shadows, at which even slaves paled in the past, and whence come now only faint and half-intelligible murmurs to the world beyond. (76)

The visions of the landscape turned "darker" carry the urgency of a multiplicity of meanings. Not only does the world grow darker in the views of a black population, but there is also a darkness in the way that the landscape succeeded in "paling" the slaves of the past. This area below Macon is a landscape that forgets, marked by a diffusion of the actualities of slavery that are now present, before the reader's eyes, in a landscape marked by a complicated failure. Here, Du Bois uses the image of the "veil" throughout the body of *Souls* as a dramatic complement to the "color-line," a texture that addresses the division between black and white in the United States. Zamir and Wald, among others, have read the veil as the hindering racial division—the idea of *difference* imposed by the white race—which, when lifted, reveals a self-reflection, a mirror.[33] In "Of the Black Belt," Du Bois's narrator travels within and through the veil and discovers shadows. This dramatization of the unveiling that reveals a plot of shadows is Du Bois's revision of a map containing state boundaries and the now-defunct Mason-Dixon line, which he replaces with the more nuanced color line. Thus, although the veil reveals the larger problem of race and consciousness, the shadow actually works to *emplace and emplot* that historical-racial map that is obscured by the "paling" and haunted landscape.

Du Bois's revised topography of shadows begins to home in on a historical narrative of the observed landscape that contains specific names of the subjectivities that have worked to emanate the shadow-lands. While traveling through the valley of the Flint river, "We passed the scattered box-like cabins of the brick-yard hands . . . and were soon in the open country, and on the confines of the great plantations of other days."

> There is the "Joe Fields place"; a rough old fellow was he, and had killed many a "nigger" in his day. Twelve miles his plantation used to run,—a regular barony. It is nearly all gone now; only straggling bits belong to the family, and the rest has passed to Jews and Negroes. Even the bits which are left are heavily mortgaged, and, like the rest of the land, tilled by tenants. (78)

Within this site that belonged to Joe Fields the narrator sees the house belonging to Benton, the black man who now manages the place. "He might be well-to-do, they say; but he carouses too much in Albany. And the half-desolate spirit of neglect born out of the very soil seems to have settled on these acres," writes Du Bois. "In times past there were cotton-gins and machinery here; but they have rotted away" (78). The shadows thus come to explicitly form a historical web of tragedies within this specific "spot" within the Black Belt: a past history of murder and the violence of slavery, a contemporary situation of "heavily mortgaged" land become ruin, and suffering tenant families riddled with heavy drinking and illiteracy. It is a landscape that is painfully reflective of a dialogue between a past of abusive glory and wealth, and a present marked by stagnation. "This, then, is the Cotton Kingdom," continues the narrator, "the shadow of a marvelous dream" (79).

Strange meanings are implicit within these shadow plots of the Black Belt. It is in Dougherty County (at the "west end of the Black Belt"), for example, that Du Bois's narrator discovers "the place of the Fence in civilization" (80).

> There is little beauty in this region, only a sort of crude abandon that suggests power,—a naked grandeur, as it were. The houses are bare and straight; there are no hammocks or easy-chairs, and few flowers. So when, as here at Rawdon's, one sees a vine clinging to a little porch, and home-like windows peeping over the fences, one takes a long breath. I think I never before quite realized the place of the Fence in civilization. This is the Land of the Unfenced, where crouch on either hand scores of ugly one-room cabins, cheerless and dirty. Here lies the Negro problem in its naked dirt and penury. And here are no fences. (80)

Here, the "naked grandeur" is reminiscent of Henry James's images of the "vacant cage" and "reliquary" of the southern scene: They are narrative visions of a landscape that has been cataclysmically hollowed by years of postbellum abandon. This neglect carries varying meanings, however: The landscape of decay here echoes "the silently growing assumption of this age . . . that the probation of races is past, and that the backward races of to-day are of proven inefficiency and not worth the saving" (162). What Du Bois achieves, through his meticulous description of the journey into these counties in Georgia, is to inflect this duality of silent landscape and silent "assumption" with the urgency of the *problem*. What is more, by setting the stage in this dual manner, he reworks the idea of the passivity of shadows into an emplacement of the human question that directly stares the observer in the face. Another word that appears to acquire a different and ominous meaning in this chapter is "society." In Dougherty, Du Bois enters a school-house, containing "the ruins of a stove" and a "dim blackboard." "Back of the schoolhouse," he writes, "is a lodgehouse two stories high and not quite finished. Societies meet there,—societies 'to care for the sick and bury the dead'; and these societies grow and flourish" (80). His repeated use of the word "societies" in the space of a single sentence represents a morbid play on the idea of cohesive groups of people joined by a particular interest: Here in the land of shadows, the one cohesive interest is that of illness and death.[34]

The journey into this answerable landscape of shadows—reverberated by the musical quotations that open all the chapters in *Souls*—offers a choir of voices and anecdotes that speak from within the shadows. "'This land was a little Hell,' said a ragged, brown, and grave-faced man to me. We were seated near a roadside blacksmith-shop, and behind was the bare ruin of some master's home." At this point, Du Bois remarkably portrays the voice speaking from the ruin, in what is an intimate conversation—the man said to "*me*." "I've seen niggers drop dead in the furrow, but they were kicked aside, and the plough never stopped. And down in the guardhouse, there's where the blood ran" (82). The unnamed voice discloses a testimony that connects the time when the "plough never stopped" despite the death of a man, with the scene of ruin witnessed in *Souls'* present. This narration connects scenes of past and present with the flowing image of running "blood"—it is the visualization of a story that is ongoing and disturbingly open. After this meeting, the visitors continue moving in what becomes scene after scene of ruins, and the urgent problem of a landscape actively haunted by the past.

> So we ride on, past phantom gates and falling homes,—past the once flourishing farms of the Smiths, the Gandys, and the Lagores,—and find all dilapidated and half ruined, even there where a solitary white woman, a relic of other days, sits alone in state among miles of Negroes and rides to town in her ancient coach each day. (83)

This dynamic scene of "riding on" opposes the dynamism of the visitors' moving car with the decaying, and regressive, scenery of the ruined landscape. The white woman in her "ancient coach" is a solitary, and almost perverse, "relic" of a past moment of oppression, where the single white figure stands among its slaves—that is nevertheless disturbingly current: The "miles of Negroes" are there.

"It is a land of rapid contrasts and of curiously mingled hope and pain," writes Du Bois (83). The "rapid contrasts" are there in the ruins, in the rolling landscape that turns barren, and even in the "pretty blue-eyed quadroon" the narrator meets after making this observation, herself "curiously mingled." Whereas Henry James sought to formulate the *impression* of the simultaneity of landscapes within the American scene, Du Bois poses as a narrator coming from *within*, who reaches for a new map of shadows that, far from providing that ultimate *conclusion* that James never attempts, nevertheless directs the reader to the site of the problem. Du Bois thus involves us in the urgent and indirect narrative of his own version of "restless analysis."

The impression in Du Bois moves beyond the realm of the aesthetic to *dwell*, to remain and to reflect, on the multiple historical and cultural meanings of living in a "land of shadows." Significantly, these shadows do not refer the reader back to a world of metaphor, and they certainly do not ask for us to allegorize them. Instead, the shadows are grounded in a material history of the evils of poverty, high mortgages, and ruin that actively and materially haunts the Black Belt. "Only black tenants can stand such a system, and they only because they must," Du Bois explains (78). In *Souls of Black Folk*, the author ponders and makes the reader reflect on the ways in which seeing a landscape, experiencing it through observation, is contingent upon a *telling* of that landscape. Within these urgent shadows, Du Bois's wonder—which leads him to exclaim, "How curious a land is this,—how full of untold story" (81)—situates the possibilities for answerability. The act of witnessing a "strange land of shadows" begins to place a map of voices and landscapes that harbor an ongoing and urgent history—landscapes that point to that "spot" where the "rapid contrasts" can enunciate a haunted living story. In signaling these "contrasts" within the single region of the Black Belt, Du Bois is also inviting his readers and traveling companions to understand the wider U.S. landscape in terms of the dissonant, yet simulataneous, versions of modernity that it harbors.

Shadow Play and Empire

It is when we read texts such as *Facundo* and *Souls of Black Folk* that we wonder how Marx's ideas of the Americas (and of the ghosts of the Americas) would have evolved, had he been haunted with a proleptic spell that allowed him to look into the development of colonialism and empire at the end of the nineteenth and beginning of the twentieth centuries. For in the invocations of these shadows we have just seen—pronounced so differently, and to tell such different histories as the ones Sarmiento and Du Bois felt compelled to tell—we find two continents that, far from awaiting their moment of haunting, have their very urgent and specific "spirits of the old," and landscapes whose "many points" contain their particular conflicts between pasts, ongoing presents, and open futures.

Speaking to the American Negro Academy in 1900, a moment in history when U.S. imperialism is in full swing, Du Bois begins to see the problem of the color line "belt[ing] the world."[35] His idea of the color line in the U.S. South is simultaneously informed by the question of the people caught in the new webs of U.S. empire after the Spanish-American War. He writes:

> Most significant of all at this period is the fact that the colored population of our land is, through the new imperial policy, about to be doubled by our own ownership of Porto Rico, and Hawaii, our protectorate of Cuba, and conquest of the Philippines. This is for us and for the nation the greatest event since the Civil War and demands attention and action on our part. What is to be our attitude toward these new lands and toward the masses of dark men and women who inhabit them? (77)

In this segment of his speech, Du Bois crafts a conception of how the color line is reconceived everywhere that cataclysmic "events" result in the tragic unraveling of relationships between people of different races. He warns of the contingent problem of ethnic and racial divisions implicit in the continued push toward imperial expansion, propelled primarily by the desire for economic and military growth. Seen this way, the shadowlands evidenced within the Black Belt in *Souls* run the risk of spreading across the map of an expanding U.S. empire.

As the events of history continue to unravel, and Du Bois is a witness to them, both the "belt" of the color line and the capaciousness of the veil continue to expand. In one of his later texts, *Darkwater: Voices from within the Veil* (1920), which Amy Kaplan describes as "an internationalist revision of *Souls*,"[36] it is the First World War that leads Du Bois to contemplate an even larger map of the globe. He incisively criticizes the idea of a European War, when what he sees is a history of conflict that spreads its roots far into the reaches of a colonial map stretching into Africa, Asia, and the Middle East. Du Bois contemplates the idea of wars being fought equally and unequally, and differentiates between an idea of a European war where "under essentially equal conditions, equal armaments, and equal waste of wealth, white men are fighting white men," and the imperial wars elsewhere: "Think of the wars through which we have lived in the last decade:

in German Africa, in British Nigeria, in French and Spanish Morocco, in China, in Persia, in the Balkans, in Tripoli, in Mexico, and in a dozen lesser places—were not these horrible too?"[37]

To speak of tragic events and shadows from within is to enunciate a geography that expels amnesia. And, to visualize and reflect upon a transnational geography of shadows as cohabiting alongside the monumental, imperial sites of twentieth-century modernity is a step toward recognition of the problems that this modernity continues to gather. Du Bois's cosmopolitanism, expressed in the quote above, directs the observer of world events to the "horrible" conflicts that span a globe, but that are obscured by that enormous veil that favors a set of stories of those in power, over the stories of populations marked by difference and disempowerment. By appropriating the language used to describe the European war as "horrible," and transferring it to another context, he is attempting to open that wound of body and of narrative to include not just a small part of the world, but the *whole* of the world, which is now marked by the ubiquity of the multiple "contrasts" spurred by the movements of colonial powers. In *Souls*, Du Bois is able to make that regional wound that is home—the land of shadows, the world as it is on that *other* side of the color line in the specific site of the Black Belt—an answerable site. In the Black Belt, Du Bois needs only to look around him to see a landscape that is presently haunted, and a population that is made ghostly by a wider social and political nexus of dispossession. This is a place where haunting does not mean fright and abstract "horror." It is rather a site that, with its sights of wearied life, incites the realization that the U.S. is a country whose bloodiest conflict up to that point has brought no resolution to the problem of reconciling ethnic, social, and cultural difference. The Black Belt is the home of racial and cultural others that the powerful occlude or dismiss as being outside of the national consciousness—a landscape that is nevertheless a crucial player in the unfolding story of U.S. modernity. In this region, as in the world geographies of neocolonialism in the early twentieth century, Du Bois implores us to look out for the ways in which inherited pasts continue to run into local futures and into the "many points" of a globe covered in myriad shadowlands with important stories that await their ethical resolutions.

Epilogue

One of the story lines in Cormac McCarthy's *No Country for Old Men* narrates the apparitions of an elusive and mortifying hitman named Anton Chigurh, who roams the area around the Texas-Mexico border. Chigurh was after a simple man named Llewelyn Moss, who happened upon a drug crime scene while out hunting in the desert, and who made the unwise decision to take a satchel full of money from one of the dead bodies he found. Chigurh, as the reader comes to discover, is no ordinary hitman, but a unique form of morality, with a worldview onto his own. After murdering Moss, Chigurh's last crime before he disappears is the murder of Carla, Moss's wife. Before he shoots her, he explains to the desperate woman how there can be only one outcome to their meeting, because he is the kind of person who has "only one way to live." "You can see what a problem that must be for [people]," he says. "How to prevail over that which you refuse to acknowledge the existence of."[1] The strangeness of Chigurh's fatal enunciation is made even more puzzling by this description of who he is as that which others "refuse to acknowledge." When, toward the end of the novel, Ed Tom Bell (the sheriff who has been unable to catch Chigurh) tells a county prosecutor that the hitman is "pretty much a ghost," the reader follows Bell in his realization that any attempt to know this ghost will be futile. Like Bell, we realize that Chigurh is an excess of this tale—the question that people "may very well not be equal to" (299).

Throughout *No Country for Old Men*, Chigurh insists on describing himself as a problem that is both unexpected and incommensurable. Having finally recognized this, Bell calls that problem "a ghost." As readers of McCarthy's text, we are invited to participate in the observation of this limit of perception. Like Bell, we remain troubled by Chigurh's haunting, which here comes to mean an incompleteness of understanding. The book closed, we continue to ask what McCarthy is doing by forcing us to reckon with this problem and this ghost, as well as this depiction of a landscape we think we know.

Chigurh's apparitions throughout the complex area of the border serve only to make him a transnational conundrum, a problem within a landscape with a haunted past and ongoing present.[2] The U.S.-Mexico border has been and is the locus of perhaps the darkest episodes of what we call "hemispheric American relations." Extrapolating somewhat, we could well say that, like Chigurh, this border is the event and object that citizens of the Americas cannot equal. It is the site that waits to be made answerable, where the limits of American imagined communities are jealously guarded and violently enforced. Not surprisingly, academic considerations within this particular area of study continuously return to that open and divisive wound (to recall Gloria Anzaldúa). Critics from Amy Kaplan to José David Saldívar have maintained that the border as symbol and geography has been essential in the move toward a transnationalization of American studies.[3] This site is thus not only the exacerbation of the question of transnationalism in the Americas. It is also the haunted and haunting core where American cultures come to terms with the border as a multiplication of difference.

Despite this traumatic geography that spells out an impasse for the Americas, we should be careful not to allow a crippling conception of difference to inform our readings of literature from the hemisphere. There are several ways in which such readings that highlight divergence can be detrimental. In the past decades, critics have at times fetishized the production of their cultural others, and their contributions have run the danger of turning their objects of study into sublime figures of a dehistoricized, alternative modernity. Although "alternative" may be a useful term that describes, for example, the redemptions Western readers find in the works emerging from different cultural quarters, it should not cloud our understanding of the commonalities to be found when studying global modernities. In recent years, scholars of transnational American studies (many of whom I have referred to throughout this book) have demonstrated the innovative ways in which the Americas can be brought together in productive conversations without occluding the features that make each culture, each language, and each text distinct.

In my own discussion, I hope to have suggested another way in which we can dynamically conduct comparative readings of literature and film from the Americas. "Dynamic" may perhaps sound like an oxymoron here, given that the subjects of this study are ghosts and haunting. But, rather than reading them as reflections of the dead and extinct, we have been seeing how the appearance of these figures and these events in literary and cinematic texts announce a questioning about our present and future perceptions of landscapes that are common to a transnational American experience. In aligning haunting with the concept of simultaneity, I have diversified the temporality and the location of the ghost, shifting the focus of inquiry by reading it as an active questioning of the present. This way, we can appreciate how ghosts in literary and cinematic texts reflect a *working through* of the doubts that the present and future inspire. As I have been arguing throughout *Ghost-Watching American Modernity*, the imagination of haunting traverses the changing landscapes within and beyond preconceived national boundaries. It wonders about the socializations between the familiar and unfamiliar histories of subjects and insists on a consideration of the possible afterlives of these very socializations.

By moving beyond the kinds of theoretical paradigms that are liable to reduce haunting to a generalizable psychic symptom, I have championed a more historically attuned investigation that considers it in relation to geography instead of the unconscious. Rather than privileging a rehearsed psychoanalytic framework to study the emergence of haunting on the page or the screen, which runs the risk of rendering haunting interiorized and ultimately diagnosable, I have made the (perhaps risky) effort to read haunting not just as the portrait of a ghost's apparition, but as the emergence of a question that is inspired by a landscape in flux. In this sense, haunting signifies more than the representation of revenance, but a larger, more complex ethical question of artistic rendition—of how the creative imagination works with a potential and incomplete perception of American modernity.

This open view, as it were, also allows us to think of haunting beyond a single literary form. As I have shown, our analysis of modern hemispheric American haunting is enriched by an exploration of its occurrence throughout texts that range from journalism and chronicle writing to the novel. We have also seen how, within haunted texts, ghosts have a way of transcending the conventions of genre. Ghosts are not simply symptoms of a genre or declarations that what we are reading is a specific category of storytelling. Their noncomformity begs us to read their haunting in a different way. Although calling a text "gothic" or "magical real" may prepare us for the appearance of a ghost within a text, it is nevertheless important to be unprepared—to allow the text a certain newness by reading against the grain, to conceive of reading as an experience of unknowability (as Derek Attridge has shown). This unknowability, however, should not be confused with what some have called the "mystification" of a text, or types of texts. However bewildering a text may be, to see in mystification a text's only purpose is to run the risk of paralyzing it, or of allowing it to take off into an interpretive zone that is disengaged from the more challenging question of how we relate evolving notions of a landscape's history and politics to matters concerning the aesthetic forms by which that evolution is evoked.

Seeing how haunting works within the American hemisphere, and in the landscapes that generate different, and often opposing, visions of community within a given moment and place, is to analyze the evolution of the intertwined narratives of the self, the group, and the imagination of their history and progress. The intersections of haunting, place, and community within a reading of these histories of imaginations and imaginations of history necessarily engage in the dynamics of ethnic relations within a specific site. They allow us to see how ethics and space intersect within national fictions and how, in turn, the very idea of nation is problematized in a text. To understand haunted imaginaries as enunciations of the questions that arise out of an architectonics of landscape, history, and aesthetics, represents an acknowledgment of the complexity inherent in how we make sense of American modernity. Reading haunting and transnationalism together can ultimately serve to illuminate the problems inherent in reading the fluctuations of subjects across a global community continuously debating ideas of difference and the universal.

Although my readings of landscape, haunting, and the hemispheric imagination are necessarily discrete exercises in seeing how artists think through their present (and how they haunt the presents of those who read their texts), they open up to wider considerations of how impressions of the local begin to pronounce the disquietudes of the transnational and the transhistoric. Although my main focus has not been contemporary works, the authors studied nevertheless stand at the threshold of our current historical period in which so much knowledge is on offer at both the local and global level. Yet this is shadowed by a tendency toward historical amnesia as well as a return to what Paul Gilroy criticizes as the assertion of the "untranslatability" between and among cultures.[4] These problems pronounce the limitations we continue to face as we struggle to apprehend the simultaneities of our global landscapes. As I have tried to demonstrate throughout *Ghost-Watching American Modernity*, to read for haunting— and to watch for ghosts—means not just to explore enunciations of enclosed grief and repetitious mourning. It is to acknowledge that the things we "may very well not be equal to" demand our attention just the same.

Notes

Introduction

1. Jane Creighton, "Bierce, Fuentes, and the Critique of Reading: A Study of Carlos Fuentes's *The Old Gringo*," *South Central Review* 9, no. 2 (1992): 68.

2. Ambrose Bierce, "War Topics" (Sunday, May 29, 1898), in Bierce, *Skepticism and Dissent: Selected Journalism from 1898–1901*, ed. Lawrence I. Berkove (Ann Arbor, MI: Delmas, 1980), 39.

3. Ambrose Bierce, "The Boarded Window," in *The Complete Short Stories of Ambrose Bierce* (Lincoln: University of Nebraska Press, 1984), 227.

4. Bridget M. Marshall, "Teaching 'The Boarded Window,'" *Ambrose Bierce Project Journal* 4, no. 1 (2008), http://www.ambrosebierce.org/journal4marshall.html#note4.

5. Carlos Fuentes, *El gringo viejo* (1985; Mexico: Fondo de Cultura Económica, 1992), 19. English version: Carlos Fuentes, *The Old Gringo*, trans. Margaret Sayers Peden and Carlos Fuentes (London: André Deutsch, 1986), 11.

6. In the very first paragraph of Faulkner's novel, Miss Rosa Coldfield sits in front of Quentin Compson, "talking in that grim haggard amazed voice until at last listening would renege and hearing-sense self-confound and the long-dead object of her impotent yet indomitable frustration would appear, as though by outraged recapitulations evoked, quiet inattentive and harmless, out of the biding and dreamy and victorious dust." William Faulkner, *Absalom, Absalom!* (New York: Vintage International, 1990), 3–4.

7. "One might enumerate the items of high civilization, as it exists in other countries, which are absent from the texture of American life, until it should become a wonder to know what was left. No State, in the European sense of the word, and indeed barely a specific national name. No sovereign, no court, no personal loyalty, no aristocracy, no church, no clergy, no army, no diplomatic service, no country gentlemen, no palaces, no castles, nor manors, nor old country houses, nor parsonages, nor thatched cottages nor ivied ruins; no cathedrals, nor abbeys, nor little Norman churches; no great Universities nor public schools—no Oxford, nor Eton, nor Harrow;

no literature, no novels, no museums, no pictures, no political society, no sporting class—no Epsom nor Ascot! Some such list as that might be drawn up of the absent things in American life—especially in the American life of forty years ago, the effect of which, upon an English or a French imagination, would probably as a general thing be appalling." Henry James, *Hawthorne* (Ithaca, NY: Cornell University Press, 1997), 35.

8. Alexander Nemerov, "Seeing Ghosts: *The Turn of the Screw* and Art History," in *What Is Research in the Visual Arts?: Obsession, Archive, Encounter,* ed. Michael Ann Holly and Marquard Smith (Williamstown, MA: Clark Art Institute, 2009), 26.

9. In an unfinished article on simultaneity in the work of Heinrich von Kleist ("Simultaneity: A Narrative Figure in Kleist," *MLN* 121, no. 3 (2006): 514–21), Bianca Theisen explains the paradoxes behind Aristotle's and Zeno's conceptions of space and time to arrive at a reading of Kleist's negotiation of simultaneous events, through his use of the "eben-als" ("just when") grammatical construction, and the "Augenblick" ("instant," or "blink of an eye"). She explains that although "plot structure sequentializes events, hierarchizing them and subjecting them to chronology, the narrative principle of simultaneity defies any transitions and offers erratic contrasts instead" (516). In this suggestive argument, Theisen notes how the logic of "earlier" and "later" renders events visible given a certain sequentiality of movement, whereas the representation of the simultaneous renders present events, which often remain invisible for the sake of representing a single event or "now," *visible.* Closer to my own focus on haunted matters, in her essay "Spectrality's Secret Sharers," Gauri Viswanathan historicizes the relationship between simultaneity and the occult in spiritualistic practices of the late nineteenth century. She compellingly argues how Madame Blavatsky and Colonel Olcott's theosophical society, which had its headquarters in Madras, India, opened the possibility of constructing relationships based on "secrecy and silence" that "offered alternative possibilities for imagining colonial relations outside a formal hierarchical framework" (136). Viswanathan understands this form of the occult as "simultaneous experience," given that it involves a search for the "hidden or repressed histories that dislocate the 'local' as the time and place of immediate experience" (136, 137). Gauri Viswanathan, "Spectrality's Secret Sharers: Occultism as (Post)colonial Affect," in *Beyond the Black Atlantic: Relocating Modernization and Technology,* ed. Walter Goebel and Saskia Schabio (Oxford: Routledge, 2006), 135–45.

10. Kevin Lynch, *The Image of the City* (Cambridge, MA: MIT Press, 1960), 12.

11. Ambrose Bierce, *The Enlarged Devil's Dictionary* (London: Victor Gollancz, 1967), 113.

12. Roger Luckhurst, "The Contemporary London Gothic and the Limits of the 'Spectral Turn,'" *Textual Practice* 16, no. 3 (2002): 535.

13. Andrew Thacker, "The Idea of a Critical Literary Geography," *New Formations* 57 (Winter 2005/2006): 62.

14. Russ Castronovo and Susan Gillman, *States of Emergency: The Object of American Studies* (Chapel Hill: University of North Carolina Press, 2009), 10.

15. Deborah Cohn, *History and Memory in the Two Souths: Recent Southern and Spanish American Fiction* (Nashville: Vanderbilt University Press, 1999), 42.

16. Anita Patterson, *Race, American Literature, and Transnational Modernisms* (Cambridge: Cambridge University Press, 2008).

17. Laura Lomas, *Translating Empire: José Martí, Migrant Latino Subjects, and American Modernities* (Durham, NC: Duke University Press, 2008), 11.

18. I take the qualifier from Julio Prieto, whose book *Desencuadernados* (2002) is quoted in Chapter 3.

19. Anna Brickhouse, *Transamerican Literary Relations and the Nineteenth-Century Public Sphere* (Cambridge: Cambridge University Press, 2009), 9.

20. Caroline Levander and Robert S. Levine, eds., *Hemispheric American Studies* (New Brunswick, NJ: Rutgers University Press, 2008), 2.

21. This connects Zamora's work in *The Usable Past: The Imagination of History in Recent Fiction of the Americas* (Cambridge: Cambridge University Press, 1997) to that of Renée L. Bergland, author of *The National Uncanny: Indian Ghosts and American Subjects* (Hanover, NH: Dartmouth College/University Press of New England, 2000). Bergland traces the "obsession" of U.S. literature with Indian ghosts and the return of the repressed memory of the crimes against the Indian nation throughout the course of the country's history.

22. Jesse Alemán, "The Other Country: Mexico, the United States, and the Gothic History of Conquest," in *Hemispheric American Studies*, ed. Levander and Levine, 75–95.

23. Similarly to Alemán, in a special edition on the Americas edited by Lois Parkinson Zamora and Silvia Spitta, Enrique Dussel likens the Hispanic world to "a phantom, a specter that roams around in 'exteriority' but has recently begun showing itself with a new face." Enrique Dussel, "'Being-in-the-World-*Hispanically*': A World on the Border of Many Worlds," *Comparative Literature* 61, no. 3 (2009): 262.

24. See Introduction to *Popular Ghosts: The Haunted Spaces of Everyday Culture*, ed. María del Pilar Blanco and Esther Peeren (New York: Continuum, 2010), ix–xxiv.

25. I am thinking of the influential collection that has helped shape a transnational canon for American studies, *José Martí's "Our America": From National to Hemispheric Cultural Studies*, ed. Jeffrey Belnap and Raúl Fernández (Durham, NC: Duke University Press, 1998).

26. Andreas Huyssen, *Present Pasts: Urban Palimpsests and the Politics of Memory* (Stanford, CA: Stanford University Press, 2003), 8.

27. Avery Gordon, *Ghostly Matters: Haunting and the Sociological Imagination* (Minneapolis: University of Minnesota Press, 1997).

28. Colin Davis, "Hauntology, Spectres, and Phantoms," *French Studies* 59, no. 3 (2005): 373.

29. Dorothy E. Smith, "Review of *Ghostly Matters*," *Contemporary Sociology* 28, no. 1 (1999): 120.

30. Judith Richardson, *Possessions: The History and Uses of Haunting in the Hudson Valley* (Cambridge, MA: Harvard University Press, 2003), 4.

31. Ibid., 4.

32. Jacques Derrida, "The Law of Genre," trans. Avital Ronell, *Critical Inquiry* 7, no. 1 (1980): 64.

33. Teresa Goddu, *Gothic America: Narrative, History, and Nation* (New York: Columbia University Press, 1997), 5.

34. A successful interpretation of the ghost as chronotopic motif is Esther Peeren's "The Ghost as a Gendered Chronotope," in *Ghosts, Stories, Histories: Ghost Stories and Alternative Histories*, ed. Sladja Blazan (Newcastle: Cambridge Scholars Publishing, 2007), 81–96.

35. Janice Best, "The Chronotope and the Generation of Meaning in Novels and Paintings," *Criticism* 36, no. 2 (1994): 292.

36. Graham Pechey, *Mikhail Bakhtin: The Word in the World* (London: Routledge, 2007), 186.

37. M. M. Bakhtin, *Art and Answerability: Early Philosophical Essays by M. M. Bakhtin* (Austin: University of Texas Press, 1990), 1–2.

38. Bakhtin writes: "For myself, none of my lived experiences and strivings can recede into the absolute past, into the past of meaning, which is detached and sheltered from the future, i.e., justified and consummated independently of the future. For, insofar as I find precisely *myself* in a given lived experience, . . . as long as I am the one living in it, it does not yet exist in full" (ibid., 117.)

39. M. M. Bakhtin, *Toward a Philosophy of the Act*, trans. Vadim Liapunov (Austin: University of Texas Press, 1993), 45.

40. Henri Bergson, "Concerning the Nature of Time," in *Duration and Simultaneity: Bergson and the Einsteinian Universe*, ed. Robin Durie (1922; Manchester: Clinamen Press, 1999), 33.

1 / Unsolving Hemispheric Mystery

1. See Philip Weinstein, "Cant Matter/Must Matter: Setting Up the Loom in Faulknerian and Postcolonial Fiction," in *Look Away: The U.S. South in New World Studies*, ed. Jon Smith and Deborah Cohn (Durham, NC: Duke University Press, 2004), 355–82. The uncanny (that which was "hidden" and suddenly "comes to light") represents the major theory used to explain haunting in literary criticism. Among Freud's examples of the uncanny is the famous anecdote of the double that turns out to be his mirror image. As Priscilla Wald explains in *Constituting Americans* (1993; Durham, NC: Duke University Press, 1995), Freud, in admitting the "discomfort" produced by his initial perception of his mirror image, contradicts his earlier point about the uncanny being done away with when "primitive" beliefs are given up. Wald uses this discomfort to write about the anxiety surrounding Americans' "experience of the self" in narratives of identity in the nineteenth century. In readings of haunting such as Lois Parkinson Zamora's *The Usable Past: The Idea of History in Modern U.S. and Latin American Fiction* (Cambridge: Cambridge University Press, 1997), which I will discuss at length, the ghost incites a reading of selfhood in the American hemisphere. See also Renée Bergland's *The National Uncanny: Indian Ghosts and American Subjects* (Hanover, MA: University Press of New England, 2000), where she discusses haunting as "subjective experience" in historical and political narratives during the era of national constitution in the United States (8). For her part, Avery Gordon begins *Ghostly Matters: Haunting and the Sociological Imagination* (Minneapolis: University of Minnesota Press, 1997) with a discussion of the virtues and limitations of Freud's essay "The Uncanny." She argues that something about uncanny experiences troubles Freud, because many of them cannot be traced back to infantile psychic desires, and are instead based on a material "reality testing" (which Freud will try to cast off as superstition in the essay, although not successfully).

2. Taken from "The Catholic Novelist in the South" (1963), where O'Connor expands on the themes she touched on in "The Grotesque in Southern Fiction," in Flannery O'Connor, *Collected Works* (New York: Library of America, 1988), 861.

3. Tzvetan Todorov's structuralist model of the fantastic in literature sets an organization of genres according to temporalities in the events of the unexpected in the action of a piece of literature: "The marvelous corresponds to an unknown phenomenon, never seen as yet, still to come—hence to a future; in the uncanny, on the other hand,

we refer the inexplicable to known facts, to a previous experience, and thereby to the past. As for the fantastic itself, the hesitation which characterizes it cannot be situated, by and large, except in the present," in Tzvetan Todorov, *The Fantastic: A Structuralist Approach to a Literary Genre* (Ithaca, NY: Cornell University Press, 1975), 42. The rigidity of Todorov's approach to the "unbelievable" is something I will take up later in this chapter, but I offer it here as one example of how this effect of the unexpected in a literary text has been encased within a rather tight-fitting label.

4. The term is traced back to Franz Roh's 1925 essay "Post-Expressionism, Magical Realism" [*Nach Expressionismus, Magischer Realismus: Probleme der neusten Europäischer Malerei*].

5. "De lo real maravillosamente americano," in Alejo Carpentier, *Tientos y diferencias* (Mexico City: Universidad Autónoma de México, 1964), 135. Translation by Tanya Huntington and Lois Parkinson Zamora in *Magical Realism: Theory, History, Community*, ed. Lois Parkinson Zamora and Wendy B. Faris (1995; Durham, NC: Duke University Press, 2000), 88.

6. Roberto González Echevarría, *Alejo Carpentier: The Pilgrim at Home* (1977; Austin: University of Texas Press, 1990), 99.

7. Wendy Faris and Lois Parkinson Zamora, Introduction to *Magical Realism*, ed. Zamora and Faris: "Improbable juxtapositions and marvelous mixtures exist by virtue of Latin America's varied history, geography, demography, and politics—not by manifesto," 75.

8. Roberto González Echevarría writes that Carpentier's attack on Surrealism is based on the movement's attempt "to rule as a universal ethic and aesthetic," which was the "basis for [Carpentier's] opposing the vibrant rural world of Latin America to the limp and inanimate urban constructs of Surrealism" (*Alejo Carpentier*, 125). Chris Bongie expands on this point in his *Islands and Exiles* (Stanford, CA: Stanford University Press, 1998), where he explains that the "epiphanies of the Caribbean's marvelous reality take two apparently contradictory forms: the revelation, on the one hand, of America's still virginal *nature*, and, on the other, of its provocatively mixed *culture*," 5.

9. For a survey on the significance of faith in transnational magical realism, see Christopher Warnes, "Naturalization of the Supernatural: Faith, Irreverence, and Magical Realism," *Literature Compass* 2, no. 1 (2005): 1–16.

10. In O'Connor, *Collected Works*, 804.

11. Letter to "Miss A.," September 6, 1955, in O'Connor, *Collected Works*, 952.

12. De Torre defines the cosmopolitan writer in terms of his ability to exist simultaneously in diverse locations and to perceive different environments as "natural": "Su espíritu se halla enfocado 'naturalmente' sobre varios horizontes, dado el radio de ideas y de figuras en que se mueve ["His spirit focuses 'naturally' over various horizons"]. (Guillermo De Torre, *Literaturas europeas de vanguardia* [Madrid: Rafael Caro Raggio, 1925], 369). As I discuss further in this chapter, Carpentier's idea of the faithful perception of the marvelous real is dependent on a certain international movement that can be interpreted alongside de Torre's description of the privileged position of the cosmopolitan writer.

13. Stephanie Merrim, "Wonder and the Wounds of Southern Histories," in *Look Away!*, ed. Smith and Cohn, 323.

14. Another difference between O'Connor and Carpentier, is the former's closer cultural connection to the "gothic" conventions of self-reflexivity, which also separate her work from Carpentier's project. Her characters are beings attempting to discover

the "Truth" in a painful journey to and through faith, usually a Southern Christian faith.

15. González Echevarría's idea of the "round trip" recalls other critical contexts describing the perspectival multiplicity of the American condition, though they are by no means interchangeable terms. An example would be W. E. B. Du Bois's adaptation of the Hegelian "double consciousness" as a way to analyze the post–Civil War African American condition of simultaneously perceiving one's position from one's point of view as well as the other's, thus resulting in a state of flux and unsettledness. See also Paul Gilroy's *Black Atlantic* (1993; Cambridge, MA: Harvard University Press, 2002) for a theorization of how traveling across the ocean constitutes a transformation in consciousness.

16. In Zamora and Faris, *Magical Realism*, 116.

17. José David Saldívar, *The Dialectics of Our America: Genealogy, Cultural Critique, and Literary History* (Durham, NC: Duke University Press, 1991), 92.

18. The emphasis and subsequent "exhaustion" of difference in North American academia dealing with Latin American literature and culture resonates with the famous Fredric Jameson–Aijaz Ahmad feud revolving around Jameson's 1986 article "Third-World Literature in the Era of Multinational Capitalism," where he posits: "I don't see how a first-world intellectual can avoid this operation [of "valorizing radical otherness"] without falling back into some general liberal and humanistic universalism: it seems to me that one of our basic political tasks lies precisely in the ceaseless effort to remind the American public of the radical difference of other national situations," *Social Text* 15 (Autumn 1986): 77. See Aijaz Ahmad, "Jameson's Rhetoric of Otherness and the National Allegory," *Social Text* 17 (Fall 1987): 3–25.

19. Alberto Moreiras, *The Exhaustion of Difference: The Politics of Latin American Cultural* (Durham, NC: Duke University Press, 2001), 187.

20. Christopher Warnes, "The Hermeneutics of Vagueness: Magical Realism in Current Literary Critical Discourse," *Journal of Postcolonial Writing* 41, no. 1 (2005): 1–13.

21. Seymour Menton, "Review," *World Literature Today* 79, no. 2 (2005): 110–11.

22. See Seymour Menton, "Jorge Luis Borges, Magic Realist," *Hispanic Review* 50, no. 2 (1982): 411–26.

23. Menton, "Review," 110. Faris herself writes, regarding this matter of inclusion and exclusion of texts: "Because I wish to explore the cultural work with which magical realism as a genre is engaged, I have not been concerned with attempting to discriminate too minutely between individual texts with the aim of establishing criteria for inclusion in a canon, and excluding from the discussion texts that do not entirely fit those criteria. If in doubt, include it, has been my motto." See Wendy B. Faris, "The Question of the Other: Cultural Critiques of Magical Realism," *Janus Head* 5, no. 2 (2002): 101–2.

24. Zamora, "Ancestral Presences: Magical Romance/Magical Realism," in *Usable Past*, 80–81.

25. Translated by Wendy B. Faris, in Zamora and Faris, *Magical Realism*, 121.

26. Menton does not acknowledge a fluid continuity between Carpentier and "Magic Realism." He uses the *Random House* dictionary (which, according to him, "may well be more useful than all the aforenoted theoretical articles and books [by Tzevetan Todorov and Emir Rodríguez Monegal among others] in sharpening our perception of Magical Realism": "The two basic dictionary definitions of magic . . . reflect

clearly the dichotomy between what Carpentier has called 'lo real maravilloso' and Magic Realism. According to Carpentier (and Miguel Ángel Asturias), the Indian and African cultures have made Latin America a continent or world of magic in the dictionary sense of 'the art of producing a desired effect or result through the use of various techniques as incantation, that presumably assure human control of supernatural agencies or the forces of nature.' On the other hand, Magic Realists, like modern-day magicians, bewilder the spectators by making reality appear to be magic: 'the art of causing illusions as entertainment by the use of sleight of hand, deceptive devices, etc.'" (412–13). Interestingly, Menton calls Magic Realists "magicians," although Carpentier, in his formulation of "lo real maravilloso" accuses the Surrealists of being "dressed up as magicians" in an exclusionary move. Menton goes on to refute Carpentier's idea by imposing his thesis of Borges as synonymous with magical realism, when he writes: "Since Jorge Luis Borges is an Argentine, and a very English-oriented one at that, it would be absurd to attribute his predilection for magic to an Indian or African cultural heritage," thus making his [Menton's] argument completely separate from that of someone like González Echevarría or Moreiras, who see in "lo real maravilloso," "transculturation," and "magical realism" an attempt to establish an autochthonous ideology of a Latin American difference, a sociocultural difference which need include a racial dimension.

27. In the latter piece, he concludes: "Magic(al) realism is certainly one of the major tendencies in international twentieth-century fiction, but like romanticism, realism, naturalism, surrealism, existentialism, and other *isms*, it is best understood within its chronological limits, particular Weltanschauung, stylistic traits, and, in some cases, in its relationship to some of the other arts." Menton, "Review," 111. In his comparison of magical realism to such concepts as "realism," and "romanticism," it appears he shifts from his 1982 stance into a belief that magical realism is a genre and not a movement exclusively.

28. Interestingly, Menton adds a footnote regarding an encounter with Borges in a roundtable discussion in California on April 10, 1980, where the former offered the author his interpretation of "El Sur": "Borges accepted this metaphorical interpretation but vehemently rejected the relationship between the violence of the gauchos and the violence of the Perón dictatorship. Be that as it may, since the story was written in 1952 during the Perón dictatorship, which took special delight in victimizing Borges, the analogy is inevitable" (425n55).

29. Todorov, *Fantastic*, 27.

30. Todorov posits the fantastic as being, in essence, brief. But we should ask whether the lifespan of the necessary decision that he explains the reader must make at the end of the story is everlasting, or if it can be suspended. This recalls Walter Benjamin's "The Storyteller," where the author reflects upon the difference between telling a story and telling the news—divulging "information"—in the modern world. "The value of information," he writes, "does not survive the moment in which it was new. It lives only at that moment; it has to surrender to it completely and explain itself to it without losing any time. A story is different. It does not expend itself. It preserves and concentrates its strength and is capable of releasing it even after a long time." In Walter Benjamin, *Illuminations* (New York: Harcourt Brace Jovanovich, 1968), 90.

31. To include another genre that is arguably adjacent to magical realism into our discussion, take for example Maggie Ann Bowers's distinction between science fiction and the magical real, in her *Magic(al) Realism* volume in the Critical Idiom series

by Routledge (London, 2005): "The science fiction narrative's distinct difference from magical realism is that it is set in a world different from any known reality. . . . Unlike magical realism, it does not have a realistic setting that is recognizable in relation to any past or present reality" (30).

32. Jorge Luis Borges, "El arte narrativo y la magia," in *Discusión* (1932; Madrid: Biblioteca Borges/Alianza Editorial, 1997), 112–13. English translation of "Narrative Art and Magic" by Suzanne Jill Levine in Jorge Luis Borges, *The Total Library: Non-Fiction 1922–1986* (New York: Allen Lane/Penguin, 2000), 75–82; 80.

33. Warnes, "Hermeneutics of Vagueness," 12.

34. David Young and Keith Hollaman, eds., *Magical Realist Fiction: An Anthology* (Oberlin, OH: Oberlin College Press, 1984), cited in Faris's "The Question of the Other."

35. Amy Kaplan, *The Social Construction of American Realism* (Chicago: University of Chicago Press, 1988), 3. For an explanation of what James means by "absent things," see my discussion in note 7 of my Introduction.

36. See, for example, Alberto Fuguet and Sergio Gómez's introduction to their edited volume *McOndo* (Barcelona: Mondadori, 1996), for a critique of the extent to which this commodification has proceeded into becoming an identification of Latin American literature. Faris notes this example in her essay.

37. Theodore Dreiser, *Sister Carrie* (1900; New York: Penguin, 1994), 98.

38. Doris Sommer, *Foundational Fictions: The National Romances of Latin America* (1991; Berkeley: University of California Press, 1993), 24.

39. Bergland, to name one example, has written about Hawthorne's "obsession" with the Native American figure in her *National Uncanny*.

40. Using Northrop Frye's distinction between romance and novel, Zamora aligns the magical realist genre with the former, because of romance and magical realism's use of "Jungian archetypes and allegory." "Allegory," she explains, "like magical realism and romance, is less concerned with individual psychology than with archetypal patterns" (*Usable Past*, 87).

41. Northrop Frye, quoted in Zamora, *Usable Past*, 97.

42. "Self-referential strategies abound in the historical Baroque, and these strategies are self-consciously manipulated by Neobaroque writers, among whom I count Borges. . . . Borges's work is double in the sense that we have seen Montaigne's and Velázquez's and Pascal's to be; his stories and essays constitute a sustained contemplation of the act that engenders them, a serial reflection upon the (im)possibility of representation. But to this doubleness Borges adds irony. He self-consciously doubles the 'double discourse' of the historical Baroque in order to ironize systems of knowledge and power such as those that the Baroque historically served, and to mediate among disparate systems of meanings." In Lois Parkinson Zamora, *The Inordinate Eye: New World Baroque and Latin American Fiction* (Chicago: University of Chicago Press, 2006), 240.

43. Alejo Carpentier, "The Baroque and the Marvelous Real," trans. Tanya Huntington and Lois Parkinson Zamora, in *Magical Realism*, ed. Zamora and Faris, 100. Other major proponents of a revaluation and reappropriation of baroque aesthetic are, of course, José Lezama Lima and a Severo Sarduy.

44. Zamora, *Inordinate Eye*, 286.

45. In the chapter "Ancestral Presences" from *Usable Past*, Zamora performs a reading of Rulfo's *Pedro Páramo* as a "transitional drama" that constitutes a "self-conscious

rejection of the binarisms of modern Western culture" through an "engagement of alternative indigenous cultural models," thus conforming to her pattern of magical realism (*Usable Past*, 117). As I have been arguing, her readings of particular texts have a sort of percolating effect that forces these works into the magical realist rubric.

46. Herman Melville, *Moby-Dick, or The Whale* (1851; New York: Penguin Classics, 2003), 336–37.

2 / Desert Mournings

1. Aldous Huxley, "The Desert," in *Tomorrow and Tomorrow and Tomorrow and Other Essays* (1952; New York: Harper and Brothers, 1956), 70.

2. Some examples are Lord Byron, Eugène Delacroix, Théophile Gautier, Gérard de Nerval, Maxime Du Camp, Horace Vernet, Eugène Fromentin, and Guy de Maupassant. See Catharine Savage Brosman's "Desert," *American Scholar* 70, no. 2 (2001): 111–22.

3. James E. Goehring, "The Dark Side of Landscape: Ideology and Power in the Christian Myth of the Desert," *Journal of Medieval and Early Modern Studies* 33, no. 3 (2003): 438.

4. David Harvey, *Spaces of Hope* (2000; Edinburgh: Edinburgh University Press, 2002), 156.

5. Michel Foucault, "Of Other Spaces," *Diacritics* 16, no. 1 (1986): 27.

6. As has often been noted, it was Jorge Luis Borges's allusion to an idiosyncratic method of classifying animals in a Chinese encyclopedia in "El idioma analítico de John Wilkins," from *Otras Inquisiciones* [*Other Inquisitions*] (1952)—a text that the French philosopher cites but never refers to by name—which led to Foucault's contemplation of the idea of the heterotopia.

7. Tulio Halperín Donghi, quoted in James Dunkerley, *Americana: The Americas in the World around 1850, or "Seeing the Elephant" as the Theme for an Imaginary Western* (London: Verso, 2000), 33.

8. The work of critics such as W. J. T. Mitchell and Denis Cosgrove is instrumental in our understanding of the representation of landscape as both symbol and human process, an active relation between individual and space, rather than an empty canvas. Mitchell explains, "Landscape may be represented by painting, drawing, or engraving; by photography, film, and theatrical scenery; by writing, speech, and presumably even music and other 'sound images.' Before all this secondary representation, however, landscape is itself a physical and multi-sensory medium (earth, stone, vegetation, water, sky, sound and silence, light and darkness, etc.) in which cultural meanings and values are encoded, whether they are put there by the physical transformation of a place in landscape gardening and architecture, or found in a place formed, as we say, 'by nature.'" W. J. T. Mitchell, *Landscape and Power* (Chicago: University of Chicago Press, 2002), 14. In his *Social Formation and Symbolic Landscape* (1984; Madison: University of Wisconsin Press, 1998), Denis Cosgrove states that "landscape denotes the external world mediated through subjective human experience in a way that neither region nor area immediately suggest. Landscape is not merely the world we see, it is a construction, a composition of the world. Landscape is a way of seeing the world" (13).

9. One need only read Jean Baudrillard's observations of the American desert in *Amérique* (1986) to see the longevity of the myth of emptiness and mystery in this space. For Baudrillard, the American desert (and Death Valley in particular) is intertwined with a poetics of spectrality. He writes: "There is something mysterious about

Death Valley *in itself.* However beautiful the combined deserts of Utah and California may be, this is something else, something sublime. The haze of supernatural heat that envelops it, its inverse depth . . . , the underwater appearance of the landscape with its salt flats and mud hills, the circle of surrounding mountains, create the effect of an inner sanctuary, an initiatory site, which reflects the geological depths and the soft and spectral limbo of the scene. . . . There's nothing funereal or morbid here, just a transverberation where all is palpable. . . . It is the only place where it is possible to relive, alongside the physical spectre of colours and the spectre of the metamorphoses that preceded us, our successive potentialities" (Jean Baudrillard, translated by David Scott, in *Semiologies of Travel: From Gautier to Baudrillard* [Cambridge: Cambridge University Press, 2004], 158).

    10. Henry James, *The American Scene* (New York: Scribner's Sons, 1946), 146–47.

    11. Paul Giles notes, "Confronted with this new world of the West, James can only lapse into silence" (Paul Giles, *Virtual Americas: Transnational Fictions and the Transatlantic Imaginary* [Durham, NC: Duke University Press, 2002], 111).

    12. James's idea of "thickness" might presage Clifford Geertz's concept of "thick description," which the latter uses specifically in the field of ethnography. For Geertz the term comes to mean being able to define and separate different registers one encounters when conducting ethnographic work—for example, the recognition of irony in another cultural framework. See Geertz's *The Interpretation of Cultures: Selected Essays* (London: Fontana Press, 1973), and the first chapter of Ben Highmore's *Cityscapes: Cultural Readings in the Material and Symbolic City* (London: Palgrave Macmillan, 2005) for an analysis of how the former's concept might be helpful in other cultural fields of analysis, such as the novel and film. For the purposes of my analysis of the desert in "artful" representation, I will continue using James's definition exclusively.

    13. Jorge Luis Borges, "La pampa y el suburbio son dioses," in *El tamaño de mi esperanza* (1926; Buenos Aires: Seix Barral, 1994), 21. The original passage reads thus: "Dos presencias de Dios, dos realidades de tan segura eficacia reverencial que la sola enunciación de sus nombres basta para ensanchar cualquier verso y nos levanta el corazón con júbilo entrañable y arisco, son el arrabal y la pampa."

    14. Lois Parkinson Zamora, "Magical Romance/Magical Realism: Ghosts in U.S. and Latin American Fiction," in *Magical Realism*, ed. Zamora and Faris, 528, 531.

    15. In an interview with Rulfo in 1983, José Carlos González Boixo mentions how some critics like to address *Pedro Páramo*'s characters as "indios," to which the novelist replies that there are "no Indians" aside from one brief episode in the novel—the ones "who come down from Apango" ["los que bajan de Apango"], but the rest of the characters are "mestizos." Following this question, González Boixo asked the author if there was a "pre-Cortesian ideological background" ["algún fondo ideológico pre-cortesiano"] or an "indigenous mentality" ["mentalidad indígena"] in the novel, to which Rulfo answered negatively, citing the "difficulty" of the "indigenous mentality," a mentality that is "totally other" to his own experience: "No, la mentalidad india es muy difícil, es una mentalidad totalmente ajena. Yo he trabajado en antropología social—van más de veintitantos años—y, a pesar de leer tantos libros y de visitar las comunidades indígenas, es muy difícil entrar en la mentalidad indígena; es totalmente ajena. ["The indigenous mentality is very difficult to understand, as it is completely other. I've worked in the field of social anthropology for over twenty years now, and despite all my reading and my visits to indigenous communities, it is very difficult to

inhabit that mentality; it is completely alien"] (Juan Rulfo, *Pedro Páramo* [Madrid: Cátedra, 2004], 250–51).

16. Martí wrote about Buffalo Bill's show on separate occasions. The article "William F. Cody—Búfalo Bill" was published in *La América* (New York) in June 1884, and reprinted in *La Nación* (Buenos Aires) on August 16, 1884. A longer article on Buffalo Bill titled "¡Magnífico espectáculo!" was published in *La Nación* on September 25, 1886.

17. Joy S. Kasson, *Buffalo Bill's Wild West: Celebrity, Memory, and Popular History* (New York: Hill and Wang, 2000), 41.

18. Richard Slotkin, "Buffalo Bill's 'Wild West' and the Mythologization of the American Empire," in *Cultures of United States Imperialism*, ed. Amy Kaplan and Donald E. Pease (Durham, NC: Duke University Press, 1993), 165.

19. José Martí, *La Gran Enciclopedia Martiana*, vol. 7, ed. Ramón Cernuda (Miami: Ediciones de Cultura Cubana, 1977), 64.

20. Susana Rotker, *The American Chronicles of José Martí: Journalism and Modernity in Spanish America* (Hanover, NH: Univeristy Press of New England, 2000), 64.

21. José Martí, "Nuestra América," in *Ensayos y crónicas* (Madrid: Cátedra, 2004), 164–65.

22. José Martí, "Our América," trans. John D. Blanco, in *Divergent Modernities: Culture and Politics in Nineteenth-Century Latin America*, by Julio Ramos (Durham, NC: Duke University Press, 2001), 299.

23. Richard Slotkin writes about the intersections of Wild West spectacle and the realm of international politics and U.S. expansion in the age of Roosevelt, whose "rough riders" are a direct reference to the show. After Martí's death in 1895, at the time of the Spanish-American War of 1898, Buffalo Bill was interviewed in the *New York World* in April 1898. Slotkin explains how, in this article, Cody (Buffalo Bill) "proposed a 'Wild West' approach to the coming war." The newspaper's headline reads: "Buffalo Bill writes on 'How I Could Drive the Spaniards from Cuba with 30,000 Indians'" (Slotkin, "Buffalo Bill's 'Wild West,'" 178).

24. Gilberto Pérez, *The Material Ghost: Films and Their Medium* (Baltimore: Johns Hopkins University Press, 1998), 25.

25. Peter Cowie, *John Ford and the American West* (New York: Harry N. Abrams, 2004), 130.

26. Kevin Brownlow, quoted in Cowie, *John Ford and the American West*, 130.

27. The photographer William Henry Jackson (1843–1942), according to Cowie, produced highly popular tinted postcards "promoting the image of the West as an Eden-in-waiting" (20). Cowie quotes Andrew Wilton, curator of the 2002 exhibition *The American Sublime*, who describes the work of yet another painter of the West, Thomas Moran (1837–1926), namely his Green River paintings of the 1870s: "The Green River buttes become an equivalent for the Pyramids, and the mountains of Colorado and Utah an American Moab or Arabia" (in Cowie, 22).

28. Edward Abbey, *Desert Solitaire* (1968; New York: Ballantine Books, 1985), 1.

29. Sam Shepard, *True West* (London: Faber and Faber, 1981), 63.

30. Wim Wenders's *Paris, Texas* (1984) opens with a stunning view of the desert in Terlingua, on the Texas-Mexico border, where the protagonist has been wandering for what appears to be years. In this movie, the desert is a search for the faculties of forgetting, from which the main character returns in shock, half-dead, and nearly mute. The Italian Sergio Leone's "spaghetti Westerns" came at a time when

the western in the American film industry was in decline (although rising in popularity, however, on television). Christopher Frayling mentions in his 1985 interview with Clint Eastwood a rather adequate description of Leone's films: "Someone once wrote that Leone's films are 'operas in which the arias aren't sung, they are stared.'" Referring to Eastwood, Frayling argues in the same interview, "It must be unique for an entire cinematic genre to depend on the fortunes of one individual, but, through the 1970s and 1980s, the future of the Western has to a large extent hinged on the boxoffice [sic] performance of [Eastwood's] work." Frayling, in *Clint Eastwood Interviews*, ed. Robert E. Kapsis and Kathy Coblentz (Jackson: University of Mississippi Press, 1999), 130; 134.

31. Alexandro Jodorowsky, *El Topo* (screenplay), trans. Joanne Pottlitzer (1971; London: Calder and Boyars, 1974), 8.

32. Though Jodorowsky refers to this title in the interview, there is actually no film exactly titled *The Law of Tombstone*. Jodorowsky might have meant *Law West of Tombstone* (1938) directed by Glenn Tryon, or *Law for Tombstone* (1937) directed by W. B. Eason and Buck Jones.

33. In his tribute to this phenomenon of manifest destiny, *Ghost Towns of the American West* (1968; Athens: Ohio University Press, 1994), Robert Silverberg writes that "a true census [of American ghost towns] is impossible, for hundreds of them have gone without a trace, completely obliterated by time and the elements" (2).

34. Diane E. Davis, *Urban Leviathan: Mexico City and the Twentieth Century* (Philadelphia: Temple University Press, 1994), 21.

35. Many ghost towns in the United States have been popular tourist attractions since the early 1900s, and a guidebook industry has grown around them. State park administrations have converted ghost towns into historic sites, and, as in the case of Calico Ghost Town in California, the Knott's Berry Farm theme park bought and restored it as a living "old West" town for public diversion.

36. Walter Benjamin, *The Origin of German Tragic Drama*, trans. John Osborne (London: Verso, 2003), 177–78.

37. Chrys M. Poff writes that many of the ghost-town films produced from the 1910s to the 1950s recycle the plotline of modern people seeking shelter in an abandoned mining town, and who eventually find "hidden treasure" untapped in the town's mines. This constitutes a renewal of the nineteenth-century mythology of the west—a reactivation of the old desires of expansion and personal freedom and wealth to be found in the west. In Chrys M. Poff, *The Western Ghost Town in American Culture* (Ann Arbor: Dissertation Abstracts International, 2004), 220.

38. Derek Attridge, *J. M. Coetzee and the Ethics of Reading Literature in the Event* (Chicago: University of Chicago Press, 2004), 64.

39. Patricia Limerick, "Haunted by Rhyolite: Learning from the Landscape of Failure," *American Art* 6, no. 4 (1992): 22.

40. Carlos Monsiváis, *Mexican Postcards*, trans. John Kraniauskas (1997; London: Verso, 2000), 58.

41. Jean Franco, "Journey to the Land of the Dead," in *Critical Passions*, ed. Mary Louise Pratt and Kathleen Newman (Durham, NC: Duke University Press, 1999), 437.

42. Rulfo, *Pedro Páramo*, 111.

43. "Desviviéndonos" literally translates to "un-" or, perhaps "dis-living."

44. Margaret Sayers Peden translates this line as follows: "The stillness seemed to be waiting for something." In the following sections, the original, Spanish, version by

Rulfo will be coupled with Sayers's translation from 1993. Juan Rulfo, *Pedro Páramo*, trans. Margaret Sayers Peden (London: Serpent's Tail, 1993).

45. Toward the novel's denouement, we learn that Rentería joins the Cristero War when the character *El Tilcuate* tells Páramo, "Se ha levantado en armas el padre Rentería" ["Father Rentería's fighting now"] (171; 115). According to Monsiváis, this conflict was "an effect of clerical anger at the policies of the post-Revolutionary State, whose monopolization of power entailed the secularization of education, and thus an anticlerical offensive. The State put a limit on the number of priests in the country, closed down temples, expelled a good number of Spanish priests and nuns, and defied the authority of the Church hierarchy in a variety of ways." In the essay Carlos Monsiváis, "Millenarianisms in Mexico," in *Mexican Postcards*, by Monsiváis, 131.

46. Bakhtin, *Toward a Philosophy of the Act*, 32.

47. Patrick Dove argues that Rulfo's work "mark[s] the limit" of the "ideological narratives" of a teleological modernity. See Patrick Dove, *The Catastrophe of Modernity* (Lewisburg, PA: Bucknell University Press, 2004), 99.

48. The score's composer was Dee Barton. Eastwood was an admirer of Japanese ghost-story films, and *High Plains Drifter*, one could argue, pays visual and aural homage to this genre.

49. Michael Henry, "Interview with Clint Eastwood," *Eastwood Interviews*, ed. Robert E. Kapsis and Kathy Coblentz (Jackson: University of Mississippi Press, 1999), 100–101. Over a century before Eastwood arrived in Mono Lake, Mark Twain, in *Roughing It* (1872), his pseudo-autobiographical about his travels in the U.S. West between 1862 and 1867, devotes a chapter (chapter 38) to this location.

50. *Shane* has been read as a film that is already reflecting on the mythology of the U.S. West, where the main character is a metonym for the immensity of the ideology that surrounds the region. In the novel *Shane* (written by Jack Schaefer), the eponymous hero is described as being "as self-sufficient as the mountains," and at one point, "Attention was on him as a sort of symbol." Jack Schaefer, *Shane* (1949; Lincoln: University of Nebraska Press, 1984), 161, 148.

51. Michael Henry, "Interview with Clint Eastwood," *Eastwood Interviews*, 99–100.

52. Paul Smith, *Clint Eastwood: A Cultural Production* (London: University College London Press, 1993), 21.

53. See Raymond Williams, *The Country and the City* (Cambridge: Cambridge University Press, 1973). I discuss Williams's work further in the next chapter.

3 / Urban Indiscretions

1. "The city is a cage of dead doves / and avid hunters! If men's bosoms / were to open and their torn flesh / fall to the earth, inside would be / nothing but a scatter of small, crushed fruit! [. . .] The city appalls me! Full / of cups to be emptied, and empty cups! / I fear—ah me!—that this wine / may be poison, and sink its teeth, / vengeful imp, in my veins! / I thirst—but for a wine that none on earth / knows how to drink! I have not yet / endured enough to break through the wall / that keeps me, ah grief!, / from my vineyard! / Take, oh squalid tasters / of humble human wines, these cups / from which, with no fear or pity, / you swill the lily's juice! / Take them! I am honorable, and I am afraid!" José Martí, "Love in the City," trans. Esther Allen, in *The Norton Anthology of Latino Literature*, ed. Ilan Stavans et al. (New York: W. W. Norton, 2011), 272–73.

2. Henry James, *Henry James: Stories of the Supernatural*, ed. Leon Edel (London: Barrie and Jenkins, 1971), 103–40.

3. Henry James, *The Complete Notebooks of Henry James*, ed. Leon Edel and Lyall Powers (New York: Oxford University Press, 1987), 10. In *Henry James and the Ghostly* (Cambridge: Cambridge University Press, 1994), Tim Lustig focuses on James's long-standing interest in developing a poetics of "boundaries": "Boundaries certainly do proliferate in the Jamesian text," Lustig notes, arguing that there is an "uncanny charge" attached "to those scenes in James's work which turn on thresholds, per-spectives, windows, doors, on those isolated moments of heightened attention which amount, at times, to encounters with the margins of the text" (7).

4. Henry James, "Preface to 'The Altar of the Dead,'" in *Art of the Novel*, ed. R. P. Blackmur (New York: Scribner's, 1934), 257.

5. Quoted in Ángel Rama, *The Lettered City*, trans. John Charles Chasteen (Dur-ham, NC: Duke University Press, 1996), 132n20.

6. Ibid., 72. In addressing these "fictitious" chronicles of Latin American urban pasts, he cites the examples of Ricardo Palma's *Tradiciones peruanas*, Vicente Riva Palacio's *México a través de los siglos*, Chilean Vicente Pérez Rosales's *Recuerdos del pasado*, and Lucio V. López *La gran aldea*, about Buenos Aires (71).

7. Raymond Williams, *The Country and the City* (Cambridge: Cambridge Univer-sity Press, 1973), 188.

8. Mauricio Tenorio-Trillo, *Mexico at the World's Fairs: Crafting the Modern Na-tion* (Berkeley: University of California Press, 1996), 2. Tenorio-Trillo also notes how involvement in the world's fairs describes a nineteenth-century belief in progress as the main driver of modernity. Included in this belief there is also, according to the author, a faith in a "positive, universal, and homogeneous truth," as well as a "recapitulat[ion] of the past" by the optimistic present that aims to "control" the course of the future (2).

9. Richard Ruland and Malcolm Bradbury, *From Puritanism to Postmodernism: A History of American Literature* (1991; New York: Penguin, 1992), 188.

10. Jorge Larrain, *Identity and Modernity in Latin America* (Cambridge: Polity Press, 2000), 79.

11. In the case of Cuba, for example, Spain officially decreed the abolition of slavery in 1886. Louis A. Pérez Jr. explains how the process of the official abolition of slavery in the island was a result of the Ten Years War, which had "destroyed the plantation economy in many regions, ending further need for slave labor." The 1870s saw the adaptation of the Spanish Moret Law, which "freed few economically pro-ductive slaves," but kept "free-born blacks . . . subject to the *patronato* of their former slave owners, for whom they worked without wages until the age of eighteen." In 1879, the liberal government of Arsenio Martínez Campos worked to implement the law, and in 1880 it was decreed as a "compromise between abolitionists and slaveholders" to use the "*patronato* as a means of gradual adjustment and adaptation" throughout an eight-year period of transition. In 1886, however, two years before the end of this period, Spain abolished slavery by royal decree. Pérez notes how "at the time of this proclamation, fewer than 30,000 slaves remained in a condition of compulsory labor." In Louis A. Pérez Jr., *Cuba: Between Reform and Revolution* (1988; New York: Oxford University Press, 1995), 126–28.

12. See Jennifer French, *Nature, Neo-Colonialism, and the Spanish American Regional Writers* (Lebanon, NH: Dartmouth College Press/University Press of New England, 2005).

13. James Dunkerley, *Americana: The Americas in the World Around, or "Seeing the Elephant" as the Theme for an Imaginary Western* (London: Verso, 2000), 44.

14. Jorge Paez, quoted in Dunkerley, *Americana*, 45n121.

15. Julio Ramos, *Divergent Modernities: Culture and Politics in Nineteenth-Century Latin America*, translated by John D. Blanco (Durham, NC: Duke University Press, 2001), 60.

16. William H. Katra discusses the United States as the model for Sarmiento's utopia in his essay "Rereading *Viajes*," in *Sarmiento: Author of a Nation*, ed. Tulio Halperín Donghi, Tulio, Iván Jaksic, Gwen Kirkpatrick, and Francine Masiello (Berkeley: University of California Press, 1994), 73–100.

17. Domingo Sarmiento, *Viajes por Europa, Africa i América, 1845–1847* (1993; Madrid: ALLCA XX, 1996), 292. This 1996 edition cites the original text, using the nineteenth-century grammar. English translation quoted from *Sarmiento's Travels in the United States in 1847*, ed. Michael Rockland (Princeton, NJ: Princeton University Press, 1970), 118–19. Throughout the rest of the chapter, translations from Rockland's text (marked with their particular page numbers) will follow the original citations from the Spanish.

18. In Sarmiento's *Conflicto y armonía de las razas en América Latina*, qtd. in Ramos, *Divergent Modernities*, 154.

19. See Ramos, *Divergent Modernities*, 11.

20. Domingo Sarmiento, *Facundo: Civilización y barbarie* (Madrid: Cátedra, 1990), 114.

21. Domingo Sarmiento, *Facundo: Civilization and Barbarism*, trans. Kathleen Ross (Berkeley: University of California Press, 2003), 83.

22. Sarmiento, *Viajes*, 4.

23. Sylvia Molloy, "The Unquiet Self: Mnemonic Strategies in Sarmiento's Autobiographies," in *Sarmiento: Author of a Nation*, ed. Halperín Donghi et al., 195.

24. As Katra has noted, *Viajes* is mostly an "impressionistic" and "highly plagiarized" account of an expeditious tour: He traveled to twenty-one states and Montreal in just six weeks (73).

25. See, for example, Doris Sommer, *Foundational Fictions: The National Romances of Latin America* (1991; Berkeley: University of California Press, 1993).

26. See Thoreau's "Sounds" chapter in *Walden* (1854). In some ways Sarmiento's narrative is echoed by Frederick Jackson Turner's argument in *The Frontier in American History* (1893), which shifted the meaning of "frontier" from a zone of war to an American zone of reinvention. In his discussion of Frederick Jackson Turner, José Martí and the U.S. frontier, Brook Thomas describes Turner's redefinition of the frontier in the country as an "account of the making of Americans through a dynamic, forward-looking process rather than one that looks backward toward natural origins," as well as the opening of the possible "narrative of American history in which conflicts could be endlessly deferred rather than dialectically solved." Brook Thomas, "Frederick Jackson Turner, José Martí, and Finding a Home on the Range," in *José Martí's "Our America": From National to Hemispheric Cultural Studies,* ed. Jeffrey Belnap and Raúl Fernández (Durham, NC: Duke University Press, 1998), 285, 279.

27. In this passage, Sarmiento's mention of a "declining" civilization appears to open up the possibility of an analogy with the Argentine pampas. He attempts to overcome this by alluding to the North American sense of thrift, the ability to live on the

"bare" essentials, as well as the opening up of an objective discussion of architecture, and the varieties of dwellings in different parts of the United States.

28. During his fifteen years in the United States, Martí's chronicles detailing life, art, and politics in this country were published in newspapers in Latin America, such as Buenos Aires's *La Nación* and Spanish-language publications in the United States; he also wrote in English for the *New York Sun*. Roberto González Echevarría, Introduction to José Martí, *Selected Writings*, trans. Esther Allen (New York: Penguin Classics, 2002), xv.

29. Gerard Aching, "Against 'Library-Shelf-Races': José Martí's Critique of Excessive Imitation," in *Geomodernisms: Race, Modernism, Modernity*, ed. Laura Doyle and Laura Winkiel (Bloomington: Indiana University Press, 2005), 155.

30. José Martí, "Nuestra América," in *Ensayos y crónicas* (Madrid: Cátedra, 2004), 159. English excerpt quoted from John D. Blanco's translation in Ramos, *Divergent Modernities*, 296.

31. In *Politics of Spanish American* Modernismo (Cambridge: Cambridge University Press, 1997), Gerard Aching discusses Darío's performative pan-Hispanism, the "rejuvenation of Hispanic culture" after Spain's imperial losses of 1898, as an "ambivalent strategy" that produces a single transatlantic Hispanic lineage, although implicitly excluding the indigenous subjects of the Spanish American landscape: "The the poetic voice [in Darío's "Salutación del optimista" from 1905] ignores indigenous contributions to American culture and concomitantly cherishes a European heritage. Yet this move complicates the poem's representation of identity politics because its deferential treatment of Spain's past is double-edged. Although it may have provided patriotic Spaniards and their Spanish American supporters with motives for reminiscing about past glories, this treatment implicitly draws an analogy between Spanish America's descendance from Spain and Spain's from Imperial Rome. Consequently, by eliminating the indigenous—the very presence of whom helps to make America unique—from this preferred social memory, the poetic voice creates a homogenous community of nations on both sides of the Atlantic with equal claims to direct lineage from one source. Inadvertently proposed or not, this notion of sibling nations stands as a direct challenge to the hierarchy of the former Spanish empire" (60).

32. Susana Rotker, "The (Political) Exile Gaze in Martí's Writing on the United States," in *José Martí's "Our America,"* ed. Belnap and Fernández, 64.

33. José Martí, "El terremoto de Charleston," in Martí, *La Gran Enciclopedia Martiana*, ed. Cernuda, 7:78. English translation by Louis A. Baralt, in *Norton Anthology of Latino Literature*, ed. Ilan Stavans et al., 273. The chronicle appeared in *La Nación* (Buenos Aires) on September 10, 1886.

34. For an exploration of Martí's involvement in freemasonry, see Jossiana Arroyo, "Tecnologías de la palabra: el secreto y la escritura en José Martí," *Encuentro de la cultura cubana* 30–31 (Autumn 2003/Winter 2004): 161–73. Louis A. Baralt's translation of "The Charleston Earthquake" reads: "That night the woods were filled with city people who, fleeing from their shaken dwellings, took refuge among the trees, and gathered in the darkness to kneel and sing out their praises to the Lord, imploring His mercy. The earth also shook and was rent in Illinois, Kentucky, Missouri, and Ohio. A man who was being initiated in a Masonic lodge stampeded out to the street with a rope around his waist. A Cherokee Indian who was brutally beating his poor wife, on feeling the ground move under his feet, fell on his knees and swore to the Lord

he would never punish her again" ("Charleston Earthquake," in *Norton Anthology of Latino Literature*, 278).

35. In an analysis of Hölderlin's theorization of the caesura, Patrick Dove writes that this literary break launches what the German writer describes as "the pure word," which Dove explains as "a remainder that perhaps cannot be recuperated by any dialectical thought of identity and difference." Patrick Dove, *The Catastrophe of Modernity* (Lewisburg, PA: Bucknell University Press, 2004), 37.

36. José Martí, "El indio en los Estados Unidos," in *Gran Enciclopedia Martiana*, ed. Ramón Cernuda (Miami: Ediciones de Cultura Cubana, 1977), 6:378.

37. Jeffrey Belnap, "Headbands, Hemp Sandals, and Headdresses: The Dialectics of Dress and Self-Conception in Martí's 'Our America,'" in *José Martí's "Our America,"* ed. Belnap and Fernández, 203.

38. In *Translating Empire: José Martí, Migrant Latino Subjects, and American Modernities* (Durham, NC: Duke University Press, 2008), Laura Lomas briefly touches upon Martí's and James's criticism of Emerson's individualism (172–73).

39. See Philip Horne, "'Reinstated': Henry James in Roosevelt's Washington," *Cambridge Quarterly* 37, no. 1 (2008): 47–63.

40. José Martí, "Carta a Bartolomé Mitre y Vedia" (December 19, 1882), in Martí, *Gran Enciclopedia Martiana*, 6:10.

41. Robert E. Abrams, *Landscape and Ideology in American Renaissance Literature: Topographies of Skepticism* (Cambridge: Cambridge University Press, 2004), 9.

42. Henry James, "Nathaniel Hawthorne," in *Henry James: The American Essays*, ed. Leon Edel (New York: Vintage, 1956), 13.

43. Neill Matheson argues that James's insistence on Hawthorne's charm as an "irreducibly relational" quality in the novelist's oeuvre connects James the critic and James the novelist. Matheson argues that, in James, "acquiring a taste for Hawthorne would require looking and reading differently, as if through the grafting of a new mode of vision, a new set of eyes." See Neill Matheson, "Intimacy and Form: James on Hawthorne's Charm," *Henry James Review* 28, no. 2 (2007): 127.

44. Henry James, *The American Scene* (New York: Scribner's Sons, 1946), 397.

45. The letter concerns the publication of Wells's *The Future in America*. In *Henry James: A Life in Letters*, ed. Philip Horne (London: Allen Lane, 1999), 442. In *The Trial of Curiosity: Henry James, William James, and the Challenge of Modernity* (New York, Oxford: Oxford University Press, 1991), Ross Posnock notes Wells's reaction to *The American Scene*, which the former describes as "posit[ing] a frightened James evading history, politics, and science and embracing 'social fancies' as a way of 'disowning the shame of power'" (147).

46. From "Preface to 'Lady Barbarina,'" in James, *Art of the Novel*, 215. For discussions of James's analyses of multiracial and multicultural North America, see, for example, Sara Blair, *Henry James and the Writing of Race and Nation* (Cambridge: Cambridge University Press, 1996); Patricia McKee, *Producing American Races: James, Faulkner, and Morrison* (Durham, NC: Duke University Press, 1999); Gert Beulens, "James's 'Aliens': Consuming, Performing, and Judging the American Scene," *Modern Philology* 96, no. 3 (1999), 347–63; James C. Davis, "Solid, Liquid, or Gas?: Race as a State of Matter," *Henry James Review* 21, no. 3 (2000): 261–69; and Kendall Johnson, "The Scarlet Feather: Racial Phantasmagoria in *What Maisie Knew*," *The Henry James Review* 22, no. 2 (2001): 128–46. See also the "Race Forum" edition of *The Henry James Review* (vol. 16) from 1995.

47. Flannery O'Connor, who was an avid and incisively critical reader of James, found a compelling and fierce way of turning this image of the "sick lioness" into the subject of her fiction. See her essay "Some Aspects of the Grotesque in Southern Fiction" (1960) in her *Collected Works* (New York: Library of America, 1988), which I discuss in Chapter 1.

48. Beverly Haviland explains in *Henry James's Last Romance: Making Sense of the Past and the American Scene* (Cambridge: Cambridge University Press, 1997) that this impersonation "was not published in the first American edition of *The American Scene* because of confusion—or cowardice—at Harper's" (59).

49. Ibid., 136.

50. Paul Giles, *Virtual Americas: Transnational Fictions and the Transatlantic Imaginary* (Durham, NC: Duke University Press, 2002), 114–15.

51. Blair, *Henry James and the Writing of Race and Nation*, 5.

52. José Martí, "Autores americanos aborígenes," in Martí, *La Gran Enciclopedia Martiana*, 5:303.

53. Haviland engages in an interesting discussion of romance and genre in her second chapter, aptly titled "Genre Trouble," where she discusses the interpolated texts of *American Scene* and James's unfinished novel *The Sense of the Past* (1900).

54. Rotker, "(Political) Exile Gaze, in *José Martí's "Our America,"* ed. Belnap and Fernández, 64; 66.

55. Doris Sommer has critiqued Martí's *"cubanidad"* in "Our America" because of the negative string of possibilities of neutralization as well as a constant proliferation of "competing positionalities" of that "our": "First, the possessive pronoun neutralizes internal differences and claims ownership in monocultural ways that now seem unproductive. Martí's nineteenth-century nationalism needed to focus on victory by squinting at Cuba, compressing its complexity into a thin but homogenous *cubanidad*. The other problem is that the discriminating pronoun 'Our' is so shifty, so available for competing positionalities and equivocal meanings." Doris Sommer, *Proceed with Caution, When Engaged by Minority Writing in the Americas* (Cambridge, MA: Harvard University Press, 1999), 108.

56. The process of professionalization of writers in nineteenth-century Latin America, is, of course, very different from the career paths of those in Europe and the United States, where writers found an autonomous sphere for their vocation (see Rama's *Lettered City* and Ramos's *Divergent Modernities*). James's letters throughout his career often reveal the pecuniary realities of his aesthetic work (see Horne's *Henry James: A Life in Letters*). During the journey that inspired *The American Scene,* James recognized, for example, that offering lectures at universities proved to be particularly favorable for his finances.

57. From Martí's "Coney Island" chronicle, included in Ramos, *Divergent Modernities* (translated by John D. Blanco), 320.

58. Jesse Matz, "Cultures of Impression," in *Bad Modernisms*, ed. Douglas Mao and Rebecca L. Walkowitz (Durham, NC: Duke University Press, 2006), 312.

59. Posnock, *Trial of Curiosity*, 74.

60. Martí, *La Gran Enciclopedia Martiana*, 8:292.

61. It was not until 1895 that the Lumière brothers patented the *cinématographe*. See Jonathan Crary, *Suspensions of Perception: Attention, Spectacle, and Modern Culture* (1999; Cambridge, MA: MIT Press, 2001) for a study of how visual culture was reorganized in the nineteenth century through the introduction of modern practices

of attention. In his discussion of the early motion-picture work of Eadweard Mud-bridge in the late 1870s (most famously *The Horse in Motion* from 1879), Crary argues that "the demise of the punctual or anchored classical observer begins in the early nineteenth century, increasingly displaced by the unstable attentive subject. . . . It is a subject competent to be both a consumer of and an agent in the synthesis of all the proliferating diversity of 'reality effects,' and a subject who will become the object of all the proliferating demands and enticements of technological culture in the twenti-eth century" (148).

62. M. M. Bakhtin, *Toward a Philosophy of the Act*, trans. Vadim Liapunov (Aus-tin: University of Texas Press, 1993), 36.

63. M. M. Bakhtin, *Art and Answerability: Early Philosophical Essays by M. M. Bakhtin* (Austin: University of Texas Press, 1990),117.

64. From letter to William Dean Howells on August 9, 1900, in Horne, *Henry James: A Life in Letters*, 340.

65. James, "Preface to 'The Altar of the Dead,'" in *Art of the Novel*, 257.

66. Henry James, "The Jolly Corner," in *The New York Stories of Henry James* (New York: New York Review of Books, 2006), 463.

67. Other stories from James's so-called "fourth phase," such as "The Altar of the Dead" and "The Beast in the Jungle" offer different representations of characters ob-sessed almost perversely with the eventuality, the "waiting to see," of life.

68. In the "Altar of the Dead" preface, James describes his motive behind the cre-ation of the character of Spencer Brydon in the following description of an attenuated indiscretion: "I was moved to adopt as my motive an analysis of some one of the con-ceivably rarest and intensest grounds for an 'unnatural' anxiety, a *malaise* so incon-gruous and discordant, in the given prosaic prosperous conditions, as almost to be compromising" (262).

69. The story was initially called "The Second House." James describes the nar-rative in a letter from August 28, 1906, as "the best thing of this sort I've ever done." Horne, *Henry James: A Life in Letters*, 437.

70. For a reading of how the supernatural is intercepted by modern market cul-ture in "The Jolly Corner," see Geoffrey Gilbert, "The Origins of Modernism in the Haunted Properties of Literature," in *The Victorian Supernatural*, ed. Nicola Bown, Carolyn Burdett and Pamela Thurschwell (Cambridge: Cambridge University Press, 2004), 239–57.

71. Haviland has read this entry of the house in "The Jolly Corner" as an image of the "invasion" of aliens into the U.S. landscape. Yet, her reading does not take into consideration the formal qualities of James's story that lead the reader to understand Brydon's own hand in the manufacturing of his haunting. Her analysis lingers on plot summary to arrive at an interpretation of James's attitude toward aliens in New York: "The absentee returns home to find his splendid house haunted by the spirit of what he might have become had he stayed in America and become a businessman. This ghost, whom the hero finally turns on and chases, is both the perpetrator of horrors and himself a horror. . . . Spencer Brydon triumphs over this alien self only when he recognizes it as himself and accepts the possibility of guilt without, for that, accepting the responsibility for the possible violence" (Haviland, *Henry James's Last Romance*, 161).

72. John Carlos Rowe, *The Other Henry James* (Durham, NC: Duke University Press, 1998), 53.

73. Chateaubriand's early frontier rhetoric, according to Slotkin, recalls John Filson's depictions of Daniel Boone's adventures in *The Discovery, Settlement and Present State of Kentucke* (1784): "Pourquoi trouve-t-on tant de charme à la vie sauvage? Pourquoi l'homme le plus accoutumé à éxercer sa pensée s'oublie t-il joyeusement dans le tumulte d'un chasse? Courir dans les bois, poursuivre des bêtes sauvages, bâtir sa hutte, allumer son feu . . . est certainement un très grand plaisir . . . Cela prouve que l'homme est plutôt un être actif, qu'un être contemplatif, que dans sa condition naturelle, il lui faut peu de chose, et que la simplicité de l'âme est un source inépuisable de Bonheur" ["Why should one find the savage life so charming? Why do men who are accustomed to the intellectual life forget themselves during the thrill of the hunt? To run in the forests, chasing after savage beasts, to build one's hut, light one's fire . . . are certainly great pleasures. . . . It proves that man is more an active being than a contemplative one, that in his natural condition he does not want for much, and that the simplicity of the soul is an unending source of happiness"]. My translation of the French version, quoted in Richard Slotkin, *Regeneration through Violence: The Mythology of the American Frontier, 1600–1860* (Norman: University of Oklahoma Press, 1973), 374.

74. Slotkin, *Regeneration through Violence*, 392.

75. Amy Kaplan, *The Anarchy of Empire in the Making of U.S. Culture* (Cambridge, MA: Harvard University Press, 2002), 96–97.

76. From Brown's Introduction to *Edgar Huntly* (qtd. in Slotkin, 375).

77. By using the terms of "embodiment" I do not intend to appropriate Amy Kaplan's analysis in order to perform an allegorization of James's ghost story as simply an anxiety of imperialist expansion, primarily because the fictionalization of the cosmopolitan return introduces a more discrete reading of national spaces and their imaginations that is not necessarily aligned with the fictions created by the writers of historical romances in the 1890s.

78. *Return of the Native* was James's first choice as a title for what was to become *The American Scene*. However, as he explains in a letter from October 22, 1904, "If Thomas Hardy hadn't long ago made that impossible I should simply give the whole series of papers the title of *The Return of the Native*. But as that's out of the question I have found myself thinking of, and liking even better—*The Return of the Novelist*." Horne, *Henry James: A Life in Letters*, 404–5.

79. Jean Franco, *The Decline and Fall of the Lettered City: Latin America in the Cold War* (Cambridge, MA: Harvard University Press, 2002), 160.

80. Carlos Ramela, "Cuentos de Felisberto Hernández," *Marcha*, April 9, 1948, 14. On the importance of the weekly magazine *Marcha* as a space in which great literary and critical figures from Latin America in the first decades of the twentieth century came together until its closure in the 1970s, see Ángel Rama's essay "Uruguay: La generación crítica (1939–1969)," in Ángel Rama, *Crítica literaria y utopía en América Latina* (Medellín: Editorial Universidad de Antioquia, 2006). Rama notes that it was through *Marcha* that many writers of the past were reappraised and given "magisterial status." Among these figures are Eduardo Acevedo Díaz, Horacio Quiroga, Juan José Morosoli, and Felisberto Hernández (421–22).

81. In Rosario Ferré, *El acomodador: Una lectura fantástica de Felisberto Hernández* (Mexico City: Tierra Firme/Fondo de Cultura Económica, 1986), 21.

82. One example is Frank Graziano's *The Lust of Seeing: Themes of the Gaze and Sexual Rituals in the Fiction of Felisberto Hernández* (Lewisburg, PA: Bucknell University Press, 1997), in which the critic reads Hernández's fiction as symptomatic of

different pathologies. More recently, Patrick O'Connor describes Hernández's first-person narrations (which make up most of his oeuvre) as "the stuff of which psychoanalytic sessions are made." Patrick O'Connor, *Latin American Literature and the Narratives of the Perverse: Paper Dolls and Spider Women* (New York: Palgrave Macmillan, 2004), 76.

83. Rama, quoted in Mario Rivas Cortés, "Felisberto Hernández visto por Ángel Rama," *Revista Iberoamericana* 71, no. 211 (2005): 382. Rama's essays on Hernández include the titles "Burlón poeta de la materia" (1964) and "La magia de la materia" (1967).

84. Ida Vitale, quoted in Ferré, *El acomodador,* 21.

85. Julio Prieto, *Desencuadernados: Vanguardias ex-céntricas en el Río de la Plata. Macedonio Fernández y Felisberto Hernández* (Rosario, Argentina: Beatriz Viterbo, 2002), 368.

86. Feliberto Hernández, *Obras completas de Felisberto Hernández* (Mexico: Siglo XXI, 1983), 32.

87. Borges's defends this method in his 1951 essay "El escritor argentino y la tradición" ("The Argentine Writer and Tradition"). See note 16 in Chapter 4.

88. Felisberto Hernández, "El acomodador," *Nadie encendía las lámparas* (Barcelona: Editorial Lumen/Palabra Menor, 1982), 37.

89. Santiago Colás, "Toward an Ethics of Close Reading in an Age of Neo-Liberalism," *New Centennial Review* 7, no. 3 (2007): 173.

90. Carlos Martínez Moreno, one of Hernández's harshest critics in the Generación Crítica, borrowed the phrase "misterio de su estupidez" to describe the fiction writer's talents (qtd. in Ferré, *El acomodador,* 22).

91. Feliberto Hernández, "La cara de Ana" (1931), in *Obras completas,* 55.

92. According to Martin Weinstein, in Uruguay's first census of 1908, 42 percent of the population of Montevideo was foreign born. Martin Weinstein, *Uruguay: Democracy at the Crossroads* (Boulder, CO: Westview Press, 1988), 4.

93. *Marcha,* December 10, 1948, 15.

94. Feliberto Hernández, "Tal vez un movimiento," in *Obras completas,* 132.

4 / Transnational Shadows

1. "The Poet Walt Whitman" chronicle was first published in *La Nación* on June 26, 1887. In José Martí, *Selected Writings*, trans. Esther Allen (New York: Penguin, 2002), 192; 194. The original text for the second passage cited is: "Acumular le parece el mejor modo de describir, y su raciocinio no toma jamás las formas pedestres del argumento ni las altisonantes de la oratoria, sino el misterio de la insinuación, el fervor de la certidumbre y el giro ígneo de la profesía," from José Martí, *La Gran Enciclopedia Martiana,* 8:217.

2. Benedict Anderson, *The Spectre of Comparisons: Nationalism, Southeast Asia and the World* (London: Verso, 1998), 74.

3. Peter Hitchcock, *The Long Space: Transnationalism and Postcolonial Form* (Stanford, CA: Stanford University Press, 2010), 186.

4. For an analysis of the relation between the regional and the international in Du Bois, see Harry Stecopoulos's chapter ("'Take Your Geography and Trace It': W. E. B. Du Bois and the Reconstruction of the South") in his *Reconstructing the World: Southern Fictions and U.S. Imperialisms, 1898–1976* (Ithaca, NY: Cornell University Press, 2008), 77–100.

5. Whitman, quoted in Shamoon Zamir, *Dark Voices: W. E. B. Du Bois and American Thought, 1888–1903* (Chicago: University of Chicago Press, 1995), 125. In this excellent text that explores U.S. intellectual history during Du Bois's formative years at Harvard University (where he studied under William James and George Santayana), Zamir contextualizes Du Bois within a period in which German philosophy was at the height of popularity among North American intellectuals. Zamir critiques Whitman's and the St. Louis Hegelians' (proponents of American Hegelianism, the group existed from 1865 into the mid-1880s) ahistorical appropriation of Hegel—part of what was called a "Teutonic nationalism"—for seeking to "reduce the concrete facts of history to an abstract schema of thesis, antithesis, and synthesis, an essentially static conceptualization of dialectic that Hegel himself had in fact rejected." This use of Hegel reaches controversial heights with the group's "interpretation of the Civil War as a necessary part of the dialectic process of history in which America would assume its rightful and leading place in the onward movement of thought and culture" (125).

6. G. W. F. Hegel, *Philosophy of History* (New York: Dover, 1956), 80.

7. Ibid., 83, 84.

8. Engels, quoted in James Dunkerley, *Americana: The Americas in the World around 1850, or "Seeing the Elephant" as the Theme for an Imaginary Western* (London: Verso, 2000), 239.

9. Marx, letter to Engels from December 2, 1854, quoted in Dunkerley, *Americana*, 491.

10. Dunkerley attributes this shift in Marx's approach to Mexico after the English Lord Palmerston became reportedly involved in the planning of "an intervention in Mexico" where, according to Marx, the "political" would be placed above the "economic" (*Americana*, 240). As is evident in Marx's "Simón Bolivar" entry for Charles Dana's *New American Cyclopaedia*, the economic thinker has a tendency to demonize any figure resembling a Bonaparte. In this entry, Marx chooses three texts over all the others available to him (Marx was able to read Spanish, after all, and had a rather vast number of texts to choose from as a reader in the British Museum). Most important, he selects Henry Ducaudray's, who was rebuffed by Bolívar during the independence campaigns. This leads Dunkerley to argue that Marx strategically selected a text that vilified this South American "Bonaparte."

11. Karl Marx, *Marx's "Eighteenth Brumaire,"* ed. Mark Cowling and James Martin (London: Pluto Press, 2002), 26–27. See Martin Harries, *Scare Quotes from Shakespeare: Marx, Keynes, and the Language of Reenchantment* (Stanford, CA: Stanford University Press, 2000), 78.

12. González Echevarría, "A Lost World Rediscovered: Sarmiento's *Facundo*," in Halperín Donghi et al., *Sarmiento: Author of a Nation* (Berkeley: University of California Press, 1994), 224.

13. Diana Sorensen discusses how Juan Bautista Alberdi, Sarmiento's intellectual rival and avid critic, refutes the latter's historical formulations of country and city in *Facundo* through the use of theoretical frameworks influenced by Alberdi's readings of Herder, Savigny, Lerminier, and Cousin, authors through which he reached the writings of Marx and Hegel. Sorensen, "The Wiles of Disputation: Alberdi Reads *Facundo*," in *Sarmiento: Author of a Nation*, ed. Halperín Donghi et al., 309.

14. See Priscilla Wald, *Constituting Americans: Cultural Anxiety and Narrative Form* (Durham, NC: Duke University Press, 1995).

15. See Carlos Alonso, *The Spanish-American Regional Novel: Modernity and Autochthony* (Cambridge: Cambridge University Press, 1990). Jean Franco explains how Güiraldes's search for a native Argentine expression constitutes a departure for an author of "sophisticated" influences ranging from Nietzsche to Dostoevsky to Zola. She writes that Güiraldes "felt Europe had taken the wrong direction." It stems from "his conviction that American experience could give a man a valid set of standards to guide his life" as well as a belief that "American experience had never been recorded." In Jean Franco, *An Introduction to Spanish-American Literature* (1968; Cambridge: Cambridge University Press, 1994), 224.

16. As the author himself would have it, the 1926 Borges is different from the Borges of the 1950s who wrote "El escritor argentino y la tradición" ("The Argentine Writer and Tradition"). In this seminal essay, Borges makes the case for the Latin American writer as a universal writer, and he visualizes the idea of an autochthony as an impossibility, for the writer encapsulates a whole world. In the following passage, he refers to Güiraldes specifically: "Now I want to speak of a justly illustrious work which the nationalists often invoke. I refer to Güiraldes' *Don Segundo Sombra*. The nationalists tell us that *Don Segundo Sombra* is the model of a national book; but if we compare it with the works of the gauchesque tradition, the first thing we note are differences. *Don Segundo Sombra* abounds in metaphors of a kind having nothing to do with country speech but a great deal to do with the metaphors of the then current literary circles of Montmartre. As for the fable, the story, it is easy to find in it the influence of Kipling's *Kim*, whose action is set in India and which was, in turn, written under the influence of Mark Twain's *Huckleberry Finn*, the epic of the Mississippi. When I make this observation, I do not wish to lessen the value of *Don Segundo Sombra*; on the contrary, I want to emphasize the fact that, in order that we might have this book, it was necessary for Güiraldes to recall the poetic technique of the French circles of his time and the work of Kipling which he had read many years before; in other words, Kipling and Mark Twain and the metaphors of French poets were necessary for this Argentine book which, I repeat, is no less Argentine for having accepted such influences." Borges, "The Argentine Writer and Tradition," trans. James E. Irby in Borges, *Labyrinths: Selected Stories and Other Writings*, ed. Donald A. Yates and James E. Irby (1962; New York: New Directions, 1964), 182.

17. Ricardo Güiraldes, *Don Segundo Sombra* (1926; Buenos Aires: Losada, 1978), 55.

18. Ralph Ellison, *Invisible Man* (1947; New York: Vintage, 1995), 7.

19. M. M. Bakhtin, *Toward a Philosophy of the Act*, trans. Vadim Liapunov (Austin: University of Texas Press, 1993), 32.

20. Ann Laura Stoler, "Intimidations of Empire: Predicaments of the Tactile and Unseen," in *Haunted by Empire: Geographies of Intimacy in North American History* (Durham, NC: Duke University Press, 2006), 1.

21. Sarmiento was a devout reader of the Leatherstocking tales of James Fenimore Cooper, a relationship of admiration that has been widely and compellingly discussed most recently by critics such as Doris Sommer, Ricardo Piglia, and William Katra.

22. The translation of the 1845 title is the following: *Civilization and Barbarism. Life of Juan Facundo Quiroga, and Physical Aspect, Mores, and Habits of the Argentine Republic*. In the United States it has commonly been referred to as *Life in the Argentine Republic in the Days of the Tyrants*.

23. Domingo Sarmiento, *Facundo: Civilización y barbarie* (1845; Madrid: Cátedra, 1990), 51. Translated version by Kathleen Ross, *Facundo: Civilization and Barbarism* (Berkeley: University of California Press, 2003), 40.

24. Carlos Alonso, *The Burden of Modernity: The Rhetoric of Cultural Discourse in Spanish America* (New York: Oxford University Press, 1998), 54.

25. Julio Ramos, *Divergent Modernities: Culture and Politics in Nineteenth-Century Latin America*, trans. John D. Blanco (Durham, NC: Duke University Press, 2001), 265n10. Ramos reads this alongside Foucault's take on *Oedipus Rex*. In *La verdad y las formas jurídicas*, Foucault reads Oedipus's act of solving the riddle in the following manner (which I quote from Ramos): "The role played by the tyrant is not only characterized by power but also by a certain knowledge. . . . Oedipus is the one who manages, with his thought and his knowledge, to solve the famous riddle of the sphinx, that he cured the city."

26. In *El tamaño de mi esperanza,* Borges—at the time an admirer of the expressions of autochthony created by his contemporaries like Güiraldes—addresses the nineteenth-century writer in the following manner: "Sarmiento (norteamericanizado indio bravo, gran odiador y desentendedor de lo criollo) nos europeizó con su fe de hombre recién venido a la cultura y que espera milagros de ella" ["Sarmiento (North-Americanized brave Indian, great hater and 'misunderstander' of what is *criollo*), Europeanized us with the faith of a man newly arrived in the realm of culture, who expects miracles from it"], 12.

27. See, for example, Gwen Kirkpatrick and Francine Masiello's "Introduction" to *Sarmiento: Author of a Nation*, ed. Tulio Halperín Donghi et al. (Berkeley: University of California Press, 1994), 1.

28. Ricardo Piglia, "Sarmiento the Writer," in *Sarmiento: Author of a Nation*, ed. Tulio Halperín Donghi et. al., 138.

29. Sommer, *Foundational Fictions: The National Romances of Latin America* (Berkeley: University of California Press, 1993), 63.

30. Ilan Stavans, Introduction to Sarmiento, *Facundo: or, Civilization and Barbarism* (New York: Penguin, 1998), xxix. This edition is a reprint of Mary Mann's 1868 translation. In this same year, Sarmiento became president of the Argentine Republic.

31. For a discussion of multigenre works of Du Bois, set against a history of the development of what Susan Gillman calls a "racial occult" (multidisciplinary practices that seek to historicize racial consciousness in the United States during the fin de siècle), see Susan Gillman, *Blood Talk: American Race Melodrama and the Culture of the Occult* (Chicago: University of Chicago Press, 2003).

32. Wald, *Constituting Americans,* 218; 236.

33. See Wald's third chapter on Du Bois in *Constituting Americans* (181–90), and Zamir's "A Prosody of Dark Voices" chapter in *Dark Voices*, 169–206.

34. In her essay on the reception of death and sociality across racial boundaries, "Neighbors, Strangers, Corpses: Death and Sympathy in the Early Writings of W. E. B. Du Bois," Susan Mizruchi argues that "Du Bois . . . portrays death as a problem of reception." In the chapter in *Souls* where Du Bois describes the death of his son, he recalls how the whites have no sympathy for the mourners. Mizruchi argues that, "in Du Bois's America, partly in response to the post-Emancipation gains and challenges of Blacks," there is "an attempt to reinvent their 'social death' under slavery in a new, more intensely metaphorical form." Mizruchi, in W. E. B. Du Bois, *Souls of Black Folk*, ed. Henry Louis Gates Jr. and Terri Hume Oliver (New York: W. W. Norton, 1999),

280, 286. Also available in *Centuries' Ends, Narrative Means*, ed. Robert Newman (Stanford, CA: Stanford University Press, 1996), 191–211.

35. W. E. B. Du Bois, "The Present Outlook for the Dark Races of Mankind," in *Writings of W. E. B. Du Bois in Periodicals Edited by Others*, vol. 1, no. 73, ed. Herbert Aptheker (Millwood, NY: Kraus-Thomson Organization, 1982).

36. Amy Kaplan, *The Anarchy of U.S. Empire and the Making of U.S. Culture* (Cambridge, MA: Harvard University Press, 2002), 183.

37. W. E. B. Du Bois, *Darkwater*, in *The Oxford W. E. B. Du Bois Reader*, ed. Eric Sundquist (New York: Oxford University Press), 502.

Epilogue

1. Cormac McCarthy, *No Country for Old Men* (New York: Knopf, 2005), 259–60.

2. For a discussion of the tension between the symbolic and material representations of this border, see the chapter on "'Real' Ethnographies," in *Contemporary Travel Writing of Latin America*, by Claire Lindsay (New York: Routledge, 2010), 92–114.

3. See Ramón David Saldívar, *Border Matters: Remapping American Cultural Studies* (Berkeley: University of California Press, 1997).

4. Paul Gilroy, *After Empire: Melancholia or Convivial Culture?* (London: Routledge, 2004), 9.

BIBLIOGRAPHY

Abbey, Edward. *Desert Solitaire*. 1968. New York: Ballantine Books, 1985.

Abrams, Robert E. *Landscape and Ideology in American Renaissance Literature: Topographies of Skepticism*. Cambridge: Cambridge University Press, 2004.

Aching, Gerard, "Against 'Library-Shelf-Races': José Martí's Critique of Excessive Imitation." In *Geomodernisms: Race, Modernism, Modernity*, edited by Laura Doyle and Laura Winkiel, 151–69. Bloomington: Indiana University Press, 2005.

———. *The Politics of Spanish American* Modernismo: *By Exquisite Design*. Cambridge: Cambridge University Press, 1997.

Ahmad, Aijaz. "Jameson's Rhetoric of Otherness and the National Allegory." *Social Text* 17 (Fall 1987): 3–25.

Alonso, Carlos. *The Burden of Modernity: The Rhetoric of Cultural Discourse in Spanish America*. New York: Oxford University Press, 1998.

———. *The Spanish-American Regional Novel: Modernity and Autochthony*. Cambridge: Cambridge University Press, 1990.

Anderson, Benedict. *Imagined Communities: Reflections on the Origin and Spread of Nationalism*. 1983. London: Verso, 1998.

———. *The Spectre of Comparisons: Nationalism, Southeast Asia and the World*. London: Verso, 1998.

Appiah, Anthony Kwame. *Cosmopolitanism: Ethics in a World of Strangers*. New York: Norton, 2006.

Arac, Jonathan. *The Emergence of American Literary Narrative, 1820–1860*. 1995. Cambridge: Harvard University Press, 2005.

Arroyo, Jossiana. "Tecnologías de la palabra: el secreto y la escritura en José Martí." *Encuentro de la cultura cubana* 30–31 (2003): 161–73.

Attridge, Derek. *J. M. Coetzee and the Ethics of Reading: Literature in the Event.* Chicago: University of Chicago Press, 2004.

Bakhtin, Mikhail M. *Art and Answerability: Early Philosophical Essays by M. M. Bakhtin.* Translated by Vadim Liapunov. Austin: University of Texas Press, 1990.

———. *The Dialogic Imagination.* 1981. Translated by Caryl Emerson and Michael Holquist. Austin: University of Texas Press, 2000.

———. *Toward a Philosophy of the Act.* Translated by Vadim Liapunov. Austin: University of Texas Press, 1993.

Belnap, Jeffrey, and Raúl Fernández, eds. *José Martí's "Our America": From National to Hemispheric Cultural Studies.* Durham, NC: Duke University Press, 1998.

Benjamin, Walter. *The Arcades Project.* Translated by Howard Eiland and Kevin McLaughlin. Cambridge, MA: Harvard University Press, 2003.

———. *Illuminations.* New York: Harcourt Brace Jovanovich, 1968.

———. *The Origin of German Tragic Drama.* Translated by John Osborne. London: Verso, 2003.

Bergland, Renée. *The National Uncanny: Indian Ghosts and American Subjects.* Hanover, NH: Dartmouth/University Press of New England, 2000.

Bergson, Henri. *Duration and Simultaneity: Bergson and the Einsteinian Universe.* Edited by Robin Durie. 1922. Manchester: Clinamen Press, 1999.

Best, Janice. "The Chronotope and the Generation of Meaning in Novels and Paintings." *Criticism* 36, no. 2 (1994): 291–317.

Beulens, Gert. "James's 'Aliens': Consuming, Performing, and Judging the American Scene." *Modern Philology* 96, no. 3 (1999): 347–63.

Bierce, Ambrose. *The Complete Short Stories of Ambrose Bierce.* Compiled by Ernest Jerome Hopkins. 1970. Lincoln: University of Nebraska Press, 1984.

———. *The Enlarged Devil's Dictionary.* Edited by Ernest Jerome Hopkins. London: Victor Gollancz, 1967.

———. *Skepticism and Dissent: Selected Journalism from 1898–1901.* Edited by Lawrence I. Berkove. Ann Arbor, MI: Delmas, 1980.

Blair, Sara. *Henry James and the Writing of Race and Nation.* Cambridge: Cambridge University Press, 1996.

Blanco, María del Pilar, and Esther Peeren, eds. *Popular Ghosts: The Haunted Spaces of Everyday Culture.* New York: Continuum, 2010.

Bongie, Chris. *Islands and Exiles: The Creole Identities of Post/Colonial Literature.* Stanford, CA: Stanford University Press, 1998.

Borges, Jorge Luis. *Collected Fictions.* Translated by Andrew Hurley. New York: Penguin Putnam, 1998.

———. *Discusión.* 1932. Madrid: Biblioteca Borges/Alianza Editorial, 1997.

———. *El tamaño de mi esperanza.* 1926. Buenos Aires: Seix Barral, 1994.

———. *Labyrinths: Selected Stories and Other Writings.* 1962. Edited by Donald A. Yates and James E. Irby. New York: New Directions, 1964.

———. *Otras inquisiciones.* 1952. Madrid: Biblioteca Borges/Alianza Editorial, 1976.

———. *The Total Library: Non-Fiction 1922–1986.* Translated by Esther Allen, Suzanne Jill Levine, and Eliot Weinberger. London, New York: Allen Lane/Penguin, 2000.

Bowers, Maggie Ann. *Magic(al) Realism.* London: Routledge, 2005.

Brickhouse, Anna. *Transamerican Literary Relations and the Nineteenth-Century Public Sphere.* 2004. Cambridge: Cambridge University Press, 2009.

Brosman, Catharine Savage. "Desert." *American Scholar* 70, no. 2 (2001): 111–22.

Carpentier, Alejo. *Tientos y diferencias.* Mexico, D.F.: Universidad Nacional Autónoma de México, 1964.

Castronovo, Russ, and Susan Gillman, eds. *States of Emergency: The Object of American Studies.* Chapel Hill: University of North Carolina Press, 2009.

Cohn, Deborah. *History and Memory in the Two Souths: Recent Southern and Spanish American Fiction.* Nashville: Vanderbilt University Press, 1999.

Colás, Santiago. "Toward an Ethics of Close Reading in the Age of Neo-Liberalism." *New Centennial Review* 7, no. 3 (2007): 171–211.

Conway, Christopher. "José Martí frente al Wild West de Buffalo Bill: frontera, raza y arte en la civilización y barbarie norteamericana." *Hispanic Journal* 19, no. 1 (1998): 129–42.

Cortés, Mario Rivas. "Felisberto Hernández visto por Ángel Rama." *Revista iberoamericana* 71, no. 211 (2005): 381–85.

Cosgrove, Denis E. *Social Formation and Symbolic Landscape.* 1984. Madison: University of Wisconsin Press, 1998.

Cowie, Peter. *John Ford and the American West.* New York: Harry N. Abrams, 2004.

Crary, Jonathan. *Suspensions of Perception: Attention, Spectacle, and Modern Culture.* 1999. Cambridge, MA: MIT Press, 2001.

Creighton, Jane. "Bierce, Fuentes, and the Critique of Reading: A Study of Carlos Fuentes's *The Old Gringo.*" *South Central Review* 9, no. 2 (1992): 65–79.

Davis, Colin. "Hauntology, Spectres, and Phantoms." *French Studies* 59, no. 3 (2005): 373–79.

Davis, Diane E. *Urban Leviathan: Mexico City in the Twentieth Century.* Philadelphia: Temple University Press, 1994.

Davis, James C. "Solid, Liquid, or Gas?: Race as a State of Matter." *Henry James Review* 21, no. 3 (2000): 261–69.

Derrida, Jacques. "The Law of Genre." Translated by Avital Ronell. *Critical Inquiry* 7, no. 1 (1980): 55–81.

———. *Specters of Marx: The State of the Debt, the Work of Mourning, and the New International.* 1993. Translated by Peggy Kamuf. London: Routledge, 1994.

De Torre, Guillermo. *Literaturas europeas de vanguardia.* Madrid: Rafael Caro Raggio, 1925.

Dove, Patrick. *The Catastrophe of Modernity: Tragedy and the Nation in Latin American Literature.* Lewisburg, PA: Bucknell University Press, 2004.

Doyle, Laura, and Laura Winkiel, eds. *Geomodernisms: Race, Modernism, Modernity.* Bloomington: Indiana University Press, 2005.

Dreiser, Theodore. *Sister Carrie.* 1900. New York: Penguin, 1994.

Du Bois, W. E. B. *The Oxford W. E. B. Du Bois Reader.* Edited by Eric Sundquist. New York: Oxford University Press, 1996.

———. *The Souls of Black Folk.* Edited by Henry Louis Gates Jr. and Terri Hume Oliver. New York: W. W. Norton, 1999.

———. *Writings by W. E. B. Du Bois in Periodicals Edited by Others.* Vol. 1. Edited by Herbert Aptheker. Millwood, NY: Kraus-Thomson, 1982.

Dunkerley, James. *Americana: The Americas in the World around 1850, or "Seeing the Elephant" as the Theme for an Imaginary Western.* London: Verso, 2000.

Dussel, Enrique, "'Being-in-the-World-*Hispanically*': A World on the Border of Many Worlds." *Comparative Literature* 61, no. 3 (2009): 256–73.

Ellison, Ralph. *Invisible Man.* 1947. New York: Vintage, 1995.

El Topo. Screenplay by Alexandro Jodorowsky. Directed by Alexandro Jodorowksy. Perf. Alejandro Jodorowsky, Jacqueline Luis, and Mara Lorenzio. Producciones Pánicas, 1970.

Faris, Wendy B. *Ordinary Enchantments: Magical Realism and the Remystification of Narrative.* Nashville: Vanderbilt University Press, 2004.

———. "The Question of the Other: Cultural Critiques of Magical Realism." *Janus Head* 5, no. 2 (2002): 101–19.

Faulkner, William. *Absalom, Absalom!* New York: Vintage International, 1990.

Ferré, Rosario. *El acomodador: una lectura fantástica de Felisberto Hernández.* Mexico City: Tierra Firme/Fondo de Cultura Económica, 1986.

Foucault, Michel. "Of Other Spaces." *Diacritics* 16, no. 1 (1986): 22–27.

———. *The Order of Things.* 1966. London: Routledge, 2006.

Franco, Jean. *Critical Passions.* Edited by Mary Louise Pratt and Kathleen Newman. Durham, NC: Duke University Press, 1999.

———. *The Decline and Fall of the Lettered City: Latin America in the Cold War.* Cambridge, MA: Harvard University Press, 2002.

———. *An Introduction to Spanish-American Literature.* 1968. Cambridge: Cambridge University Press, 1994.

French, Jennifer L. *Nature, Neo-Colonialism, and the Spanish-American Regional Writers.* Lebanon, NH: Dartmouth College Press/University Press of New England, 2005.

Freud, Sigmund. *The Uncanny.* 1919. New York: Penguin, 2003.

Fuentes, Carlos. *El gringo viejo.* 1985. Mexico: Fondo de Cultura Económica, 1992.

———. *The Old Gringo.* Translated by Margaret Sayers Peden and Carlos Fuentes. London: André Deutsch, 1986.

Fuguet, Alberto, and Sergio Gómez, eds. *McOndo.* Barcelona: Mondadori, 1996.

Geertz, Clifford. *The Interpretation of Cultures: Selected Essays*. London: Fontana Press, 1973.

Gilbert, Geoffrey, "The Origins of Modernism in the Haunted Properties of Literature." In *The Victorian Supernatural*, edited by Nicola Bown, Carolyn Burdett and Pamela Thurschwell, 239–57. Cambridge: Cambridge University Press, 2004.

Giles, Paul. *Virtual Americas: Transnational Fictions and the Transatlantic Imaginary*. Durham, NC: Duke University Press, 2002.

Gillman, Susan. *Blood Talk: American Race Melodrama and the Culture of the Occult*. Chicago: University of Chicago Press, 2003.

Gilroy, Paul. *After Empire: Melancholia or Convivial Culture?* London: Routledge, 2004.

———. *The Black Atlantic: Modernity and Double Consciousness*. 1993. Cambridge, MA: Harvard University Press, 2002.

Goddu, Teresa A. *Gothic America: Narrative, History, and Nation*. New York: Columbia University Press, 1997.

Goehring, James E. "The Dark Side of Landscape: Ideology and Power in the Christian Myth of the Desert." *Journal of Medieval and Early Modern Studies* 33, no. 3 (2003): 437–51.

González Echevarría, Roberto. *Alejo Carpentier: The Pilgrim at Home*. 1977. Austin: University of Texas Press, 1990.

Gordon, Avery. *Ghostly Matters: Haunting and the Sociological Imagination*. Minneapolis: University of Minnesota Press, 1997.

Graziano, Frank. *The Lust of Seeing: Themes of the Gaze and Sexual Rituals in the Fiction of Felisberto Hernández*. Lewisburg, PA: Bucknell University Press, 1997.

———. "La lujuria de ver; la proyección fantástica en 'El acomodador.'" *Revista iberoamericana* 58, no. 160–61 (1992): 1027–39.

Greenblatt, Stephen. *Marvelous Possessions: The Wonders of the New World*. Chicago: University of Chicago Press, 1991.

Gruesz, Kirsten Silva. *Ambassadors of Culture: The Transamerican Origins of Latino Writing*. Princeton, NJ: Princeton University Press, 2002.

Güiraldes, Ricardo. *Don Segundo Sombra*. 1926. Buenos Aires: Losada, 1978.

Halperín Donghi, Tulio, Iván Jaksic, Gwen Kirkpatrick, and Francine Masiello, eds. *Sarmiento: Author of a Nation*. Berkeley: University of California Press, 1994.

Harries, Martin. *Scare Quotes from Shakespeare: Marx, Keynes, and the Language of Reenchantment*. Stanford, CA: Stanford University Press, 2000.

Harvey, David. *Spaces of Hope*. 2000. Edinburgh: Edinburgh University Press, 2002.

Haviland, Beverly. *Henry James's Last Romance: Making Sense of the Past and the American Scene*. New York: Cambridge University Press, 1997.

Hegel, G. W. F. *The Philosophy of History*. 1831. New York: Dover, 1956.

Hernández, Feliberto. *Nadie encendía las lámparas y otros cuentos*. Barcelona: Editorial Lumen/Palabra Menor, 1982.

———. *Obras Completas de Felisberto Hernández*. Edited by María Luisa Puga. Mexico City: Siglo XXI, 1983.

Highmore, Ben. *Cityscapes: Cultural Readings in the Material and Symbolic City*. London: Palgrave Macmillan, 2005.

High Plains Drifter. Screenplay by Ernest Tidyman and Dean Riesner. Directed by Clint Eastwood. Perf. Clint Eastwood, Verna Bloom, and Billy Curtis. Malpaso Pictures, 1972/3.

Hitchcock, Peter. *The Long Space: Transnationalism and Postcolonial Form*. Stanford, CA: Stanford University Press, 2010.

Hollinger, David. *Postethnic America: Beyond Multiculturalism*. 1995. New York: Basic Books, 2005.

Horne, Philip, ed. *Henry James: A Life in Letters*. London: Allen Lane, 1999.

———. "'Reinstated': Henry James in Roosevelt's Washington." *Cambridge Quarterly* 37, no. 1 (2008): 47–63.

Huxley, Aldous. *Tomorrow, and Tomorrow and Tomorrow and Other Essays*. 1952. New York: Harper and Brothers, 1956.

Huyssen, Andreas. *Present Pasts: Urban Palimpsests and the Politics of Memory*. Stanford, CA: Stanford University Press, 2003.

James, Henry. *The American Scene*. Edited by W. H. Auden. New York: Scribner's Sons, 1946.

———. *The Art of the Novel*. Edited by R.P. Blackmur. New York: Scribner's, 1934.

———. *The Complete Notebooks of Henry James*. Edited by Leon Edel and Lyall Powers. New York: Oxford University Press, 1987.

———. *Hawthorne*. Ithaca, NY: Cornell University Press, 1997.

———. *Henry James: The American Essays*. Edited by Leon Edel. New York: Vintage, 1956.

———. *Henry James: Stories of the Supernatural*. Edited by Leon Edel. London: Barrie and Jenkins, 1971.

———. *The New York Stories of Henry James*. New York: New York Review of Books, 2006.

Jameson, Fredric. *The Geopolitical Aesthetic: Cinema and Space in the World System*. 1992. Bloomington: Indiana University Press/British Film Institute, 1995.

———. "Third-World Literature in the Era of Multinational Capitalism." *Social Text* 15 (Autumn 1986): 65–88.

Jodorowsky, Alexandro. *El Topo*. Screenplay. 1971. Translated by Joanne Pottlitzer. London: Calder and Boyars, 1974.

Johnson, Kendall. "The Scarlet Feather: Racial Phantasmagoria in *What Maisie Knew*." *Henry James Review* 22, no. 2 (2001): 128–46.

Kaplan, Amy. *The Anarchy of Empire in the Making of U.S. Culture*. Cambridge, MA: Harvard University Press, 2002.

———. *The Social Construction of American Realism*. Chicago: University of Chicago Press, 1988.

Kapsis, Robert E., and Kathy Coblentz, eds. *Clint Eastwood Interviews.* Jackson: University of Mississippi Press, 1999.

Kasson, Joy S. *Buffalo Bill's Wild West: Celebrity, Memory, and Popular History.* New York: Hill and Wang, 2000.

Larrain, Jorge. *Identity and Modernity in Latin America.* Cambridge: Polity Press, 2000.

Levander, Caroline F., and Robert S. Levine, eds. *Hemispheric American Studies.* New Brunswick, NJ: Rutgers University Press, 2008.

Limerick, Patricia. "Haunted by Rhyolite: Learning from the Landscape of Failure." *American Art* 6, no. 4 (1992): 18–39.

Lindsay, Claire. *Contemporary Travel Writing of Latin America.* New York: Routledge, 2010.

Lomas, Laura. *Translating Empire: José Martí, Migrant Latino Subjects, and American Modernities.* Durham, NC: Duke University Press, 2008.

Luckhurst, Roger. "The Contemporary London Gothic and the Limits of the 'Spectral Turn.'" *Textual Practice* 16 no. 3 (2002): 527–47.

Lustig, T. J. *Henry James and the Ghostly.* Cambridge: Cambridge University Press, 1994.

Lynch, Kevin. *The Image of the City.* Cambridge, MA: MIT Press, 1960.

Mao, Douglas, and Rebecca L. Walkowitz, eds. *Bad Modernisms.* Durham, NC: Duke University Press, 2006.

Marshall, Bridget M. "Teaching 'The Boarded Window.'" *Ambrose Bierce Project Journal* 4, no. 1 (2008). http://www.ambrosebierce.org/journal4marshall.html.

Martí, José. *Ensayos y crónicas.* Madrid: Cátedra, 2004.

———. *La Gran Enciclopedia Martiana.* Edited by Ramón Cernuda. Miami: Ediciones de Cultura Cubana, 1977.

———. *Selected Writings.* Translated by Esther Allen. New York: Penguin, 2002.

Marx, Karl. *Marx's "Eighteenth Brumaire."* Edited by Mark Cowling and James Martin. London: Pluto Press, 2002.

Matheson, Neill. "Intimacy and Form: James on Hawthorne's Charm." *Henry James Review* 28, no. 2 (2007): 120–39.

McCarthy, Cormac. *No Country for Old Men.* New York: Alfred Knopf, 2005.

McKee, Patricia. *Producing American Races: Henry James, William Faulkner, Toni Morrison.* Durham, NC: Duke University Press, 1999.

Melville, Herman. *Moby-Dick, or the Whale.* 1851. New York: Penguin Classics, 2003.

Menton, Seymour, "Jorge Luis Borges: Magic Realist," *Hispanic Review* 50, no. 2 (1982): 411–26.

———. "Review of Wendy B. Faris's *Ordinary Enchantments.*" *World Literature Today* 79, no. 2 (2005): 110–11.

Mitchell, W. J. T. *Landscape and Power.* Chicago: University of Chicago Press, 2002.

Mizruchi, Susan. "Neighbors, Strangers, Corpses: Death and Sympathy in the Early Writings of W. E. B. Du Bois." In W. E. B. Du Bois, *Souls of Black Folk,* edited by Henry Louis Gates Jr. and Terri Hume Oliver. New York: W. W. Norton, 1999.

Monsiváis, Carlos. *Mexican Postcards.* 1997. Translated by John Kraniauskas. London: Verso, 2000.

Moreiras, Alberto. *The Exhaustion of Difference: The Politics of Latin American Cultural Studies.* Durham, NC: Duke University Press, 2001.

Moya, Paula, and Ramón Saldívar. "Fictions of the Trans-American Imaginary." Special issue. *Modern Fiction Studies* 49, no. 1 (2003).

Nemerov, Alexander. "Seeing Ghosts: *The Turn of the Screw* and Art History." In *What Is Research in the Visual Arts?: Obsession, Archive, Encounter,* edited by Michael Ann Holly and Marquard Smith, 13–32. Williamstown, MA: Clark Art Institute, 2009.

Newman, Robert, ed. *Centuries' Ends, Narrative Means.* Stanford, CA: Stanford University Press, 1996.

O'Connor, Flannery. *Collected Works.* New York: Library of America, 1988.

O'Connor, Patrick. *Latin American Fiction and the Narratives of the Perverse: Paper Dolls and Spider Women.* New York: Palgrave Macmillan, 2004.

Paris, Texas. Screenplay by L. M. Kit Carson and Sam Shepard. Directed by Wim Wenders. Perf. Harry Dean Stanton, Natassja Kinski, and Hunter Carson. Road Movies Filmproduktion, 1984.

Patterson, Anita. *Race, American Literature, and Transnational Modernisms.* Cambridge: Cambridge University Press, 2008.

Pechey, Graham. *Mikhail Bakhtin: The Word in the World.* London: Routledge, 2007.

Peeren, Esther, "The Ghost as a Gendered Chronotope." In *Ghosts, Stories, Histories: Ghost Stories and Alternative Histories,* edited by Sladja Blazan, 81–96. Newcastle: Cambridge Scholars Publishing, 2007.

Pérez, Gilberto. *The Material Ghost: Films and Their Medium.* Baltimore: Johns Hopkins University Press, 1998.

Pérez, Louis A., Jr. *Cuba: Between Reform and Revolution.* 1988. New York: Oxford University Press, 1995.

Pérez-Firmat, Gustavo, ed. *Do the Americas Have a Common Literature?* Durham, NC: Duke University Press, 1990.

Poff, Chrys M. *The Western Ghost Town in American Culture, 1869–1950.* Ann Arbor: Dissertation Abstracts International, 2004.

Posnock, Ross. *The Trial of Curiosity: Henry James, William James, and the Challenge of Modernity.* New York: Oxford University Press, 1991.

Prieto, Julio. *Desencuadernados: vanguardias ex-céntricas en el Río de la Plata. Macedonio Fernández y Felisberto Hernández.* Rosario, Argentina: Beatriz Viterbo, 2002.

Rama, Ángel. *Aquí Montevideo: gentes y lugares.* Montevideo: Arca, 1966.

———. *Crítica literaria y utopía en América Latina.* Medellín: Editorial Universidad de Antioquia, 2006.

———. *The Lettered City.* Translated by John Charles Chasteen. Durham, NC: Duke University Press, 1996.

Ramela, Carlos. "Cuentos de Felisberto Hernández." *Marcha*, April 9, 1948, 14.

Ramela, Carlos, and Homero Alsina Theveret. "El jurado que falló." *Marcha*, December 10, 1948, 15.

Ramos, Julio. *Divergent Modernities: Culture and Politics in Nineteenth-Century Latin America.* Translated by John D. Blanco. Durham, NC: Duke University Press, 2001.

Richardson, Judith. *Possessions: The History and Uses of Haunting in the Hudson Valley.* Cambridge, MA: Harvard University Press, 2003.

Rivas Cortés, Mario. "Felisberto Hernández visto por Ángel Rama." *Revista Iberoamericana* 71, no. 211 (2005): 381–85.

Rockland, Michael, ed. *Sarmiento's Travels in the United States in 1847.* Princeton, NJ: Princeton University Press, 1970.

Rotker, Susana. *The American Chronicles of José Martí: Journalism and Modernity in Spanish America.* Hanover, NH: University Press of New England, 2000.

Rowe, John Carlos. *The Other Henry James.* Durham, NC: Duke University Press, 1998.

Ruland, Richard, and Malcolm Bradbury. *From Puritanism to Postmodernism: A History of American Literature.* 1991. New York: Penguin, 1992.

Rulfo, Juan. *Pedro Páramo.* 1955. Madrid: Cátedra Letras Hispánicas, 2004.

———. *Pedro Páramo.* Translated by Margaret Sayers Peden. London: Serpent's Tail, 1993.

Saldívar, José David. *Border Matters: Remapping American Cultural Studies.* Berkeley: University of California Press, 1997.

———. *The Dialectics of Our America: Genealogy, Cultural Critique, and Literary History.* Durham, NC: Duke University Press, 1991.

Sarmiento, Domingo Faustino. *Facundo: Civilización y barbarie.* 1845. Madrid: Cátedra, 1990.

———. *Facundo: or, Civilization and Barbarism.* 1868. Translated by Mary Mann. New York: Penguin Classics, 1998.

———. *Facundo: Civilization and Barbarism.* Translated by Kathleen Ross. Berkeley: University of California Press, 2003.

———. *Viajes por Europa, Africa i América, 1845–1847.* 1993. Madrid: ALLCA XX, 1996.

Schaefer, Jack. *Shane.* 1949. Lincoln: University of Nebraska Press, 1984.

Scott, David. *Semiologies of Travel: From Gautier to Baudrillard.* Cambridge: Cambridge University Press, 2004.

Shane. Screenplay by A. B. Guthrie Jr. Directed by George Stevens. Perf. Alan Ladd, Jean Arthur, and Van Heflin. Paramount Pictures, 1952.

Shepard, Sam. *True West.* London: Faber and Faber, 1981.

Silverberg, Robert. *Ghost Towns of the American West.* 1968. Athens: Ohio University Press, 1994.

Slotkin, Richard. "Buffalo Bill's 'Wild West' and the Mythologization of the American Empire." In *Cultures of United States Imperialism*, edited by Amy Kaplan and Donald E. Pease, 164–82. Durham, NC: Duke University Press, 1993.

———. *Regeneration through Violence: The Mythology of the American Frontier, 1600–1860*. Norman: University of Oklahoma Press, 1973.

Smith, Dorothy E. "Review of *Ghostly Matters*." *Contemporary Sociology* 28, no. 1 (1999): 120.

Smith, Jon, and Deborah Cohn, eds. *Look Away!: The U.S. South in New World Studies*. Durham, NC: Duke University Press, 2004.

Smith, Paul. *Clint Eastwood: A Cultural Production*. London: University College London Press, 1993.

Sommer, Doris. *Foundational Fictions: The National Romances of Latin America*. 1991. Berkeley: University of California Press, 1993.

———. *Proceed with Caution, When Engaged by Minority Writing in the Americas*. Cambridge, MA: Harvard University Press, 1999.

Stavans, Ilan, et al., eds. *The Norton Anthology of Latino Literature*. New York: W. W. Norton, 2011.

Stecopoulos, Harry. *Reconstructing the World: Southern Fictions and U.S. Imperialisms, 1898–1976*. Ithaca, NY: Cornell University Press, 2008.

Stoler, Ann Laura, ed. *Haunted by Empire: Geographies of Intimacy in North American History*. Durham, NC: Duke University Press, 2006.

Tenorio-Trillo, Mauricio. *Mexico at the World's Fairs: Crafting a Modern Nation*. Berkeley: University of California Press, 1996.

Thacker, Andrew. "The Idea of a Critical Literary Geography." *New Formations* 57 (Winter 2005/2006): 56–73.

Theisen, Bianca. "Simultaneity: A Narrative Figure in Kleist." *MLN* 121, no. 3 (2006): 514–21.

Thoreau, Henry David. *Walden and Other Writings*. New York: Barnes and Noble Books, 1993.

Todorov, Tzvetan. *The Fantastic: A Structuralist Approach to a Literary Genre*. 1970. Translated by Richard Howard. Ithaca, NY: Cornell University Press, 1975.

Turner, Frederick Jackson. *The Frontier in American History*. New York: Dover, 1996.

Twain, Mark. *Roughing It*. Stilwell, KS: Digireads, 2007.

Viswanathan, Gauri. "Spectrality's Secret Sharers: Occultism and (Post)colonial Affect." In *Beyond the Black Atlantic: Relocating Modernization and Technology*, edited by Walter Goebel and Saskia Schabio, 135–45. Oxford: Routledge, 2006.

Wald, Priscilla. *Constituting Americans: Cultural Anxiety and Narrative Form*. Durham, NC: Duke University Press, 1995.

Warnes, Christopher. "The Hermeneutics of Vagueness: Magical Realism in Current Literary Critical Discourse." *Journal of Postcolonial Writing* 41, no. 1 (2005): 1–13.

———. "Naturalizing the Supernatural: Faith, Irreverence, and Magical Realism." *Literature Compass* 2, no. 1 (2005): 1–16.

Weinstein, Martin. *Uruguay: Democracy at the Crossroads*. Boulder, CO: Westview Press, 1988.

Whitman, Walt. *Leaves of Grass*. Oxford: Oxford University Press, 1998.

Williams, Raymond. *The Country and the City*. Cambridge: Cambridge University Press, 1973.

Young, David, and Keith Hollaman, eds. *Magical Realist Fiction: An Anthology*. Oberlin, OH: Oberlin College Press, 1984.

Zabriskie Point. Screenplay by Michelangelo Antonioni, Franco Rossetti, Tonino Guerra, and Sam Shepard. Directed by Michelangelo Antonioni. Perf. Mark Frechette and Daria Halprin. MGM, 1970.

Zamir, Shamoon. *Dark Voices: W. E. B. Du Bois and American Thought, 1888–1903*. Chicago: University of Chicago Press, 1995.

Zamora, Lois Parkinson. *The Inordinate Eye: New World Baroque and Latin American Fiction*. Chicago: University of Chicago Press, 2006.

———. *The Usable Past: The Imagination of History in Recent Fiction of the Americas*. Cambridge: Cambridge University Press, 1997.

Zamora, Lois Parkinson, and Silvia Spitta, eds. "The Americas, Otherwise." Special issue. *Comparative Literature* 61, no. 3 (2009).

Zamora, Lois Parkinson, and Wendy B. Faris, eds. *Magical Realism: Theory, History, Community*. 1995. Durham, NC: Duke University Press, 2000.

Index

Reyes, Alfonso, 57
Richardson, Judith, 20, 21
Rodó, José Enrique, 50
Rodríguez Monegal, Emir, 141, 188n26
Roosevelt, Theodore, 118, 137, 193n23
Rosas, Juan Manuel de, 43, 106, 160, 161, 164
Rotker, Susana, 70, 71, 113–14, 125
Rowe, John Carlos, 135
ruins, 80; in Du Bois, 171, 175, 176; in ghost towns, 81; in post-earthquake Charleston (1886), 114–15; in Rulfo, 84, 89, 91. *See also* ghost towns; Martí, José; Rulfo, Juan
Ruland, Richard, 105
Rulfo, Juan, 6, 16, 17, 23, 29, 56, 60, 67, 68; broken community relations in, 68, 84, 85, 99; depictions of indigenous communities, 192–93n15; ghost town (Comala) in, 84, 87, 88, 92, 94; landscape depiction in, 81, 83, 84, 88; Mexican Revolution depicted in, 60, 88, 89; narrative style of, 85, 87, 91; *Pedro Páramo*, 81–82, 83–92; uncertainty in, 82, 85–86
Russell, Charles M., 75

Saco, José Antonio, 140
Saldívar, José David, 39, 180
Saldívar, Ramón, 16
Sarmiento, Domingo, 6, 23, 27, 29, 43, 64, 113, 140, 151, 205n21, 206n26; *Facundo*, 160–68; generic transgressions of, 45, 54, 167–68, 170; geographical and topographical descriptions in, 107, 109, 114, 161, 163, 164–65, 168, 204n13; literary style of, 111, 161, 162; U.S. Civil War, views on, 169; U.S. life, views on, 108–9, 111; *Viajes por Europa, África i América* (partial translation: *Sarmiento's Travels in the U.S.*), 110–12, 197n16
Schaefer, Jack: *Shane*, 195n50
Shepard, Sam, 75, 76
Silverberg, Robert, 194n33
simultaneity: Henri Bergson, views of, 26–27; Benedict Anderson, construed by, 70. *See also* haunting; landscapes; modernity
Slotkin, Richard, 64, 69, 73, 104, 136, 193n23, 202n73
Sommer, Doris, 45, 53–54, 55, 56, 168, 200n55, 205n21

Smith, Jon, 15, 16
Spanish-American War, 2, 137, 154, 177, 193n23,
Stavans, Ilan, 169
Stevens, George, 96, 97
Stoler, Ann Laura, 2, 160

Tenorio-Trillo, Mauricio, 105, 196n8
Thacker, Andrew, 9–10
Theisen, Bianca, 184n9
Thomas, Brook, 197n26
Thoreau, Henry David, 75, 111, 119, 197n26
Todorov, Tzvetan, 8, 28, 45–48, 49, 141, 186–87n3, 188n26, 189n30. *See also* genre
Torre, Guillermo de, 36, 187n12
Turner, Frederick Jackson, 197n26
Twain, Mark, 195n49, 205n16

uncanny, the (*Unheimlich*), 15, 19, 33, 186n1, 186–87n3, 196n3
urban spaces, 14, 66, 75, 127, 130; cosmopolitan sites, viewed as, 145, 146; relation to other spaces, viewed in, 64, 109–11, 114, 157, 161, 163–65; transformation in 19th and 20th centuries, 29, 103–6. *See also* Hernández, Felisberto; James, Henry; Martí, José
Uruguay, 106, 203n92
Uslar Pietri, Arturo, 55
U.S.-Mexico border, 2, 5, 29, 75, 179, 180, 193n30, 207n2

Viswanathan, Gauri, 184n9

Wald, Priscilla, 170, 171, 173, 186n1
Warnes, Christopher, 40–41, 49, 51
Weinstein, Martin, 203n92
Weinstein, Philip, 30, 51–52, 58, 186n1
Weissberg, Lilliane, 16
Wenders, Wim, 193n30
Whitman, Walt, 149, 150, 152, 204n5
Williams, Raymond, 99, 104

Young, David, 51

Zamir, Shamoon, 170, 173, 204n5
Zamora, Lois Parkinson, 14–15, 16, 28, 35, 42, 53, 54–58, 60, 68, 186n1, 190n40, 190n42, 190–91n45
Zinneman, Fred, 96